Self-Reliant Cities

Energy and the Transformation of Urban America

David Morris

Sierra Club Books
San Francisco

The Sierra Club, founded in 1892 by John Muir,
has devoted itself to the study and protection
of the earth's scenic and ecological resources—
mountains, wetlands, woodlands, wild shores and
rivers, deserts and plains. The publishing program
of the Sierra Club offers books to the public
as a nonprofit educational service in the hope
that they may enlarge the public's understanding
of the Club's basic concerns. The point of view
expressed in each book, however, does not
necessarily represent that of the Club.
The Sierra Club has some fifty chapters coast
to coast, in Canada, Hawaii, and Alaska.
For information about how you may participate in
its programs to preserve wilderness and the quality
of life, please address inquiries to Sierra Club,
530 Bush Street, San Francisco, CA 94108.

Library of Congress Cataloging in Publication Data

       Morris, David J.
          Self-Reliant Cities

          Bibliography: p. 235
          Includes index.
1. United States—Public works—Energy consumption.
2. Public utilities—United States—Energy consumption.
3. Cities and towns—United States—Energy consumption.   I. Title.
HD4605.M67   333.79'13'0973   81-18301
ISBN 0-87156-296-0   AACR2

       Jacket design by Paul Bacon
       Book design by Wolfgang Lederer
       Illustrations by Nancy Warner
       Printed in the United States of America
       10   9   8   7   6   5   4   3   2   1

for my parents, Lottie and Gus

Acknowledgments

I am grateful for the emotional and intellectual support given me by the staff of the Institute for Local Self-Reliance during the period I was writing this book. Special thanks are due Edward Hensley for talking the book through with me and for Joan Matthews for turning the manuscript into electrons. I am grateful for the assistance of my special friend and colleague, Harriet Barlow, a woman who teaches each person she touches. And my thanks to Mary Jo Sutherland—again.

If the tone of this book is optimistic it is an optimism that grows out of my personal acquaintance with hundreds of people working in every section of the country. Space does not permit me to list all their names. Some are involved in local politics; most work in small businesses and community organizations. These people, working in communities as disparate as small towns in Maine or major megalopolises in California or New York, have been a source of inspiration to me. The movement towards local self-reliance comes from below. It is a heterogeneous movement. Each community shapes its future to its specific needs. But there is a common element linking each discrete activity—the belief that the average person can shed the role of spectator and can become an actor in shaping the future of the community.

Contents

Introduction:
What Makes a City?

Without power and independence, a town
may contain good subjects but it can
contain no active citizens.

Alexis de Tocqueville

This book is about American cities and how their
shape and authority have been influenced by our changing sources and
forms of energy. It begins by describing the way the American city
evolved during the age of inexpensive fossil fuels. This age (1870–1970)
was characterized by one central feature: the price of oil fell continuously.

The book then turns its attention to cities in the age of expensive
energy. The use of concentrated fuels in increasing quantities created a
fragmented society. Cities that once produced their own food, energy,
and goods became increasingly dependent on imported materials.
Densely populated communities ignored their interrelationships with
the natural environment, paving over topsoil, rerouting rivers, dumping
human and solid wastes in nearby streams. Economic and political
power moved away from the consumer and the citizen. The factory, the
farm, the power plants, the political official became more and more
removed from the urban community.

The 2,000 percent increase in the price of world crude oil between
1970 and 1980 forced the residents of cities to reexamine their fragile
supply lines for many of their products and the way they use natural

1

resources. One way densely populated communities responded to energy and natural resource crises was to move toward energy self reliance. And in recreating the city as an energy efficient organism, they may be effecting dramatic changes in the way our urban areas look and the role they play in our economic and political systems.

A city is a collection of citizens. It has political power because its citizens have given it the authority to make basic decisions shaping the design and development of their community. But political authority should not be confused with government. This book is less about government than about governance—the process rather than the paraphernalia of governing. And it is less concerned with the public sector's ability to grow, than with the community's ability to plan comprehensively. The activities addressed here will take place in an urban environment, but not necessarily under the direct auspices of city governments.

A city is located on a finite piece of land with limited access to resources. Since, as we now know, the world has a finite resource base, the city is an excellent laboratory in which to test our ability to thrive—or at least survive—in the new age. How cities discovered and learned to manage their resources—especially energy resources—and the management problems they faced and will face in the future are the central points and issues addressed in this book.

The typical American city is not just a matter of demographic averages; it is the place where most of us live. And it is not nearly as large as the popular image of the city. Out of the over 1,500 cities with populations over 10,000, only seven have populations of one million or more. More people live in cities of 10,000 to 50,000 than in cities of more than 250,000. The typical city is not as congested as we typically imagine, either. Although urban areas on the average are five to ten times denser than nonurban areas, density varies so widely from one part of the country to another that average density figures lose their meaning. For example, Manhattan's density can be represented by about 140 people on a football field. At the average density of cities with more than 100,000 inhabitants, the football field would be shared by five to ten people. The fastest growing cities (those with populations of 25,000 to 50,000) have areas so sparsely populated that only one or two persons would be standing on the field. There is, in other words, still plenty of space in our medium and larger cities.

The choice of the city as the central focus of this book is a pragmatic one. America is a nation of cities in that about 75 percent of Americans live in or around them. But only 50 percent of our population lives under the direct political authority of cities with more than 10,000 people.

One might argue that people identify more strongly with their neighborhood than with their cities. Neighborhoods are where we walk the dog, send our children to school, talk with the neighbors, worry about crime and go shopping. Yet neighborhoods have not been given significant political authority in our federal system and therefore have only rarely been the locus of decision making. On the other hand, some argue that the city as a political jurisdiction is an anachronism. Since much of its population has spilled over political boundaries during this century, it would be more accurate to fold in the urbanized areas surrounding central and satellite cities when discussing possible urban futures. That may be true in theory. In practice, however, political jurisdictions do not coincide with population concentrations. Until they do, metropolitan areas will not become effective decision-making entities.

This book describes the history and the possible futures of both large and small municipalities. When it discusses contemporary events many of the activities described take place in what Americans would normally consider to be small cities. The reader may find it useful to think of the typical city discussed in the second part of this book as having fifty thousand residents with a density of twenty-five hundred people per square mile. That typical sized city is large enough to employ a significant portion of its population in local businesses and to have the beginnings of a strong cultural base. It is larger than the small town, where everybody knows everybody else, and is smaller than the metropolis where bureaucracy begets impersonality. It may be considered a small city by current American standards, but it is a city with a population equal to or greater than the most famous cities in history, cities such as Athens or Florence, which bequeathed the world litera-

3

ture, physical art, philosophy, and organizational forms that are still widely admired.

This book is divided into two sections. Part One, "Losing Control," traces the development of urban areas from small, independent, self-sufficing villages into large cities totally dependent on imported materials — cities that are but nodes in a much larger political and economic mesh. This part of the book is historical; each chapter is ordered chronologically.

The first two chapters treat the direct relationship of energy sources and technologies to the shape and authority of the city. The first chapter describes how the discovery of coal and the invention of the steam engine combined to develop the large industrial city. The density of those cities forced them to demand—and they eventually received— the authority to protect the health and safety of their citizens by overseeing construction of basic urban life-support systems: water supplies, waste disposal, road networks.

When the petroleum-driven internal-combustion-engine vehicle entered society, the population implosion caused by the steam engine was reversed. The automobile and truck stretched cities out of shape. They created towns with no centers. They encouraged growing segments of the urban population to relocate outside the direct political authorities of the municipal corporation, and this fragmented the metropolitan areas into dozens, even hundreds, of tiny political entities.

As the petroleum-powered vehicles allowed people to settle virtually anywhere, electricity's ready transmission over long distances at nominal cost allowed them to maintain direct linkage to the central power sources. The second chapter tells of the relationship between cities and their power sources. It relates the size of the power plant to the ability of the city to regulate the electric industry, and it describes the transformation of the electric delivery system. Once, simple neighborhood power networks were regulated by the cities; now electrical delivery is by vast and complex continental grids, which are regulated by state and federal agencies but increasingly are incomprehensible even to their own engineer-managers.

The final two chapters of Part One consider the changing role of the city within the American political and economic system. The municipal budget increased dramatically during the last century; so did the competence and authority of the city to plan its own future. But even as the city has become directly involved in the development process, it has found itself increasingly subject to forces beyond local control. The local economy is little else than a tiny branch in a global marketplace. A city's destiny often depends on decisions made in distant corporate boardrooms.

The cities' dependence on remote corporations is paralleled by cities' increasing subservience to remote governments. The layer-cake system of federalism gave each level of government the capacity to generate revenue in order to finance its own responsibilities. In the twentieth century, however, higher levels of government have preempted revenue sources, and lower levels of government have been reduced to administering programs conceived and financed by bureaucrats remote from those affected.

Part Two, "Gaining Autonomy," tells of many efforts of cities to reduce their dependency on imported energy and how that effort gradually broadened into a striving for self-reliance. It begins with the effects of a historical discontinuity—the 1973 oil embargo and the 2,000 percent increase in the price of crude oil between 1970 and 1980. That price hike and the continuing instability of international oil pipelines catalyzed communities to re-examine their resource base. The first chapter of the second part provides an overview to explain how this unprecedented change in the economics of energy marked a watershed in urban development. The book's four concluding chapters describe different facets of the municipal response to rising energy prices. The events it describes are taking place now. The use of discrete chapters allows the author to discuss in greater depth the technological, institutional, and financial changes that encourage local energy independence.

But history cannot be so neatly compartmentalized. The events and trends described in each chapter do not occur in isolation. The 2,000 percent crude oil price hike has had the effect of a boulder dropped into a relatively still lake. The initial splash spreads outward in smaller waves, rippling the effects into the social, political, technological, and commercial systems.

When the price of gasoline soars, for example, people buy more fuel efficient smaller vehicles. Smaller vehicles can operate on narrow streets. Our broad thoroughfares, laid out in an era when vehicles were getting larger, not smaller, are suddenly out of proportion to today's and tomorrow's transportation needs. Like a person's old suit of clothes after a long diet they fit loosely. People start to take more notice of the half of the city's surface (and a large part of its underground) devoted to the transportation of people, goods, and wastes. Some people encourage a return to urban villages within cities, neighborhoods where people work and shop where they play, where the functions of residence, business, and recreation are within walking or bicycle riding distance from each other.

The unprecedented price increases make direct sunlight an increasingly competitive power source with fossil fuels. The ability to intercept sunlight becomes a financial asset. Municipal building codes, zoning practices, and comprehensive plans begin to take into account the new importance of solar access. But urban planners, especially in older cities, discover that the task of finding an equitable means of designing land area to encourage energy efficiency is a complex and difficult one. Institutions, customs, and laws do not change as rapidly as do technologies or prices.

Rising energy prices encourage decentralized power plants. In part this is a function of the higher overall fuel conversion efficiencies achievable in power plants that can use the waste heat generated in nearby buildings or industrial processes. In part it is one result of the increased attractiveness of decentralized fuels, such as small streams, organic waste, or direct sunlight. Cities once again, as they did a century previously, find themselves having to design a new energy production and distribution system. It is one of history's ironies that cities undertake such a re-examination of the role of monopolistic energy utilities at precisely that moment that the first long term franchises awarded utilities come up for renewal.

The emergence of urban energy sources, as reported on in Chapter 7, lends credibility to the idea of energy self-reliance. The new technologies give cities the opportunity to seek energy independence. But the opportunity is only grasped when there is a motivation to do so. The impact of rising energy payments on the local economy has proved to be such an incentive. The collective fiscal impact of energy imports on the local economy has become increasingly harmful. By 1980 more than 20 percent of the gross income of a community is paid for energy; 90 percent of these dollars leave the local area. They are unavailable for future local investment.

Cities are beginning, as reported in Chapter 6 and Chapter 8, to examine their municipal balance of payments and to devise strategies to reduce their energy-related dollar drain. They have begun to develop financing mechanisms compatible with the different timing of benefits that flow from investments in nonconventional versus conventional energy sources. The value of an oil well, for instance, is derived from the cheap oil it can offer today. The fact that prices will increase in later years or that the resource itself will disappear in a generation is discounted by today's marketplace. The value of a storm window, however, comes after the entire investment is made. The original investment repays itself again and again over several generations. The product can be recycled after its useful life has ended, and once again provide years of energy savings. How do we take into account these long term benefits in a society and marketplace geared to short term profits?

The cost of converting to self-reliance, assuming we decide it is worth the investment, is astounding. But some of the costs would come due anyway. The physical stock of our cities, our sewers and roadways, bridges and heating systems are wearing out. This is especially true in the huge industrial city whose infrastructure was built a century ago to provide services to the flood of human beings entering the city. New York City needs tens of billions of dollars to reconstruct its foundations. Newer cities also suffer these costs. Even as Dallas sprouts new neighborhoods the older parts of the city begin to deteriorate, requiring hundreds of millions of dollars of investment. What will the public works program of an energy efficient city look like?

The reconstruction of the waste disposal and transportation systems in our densely populated communities will require huge investments. But to convert our homes and vehicles and businesses into energy producers and efficient energy consumers not only requires large investments but investments on terms not normally achievable by individual households or small businesses. Chapter 8 discusses the search by communities for ways to finance the energy transition. Increasingly communities are turning toward two institutions, the energy utility and the municipal corporation, to assist them. These two institutions leverage large sums of money, serve geographically limited areas, and are directly or indirectly controlled or regulated by the public they serve.

The last chapter weaves together the threads of the entire book. It discusses the ecological city, a city that embraces efficiency as a governing principle. It discusses the city of the near future that transforms its traditional parasitical relationship with the natural environment into a more symbiotic and mutually beneficial one. It discusses recent actions in which cities use their rooftops for energy generation, their waste products as sources of raw materials, and their land for agriculture. It raises the vision of integrated systems in which the wastes of one process become the raw materials of another, in which production and consumption are more closely linked, in which cities become producers of the basic wealth that has usually been associated with extractive industries.

PART I

Losing
Control

The older conception of the walled
city as a shared common enterprise
has been weakened by the breaching
of its walls and its transformation
into an open economy.   Norton E. Long

CHAPTER 1

Shaping the American City: From Wood to Coal to Petroleum

Cities are built and unbuilt by the forces of law and
economics, supply and demand, cash flow and the
bottom line, far more than by ideals, intentions, talents
and visions of architects and planners.

Ada Louise Huxtable

A common history links municipalities as diverse as
the giant port city of Seattle, the landlocked hill city of Elkins, West
Virginia, sprawling Phoenix, and tiny Stockbridge, Massachusetts. Each
has been buffeted as the sources and uses of energy change. First the
small, compact, preindustrial cities, driven by animal and human power,
became — or were overtaken by — giant industrial cities, fueled by coal
and driven by the steam engine. The electric streetcar pushed out the
boundaries of these giant cities. Along its tracks the first suburbs
sprouted and fought for their autonomy against the annexationist efforts
of their urban parents.

Then the giant central cities gave way, becoming metropolitan
communities in which larger and larger portions of the population lived
outside the central city. The petroleum society raised the automobile to
preeminence and further encouraged urban sprawl; cities with extremely low densities sprang up on the fringes of metropolitan areas
and in previously rural locations. Within two generations, the nation

11

had to confront the equally difficult consequences of congestion in the coal-based industrial cities and sprawl in the petroleum-based suburban communities.

In the preindustrial cities of 1850, Americans consumed the equivalent of a ton of coal per person per year. That ton per person represented less than 10 percent of the total energy consumed; our major source of energy was animal power. Wind, water, wood, and human power provided the remainder.

These cities were small and compact, rarely measuring more than four miles across. Their industry consisted of small plants, which spread along the coasts and rapid-flowing rivers encouraged by the availability of wind and water power. Of the cities' inhabitants, the vast majority lived within walking distance of the city centers. Only the rich could afford to stable horses and maintain carriages. The pedestrian cities were possible because the home was the workplace. Even in the nation's largest city, New York, of all workers in 1840 only 23 percent worked outside the home.

But after the Civil War, these small, compact cities suddenly mushroomed, joining the roster of the largest urban areas in world history. The population "imploded" — people moved from the rural areas to the cities, and millions of immigrants landed in New York and stayed there. In 1790 two dozen cities each with more than twenty-five hundred residents contained 5 percent of the nation's five million people; in 1860 two dozen cities each with more than eight thousand people contained 12 percent of the 35 million Americans. By 1900, 20 cities with populations greater than fifty thousand contained 25 percent of the 70 million Americans. And three cities alone — New York, Philadelphia, and Chicago — were home to 6.5 million Americans, or 10 percent of the country. This phenomenal migration caused Horace Greeley, then editor of *The New York Tribune*, to comment, "We cannot all live in cities, yet nearly all seem determined to do so."

From Wood to Coal

What made this urban growth possible? Energy. The groundwork was laid in rapid steps. In 1858 the first natural-gas company was formed. The next year F. L. Drake drilled the first oil well at what was named, fittingly, Oil Creek, Pennsylvania. In 1863 John D. Rockefeller quietly entered the oil industry, and the first modern locomotive began operation. In 1864 the first Bessemer steel plant opened in Wyandotte, Michigan. In 1865 Samuel Van Syckle built the first oil pipeline. In 1873 Thomas Edison inaugurated the first central power plant, and in 1878 Wanamaker's store in Philadelphia became the first to be illuminated by electric lights. Per capita energy consumption doubled between 1850 and 1880, and doubled again by 1900. This was, in the words of historian Howard Mumford Jones, "the age of energy."[1]

By 1900 coal was supplying more than 70 percent of the nation's energy; the use of coal was more pervasive in our cities then than the use of petroleum is today. Coal heated homes and ran factories. Converted to gas, and later to electricity, it lighted parlors and streets. It fueled our transportation systems: the railroads between cities and the electric streetcars within the cities.

To overestimate the impact of the steam engine on our society would be difficult. When coal replaced water as a primary source of energy and was used to fuel the steam engine, factories were freed from their river banks and cast loose to settle wherever they could attract the most capital. As Ralph Woods poetically wrote, "The little mill using water power from some otherwise indistinguishable stream became freed of its economic bondage, entertained visions of grandeur and forthwith moved to one or another of the big cities and began to use steam power."[2] It was no coincidence, then, that the city assumed its dominant role in American life in the 1880s, the same period in which steam power surpassed water power, in number of units used and total power produced, and became our dominant energy source.

The steam engine was unveiled at the Centennial Exhibition in Philadelphia in 1876. One contemporary wrote: "As Zeus subsumed all lesser deities into himself, so the steam engine now absorbed all its primitive originals. . . ."[3]

The steam engine made large, concentrated production units not only technically feasible but economically attractive. Steam power became cheaper as the industrial unit decreased in size, encouraging businesses to expand their factories as much as possible. Lewis Mumford said, "With parts of the plant no more than a quarter of a mile from the power-center, every spinning machine or loom had to tap power

13

Changing Energy Sources: 1850–1980

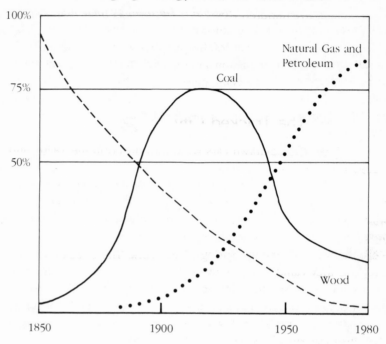

The shape of the American city was greatly influenced by its changing fuel base. When wood was supreme the cities were isolated villages. King Coal transformed them into giant industrial cities. Petroleum created the sprawling suburban cities.

---

from the belts and shafts worked by the central steam engine. The more units within a given area, the more efficient was the source of power: hence the tendency toward giantism in textile factories, which covered a large area and were usually five stories high."[4]

A single factory could employ two hundred fifty people. A dozen such factories provided the nucleus of a considerable town. Although in 1860 the country had fewer than a million and a half factory workers, by 1920 there were eight and a half million. The industrial city, or "coketown," as Lewis Mumford dubbed it, came to dominate America's landscape and culture.

By 1925 New York had six million people; Chicago, three million; and Milwaukee, five-hundred thousand. Yet even as their populations caused levels of congestion unknown in modern cities (lower Manhattan had a population density of five-hundred thousand people per square mile, about 800 people on a football field), the process of population deconcentration was taking place.

The Tracked City

Horse-drawn cars were introduced in the 1870s, and by 1890 more than twenty-eight thousand horsecars provided street railway service on 6,600 miles of track. The horsecar allowed people to live at least 4 miles from the center of a city along street railway lines, quadrupling the land area available for near-city settlement. Even more expansion followed Frank Sprague's establishment in 1888 of the first electric railway, in Saratoga Springs, New York. The streetcars — or trolleys, as they came to be known — were an immediate sensation. Fifty-one municipalities had electric streetcars by 1890; by 1895 electric trolleys operated in eight hundred fifty cities on more than 10,000 miles of track. By 1902 only 665 miles of street-railway track out of a total of 22,577 were not electrified.

The coal-powered electrification of city transportation systems greatly expanded the area available for cities' development. Because electric streetcars could travel at twice the speed of the old horsecars — up to 15 miles an hour — people could live as far as ten miles from the center of the city and still commute downtown to work.

The metropolis tended to expand along the streetcar and railroad lines that ran out of the city radially, giving the metropolis a star shape. But the same trend in development that allowed expansion also limited it; the tracks anchored population expansion to the rails. And where no track to the city existed, no suburb arose.

The historic practice of the poor living on the periphery of the cities while the rich congregated in the center now changed. A study of two thousand wealthy Detroit families found that in 1910 more than half were living within three miles of the central business district. Only one family in ten lived outside the city limits. By 1930, however, only 7 percent of the families remained within the six-mile circle, and half lived in the suburbs. "In just 20 years," a demographer comments, "the pattern of affluent neighborhoods in Detroit was turned inside out. Between 1910 and 1930 the population of community areas of Portage Park, Hermosa, Belmont-Cragin, Montclair, Garfield Ridge, Chicago Lawn and Gage Park leaped from 26,006 to 329,510."[5] One eminent historian wrote that the "wealthy and not-so-wealthy joined in fleeing from the noise and confusion of the waterfront, the dirt, the stench, and the intolerably crowded conditions of the old central city."[6]

Area Annexed by Central Cities, 1870–1940

Year	Area of Cities (square miles)	Increase in Area by Annexing (square miles)	Percent Increase
1870	985		
1890	1,432	447	45
1910	2,273	841	59
1930	3,088	815	36
1940	3,119	31	1

Source: Kenneth Fox, Better City Government
(Philadelphia: Temple University Press, 1977), p. 149.

While the population began to spread across the surrounding countryside, downtown businesses built toward the sky. In 1857 New York's Otis Elevator Company installed in a high-rise building the first passenger elevator, a hydraulic contraption that functioned effectively only to a height of 20 stories. With the introduction of the electric elevator in the 1880s, the elevator's lifting range increased considerably. By using iron and steel skeletons, one could build very tall structures with relatively thin metallic walls, unlike the thick masonry walls required for earlier buildings. The 60-story Woolworth Building became the prototype for future skyscrapers in 1913; by 1929 American cities had 337 skyscrapers of more than 20 stories. By 1975, 1,000 buildings had been built with more than 30 stories.

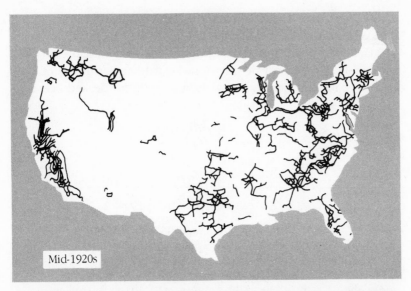

Mid-1920s

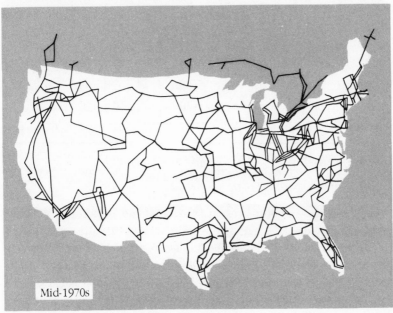

Mid-1970s

The growth of major electric interconnection on the
American continent between the 1920s and the mid-1970s.

Cities tried to maintain their tax bases, and their citizenry, by annexing large surrounding areas. New York City's territory expanded from 44 square miles in 1880 to 299 square miles in 1900. Chicago's territory increased by 500 percent between 1880 and 1900. For the 47 central cities of 44 metropolitan areas, annexation activities peaked between 1910 and 1930.

Sizes of Selected Cities, 1860–1970
(in square miles)

City	1860	1870	1880	1890	1900	1920	1930	1950	1970
Chicago	17	35	35	178	189	190	207	212	228
Cincinnati	7	7	25	25	39	50	72	75	78
Cleveland	9	12	27	28	32	46	71	81	81
Detroit	13	16	22	28	28	40	140	140	140
Los Angeles	29	29	29	29	43	101			
Minneapolis	5	8	12	53	53	53	54	54	54
New York City	22	22	22	44	299	299	299	299	299
Seattle	11	11	5	13	34	71			
Boston		13		39		39	44	46	46
Philadelphia		130		130		130	130	127	127
St. Louis		61		61		61	61	61	61

Source: Michael H. Ebner and Eugene M. Tobin, eds., *The Age of Urban Reform: New Perspectives on the Progressive Era* (Port Washington, New York: Kennikat Press, 1977), pp. 44 and 52.

This strategy temporarily kept the population dispersal from fragmenting political jurisdictions. Between 1900 and 1910 the central cities grew 50 percent faster than their suburban rings; between 1910 and 1920 the central cities still grew faster than suburban areas, although only slightly. After that, central cities lost ground. Suburban residents successfully fought annexation, and the older cities became surrounded by new, politically independent suburban communities. More and more of the nation's growth occurred not within the boundaries of the central cities but in the proliferating suburbs.

Petroleum Takes Over:
The Rise of the Suburbs

Although the proportion of the metropolitan citizenry that lived in the suburbs rose continuously, the population of the central industrial cities did not actually decline until after World War II. One reason their population did not decline sooner is that during the war the federal government pumped billions of dollars into the old manufacturing cities. Milwaukee, Minneapolis, New Orleans, Boston, Newark, New York, Chicago, Detroit, and St. Louis grew in population from 1940 through 1947, attaining peaks they may well never match again.

A different source of energy was then beginning to affect society, a form of energy that was as decentralizing in its impact as the steam engine and coal had been centralizing in the late nineteenth century.

In 1900 petroleum supplied less than 1 percent of the nation's energy; only eight thousand motor vehicles were registered. Three years after the 1911 introduction of the Model T, more than six hundred thousand cars were on the road. Nineteen fourteen was also the first year that annual gasoline consumption surpassed the demand for kerosene.

At first, motorists made their gasoline purchases in five-gallon tanks through pieces of chamois, and then in 1907 service stations opened in several cities — among them, Seattle, St. Louis, and Dallas. Ten years later fifteen thousand retail service stations had opened, and nine million cars were on the road. By 1930 there were 27 million cars, and a network of a hundred thirty-five thousand stations serviced every city and town in the nation.

Oregon became in 1919 the first state to impose a tax on gasoline, a one-cent tax for road construction and maintenance. In the 1920s, 75 percent of the federal government assistance to lower levels of government went for highway construction.

The automobile came first to the rural areas, where the need was greatest; the states with the greatest car ownership per capita in 1920 were South Dakota, Iowa, and Nebraska. The highly urban areas, such as Rhode Island and the District of Columbia, were below the national average. Starting in the 1920s the larger cities were pressed to build

19

exclusive automobile roads, called parkways. These roads, according to one urban historian, were the first limited-access roads, but they were not designed to handle rush-hour traffic.[7] That is, they were not meant to facilitate the suburbanite's access to the city. On the contrary, the parkways were built strictly for the recreation of the city dwellers. The urban motoring public could use these roads to take pleasant spins through their cities' open spaces and parks and on out into the countryside. Naturally, the roads were directed toward the nearest open country—the areas between the points of the tracked city's star pattern.

The first impact of automobile use was felt in the railroad suburbs. New housing subdivisions could be built far from the railroad stations. Lots became larger. The same historian said, "Whereas in 1900 no one dared to advertise a home that was not in easy walking distance, by the 1920s no one dared to offer a new home that did not have off-street parking and nearly always a garage."[8] One drove the car to the railroad depot. But there was still only limited auto commuting to the cities.

Ending the Tracked City: The Role of General Motors

The auto and petroleum were ready in the wings, but one more character was added before the curtain went up on the petroleum era. With electricity and mass-transit systems still the preeminent transportation systems in our cities in the 1930s, a newcomer appeared — the motor bus. One contemporary writer exclaimed, "Even in [its] crude form, the motor vehicle [is] a serious competitor of the city railway. Its flexibility, the fact that it could be on this street or on that as temporary traffic of the sidewalk in order to pick up passengers, instead of forcing them to stand in the middle of the street, all were large points in its favor."[9]

Most cities, although they recognized some advantages in using buses, liked railways for moving masses of people. City and state legislators encouraged urban transportation systems in which the bus supplemented, but did not supplant, the railway. With certain exceptions, the motor bus would not be used in the same streets as the streetcar.[10]

Policy makers failed to anticipate, however, the growing power of General Motors. Even at its birth, General Motors' founders thought of it less as a producer of automobiles than as an umbrella for remaking the country's transportation system. In 1908 Benjamin Briscoe joined with William C. Durant to organize not merely a corporation but an industry, "for the purpose of having one big concern of such dominating influence in the automobile industry, as for instance, the United States Steel Corporation exercises in the steel industry."[11]

Henry Ford's refusal to subordinate his own car company to General Motors led to initial failure for GM. But a revived GM in the 1920s recognized what Henry Ford did not — that the American automobile market was saturated, and that the future of sales lay not with new-car purchases but with replacement cars selected from among a wide variety of colors and models. By 1930 GM had gained dominance over Ford and was ready to bring the automobile into the city.

General Motors entered bus production in 1925 by acquiring Yellow Coach, which at that time was the nation's largest manufacturer of city and intercity buses. A year later GM assisted in the formation of the Greyhound Corporation (until 1948 GM was Greyhound's largest single shareholder) and soon became involved in the bus company's attempt to convert passenger rail operations to intercity bus service.

Greyhound's announcement of its intention to convert commuter rail operations to intercity bus services came in 1928. By 1939 six major railroads had agreed under pressure from Greyhound to replace substantial portions of their commuter rail services with Greyhound bus systems. By 1950, Greyhound carried roughly half as many intercity passengers as did all the nation's railroad companies combined.

General Motors also diversified into city bus and rail operations. At first its procedure consisted of directly acquiring and then scrapping local electric-transit systems in favor of GM buses. As GM general counsel Henry Hogan observed later, the corporation "decided that the only way this new market for buses could be created was for it to finance the conversion from streetcars to buses in some small cities."[12] In 1932 GM formed a holding company, United Cities Motor Transit, as a subsidiary of GM's bus division; its sole function was to acquire electric streetcar companies, convert them to GM motorbus operations and then resell the properties to local concerns that agreed to purchase GM bus replacements. The company's first targets were the electric streetcar lines of Kalamazoo and Saginaw, Michigan, and Springfield, Ohio. "In each case," Hogan stated, GM "successfully motorized the city, turned the management over to other interests and liquidated its investment."[13]

In 1936 another GM subsidiary, Omnibus Corporation, succeeded in converting New York City's immense electric railway system to GM buses. In the same year GM established National City Lines, Inc. And "during the following 14 years General Motors, together with Standard Oil of California, Firestone Tire, and two other suppliers of bus-related products, contributed more than $9 million to this holding company for the purpose of converting electric transit systems in 16 states to GM bus operations."[14] Little likelihood existed that the systems would return to electric vehicles even after they were resold by National City Lines, because GM extracted from the local transit companies contracts that prohibited their purchase of "any new equipment using any fuel or means of propulsion other than gas."[15] By 1949, more than 100 electric transit systems had been replaced with GM buses in 45 cities including New York, Philadelphia, Baltimore, St. Louis, Oakland, Salt Lake City, and Los Angeles.

In April of the same year, 1949, a Chicago federal jury convicted GM of having criminally conspired with Standard Oil of California, the Firestone Tire Company, and others to replace electric transportation with gas or diesel buses, and to monopolize the sale of buses and related products to local transportation companies throughout the country. Nonetheless,

> General Motors continued to acquire and dieselize electric transit properties through September of 1955. By then approximately 88 percent of the nation's electric streetcar network had been eliminated. In 1936, when GM organized National City Lines, 40,000 streetcars were operating in the United States; at the end of 1955 only 5,000 remained. In December of that year, GM bus chief Roger M. Keyes correctly observed, "The motor coach has supplanted the interurban systems and has for all practical purposes eliminated the trolley.[16]

Did transit passengers enjoy the switch to buses? One historian responds, "Frankly, we doubt it. Letter after letter to local editors objected to the change. Buses were decried for their fumes, their jerky starts and stops, their lack of room and even their slow speed."[17] But because buses inhibited the automobile less than did fixed streetcar tracks, the conversion made the lot of automobile drivers a great deal easier.

GM also played a vital role in replacing the railroads' steam and electric power with diesel locomotives. And later GM pushed for trucks and cars to replace the trains; while the corporation was reducing the preeminence of rail as a freight- and passenger-carrying transportation mode, it developed the most powerful economic and political coalition in history to encourage the use of the alternative — the highway. As a result, highway location began to determine the prosperity of cities the way location of railroad tracks had determined it at the turn of the century.

On June 28, 1932, Alfred P. Sloan, Jr., president of General Motors, organized the National Highway Users Conference to combine representatives from the nation's auto, oil, and tire industries in a common front against competing transportation interests. Sloan became the permanent chairman of the conference and served in that capacity until 1948, when he was succeeded by the new chairman of GM, Albert Bradley. The National Highway Users Conference brought together the Motor Vehicle Manufacturers Association, the American Petroleum Institute, the American Trucking Association, the Rubber Manufacturers Association, and the American Automobile Association.

At the state level, the conference used its twenty-eight hundred lobbying groups to persuade 44 of the nation's 50 legislatures to adopt and preserve measures that dedicated state and local gasoline-tax revenues to highway construction exclusively. From 1945 to 1970 states and localities spent more than $156 billion constructing hundreds of thousands of miles of roads. During the same period, only 16 miles of subway were constructed in the entire country.

On the federal level, the Highway Trust Fund and the Interstate Highway Act of 1956 duplicated the efforts at the state and local levels. The federal government spent approximately $70 billion for highways from 1956 through 1970 — and only $795 million, or 1 percent of that amount, for rail transit.

The roads became smoother and more numerous. Driving was simplified. In the 1950s the automatic transmission became com-

monplace, making the clutch pedal obsolete and persuading millions
more people to become auto drivers. For urban driving the technology
was particularly appropriate: "With an automatic transmission, driving
in stop-and-go traffic is far more relaxing and even the least experi-
enced and most scared learned they can start a car without making it
buck like a Texas bronco. No longer was complex foot coordination
required to drive a car, and many who previously had dreaded the
thought of urban driving were now quite willing to take the plunge."[18]

The nation's conversion to the petroleum era was now complete.
Three events took place in 1949 and 1950 that indicated the intimate
relationship between energy sources, technology, and demographics.
Petroleum surpassed coal as the nation's primary energy source. Don
Casto opened the first regional shopping center outside Columbus,
Ohio, beyond new suburban developments. And the U.S. Bureau of the
Census began identifying for the first time Standard Metropolitan Statis-
tical Areas (SMSAs).

Each SMSA had a central city or a twin central city, with a population
of at least fifty thousand, and included the surrounding county (or
counties) if the county residents were tied through business relationships to the core cities. Establishing the SMSAs was an official recognition of the suburbanization of America. Later, SMSAs would become
crucial in the distribution of federal funds.

Dedensifying America:
The Rise of Urban Sprawl

An extensive highway system, cheap gasoline, and reli-
able, relatively inexpensive automobiles made possible the dispersion
of the population. But they did not make it inevitable — that required
an active federal policy. As early as 1931 Governor Franklin Roosevelt of
New York concluded, "Farsighted men and women are at last aware of
the fact that our population is overbalanced — too many people in very
large cities, too few in the smaller communities."[19] After he was elected
president, FDR repeated the theme: "We have got to restore the balance
of population, get them out of the big centers of population."[20] The
Resettlement Administration was put in charge of creating garden cities

that would surround the central cities and form metropolitan areas where cities and the countryside would blend.

After World War II President Truman established the Federal Housing Administration, which pioneered the development of low-down-payment, long-term mortgages repayable in fixed monthly payments. In many cases, veterans needed no down payment at all. The single-family detached house as part of a suburban subdivision became synonymous with the good life; the vast majority of FHA homes have been built outside central cities. In fact, federal financing largely has been unavailable for inner-city residential construction. Indeed the government initiated an urban renewal program in the 1960s that devastated large parts of the central cores of larger cities, destroying far more housing units than it built.

Another trend affecting the growth of cities was that federal expenditures began to favor the South and the West. Southern members of Congress controlled key committees overseeing military spending, and they heavily influenced the placement of military bases and defense outlays. Neil Peirce writes, "It is almost entirely because of defense outlays, in fact, that the Frost Belt states between 1975 and 1979 sent Washington $165 billion more in taxes than they received back in overall federal spending, while 32 Sun Belt and western states had a $112 billion surplus in their 'balance of payment' with the federal government." The New York City regional planning association estimated that in 1975 its environs sent Washington $6 billion more than the area received in federal monies.

Highway expenditures, too, were geared to the western states. The interstate highway fund invested in the sparsely populated West: Montana received $2.44 worth of highway investment for each dollar it put into the fund between 1957 and 1972; Nevada received $1.98 and Wyoming $2.71 for each dollar invested. But Massachusetts and Michigan received only 77 cents, and New Jersey only 66 cents. Moreover, the highway trust fund overwhelmingly spent money to construct new roads rather than to maintain existing roads, discriminating against the northeastern and midwestern states, which had built their transportation systems decades before.

The results of federal policies and the new petroleum-based transportation systems became obvious in the 1950s and 1960s: from 1950 to

1960 about a third of the older central cities declined in population; between 1960 and 1970, more than half declined; and, between 1970 and 1980, more than 80 percent declined. In 1950 nearly 60 percent of all people residing in metropolitan areas lived in the central cities. By 1970 only a little more than 40 percent lived in the central cities, and in the 1970s the percentage continued to decline.

In the process, the large central city began to lose its influence over state politics. New York City, which in 1950 contained 55 percent of the state of New York's population, retained only 40 percent in 1980. Chicago's portion of Illinois's total population declined from 40 to 25 percent in the same time span, and Baltimore's proportion of Maryland's population plummeted from 40 percent to 15 percent, Detroit's from 29 percent to 18 percent, and Denver's from 33 percent to 18 percent. Less influence was given up by cities in the West, where they were being shaped in a new matrix; Los Angeles, for example, had the same population as Brooklyn in 1970, but had seven times Brooklyn's area. Houston, with the same population as Philadelphia in 1970, occupied a land area three times larger. And in the same year Detroit's million people lived on 138 square miles while Phoenix's million inhabitants lived on 247 square miles.

The fastest-growing municipalities now, however, were the smaller and medium-sized cities. The number of cities with populations greater than two hundred fifty thousand remained constant between 1960 and 1977, but in that period the number of cities with populations between twenty-five thousand and a hundred thousand increased by 50 percent. By 1980 more than 70 percent of all urban dwellers lived in cities with fewer than two hundred fifty thousand people.

The very concept of urbanization had changed. In the 1970s, for the first time, the areas outside the SMSAs were the fastest growing component. The migration of greater population to the suburbs developed over decades, but the flow into the small cities instead of out of them was amazingly quick: demographer William Alonso concluded, "For the past 200 years people have been leaving the small cities and for the past six years or so, that process has been reversed."[21] Now small cities were growing, as a whole, far faster than the metropolitan areas. Their densities were very low, often less than one person per acre. America was spreading over the countryside, living in urban areas that, in any other

Population and Number of Cities by Size—1900–1977

Population Size	Number of Cities					Population (millions)					Percent of Total Urban Population				
	1900	1920	1940	1960	1977	1900	1920	1940	1960	1977	1900	1920	1940	1960	1977
1,000,000 or more	3	3	5	5	6	6.4	10.1	15.9	17.5	17.7	27	23	25	18	15.8
500,000—1,000,000	3	9	9	16	20	1.6	6.2	6.4	11.1	11.2	7	14	10	11	10
250,000—500,000	9	13	23	30	33	2.9	4.5	7.8	10.8	11.5	12	10	12	11	10.3
100,000—250,000	23	43	55	81	104	3.3	6.5	7.3	11.6	16.1	14	15	12	12	14.4
50,000—100,000	40	76	107	201	249	2.7	5.3	7.3	13.8	17.4	11	12	12	14	15.6
25,000—50,000	82	143	213	432	536	2.8	5.1	7.4	14.9	18.6	12	11	12	15	16.6
10,000—25,000	280	465	665	1134	1385	4.3	7.0	10.0	14.6	19.3	18	16	16	18	17.3
TOTAL	440	752	1077	1899	2301	24	44.8	62.7	97.4	111.8					

The largest cities have a decreasing share of the urban population while the fastest growing cities have populations between 25,000 and 100,000.

Sources: Statistical Abstract of the United States, 1979;
Historical Statistics of the United States—Colonial Times to 1970.

27

nation in the world, would be designated rural. America had become victim of sprawl.

Congressional hearings held in 1980 on the future of the American city described the new American city of the eighties:

> Small towns sprawl, suburbs sprawl, big cities sprawl, and metropolitan areas stretch into giant megalopolises — formless webs of urban development like Swiss cheese with more holes than cheese. Gertrude Stein described one spread-out city by saying, "There's no there there." The lack of thereness has become pervasive in American communities.[22]

Richard Noyes, editor of *The Salem Observer*, dramatized what sprawl means in everyday terms to the 7,566 employed residents of Salem, New Hampshire. Fewer than a third of the residents worked in town. Almost a quarter drove more than 15 miles each way to work, most of them into the Boston area 30 miles away. Even when jobs were available in Salem, the commuting continued. When Digital Equipment Corporation built a large plant in Salem, the majority of the two thousand workers did not live in Salem. "They're driving here from Fitchburg, Mass., their headlights early in the morning blinding Salem residents headed the other way."[23]

Some observers, after analyzing the role of the automobile in the modern American city, concluded that the entire transportation system had begun to feed on itself. Our cities are now designed to separate work from play, shopping from homes, and people from people. Trips have begun to beget trips. In the mid-1970s recreational trips had decreased in number sharply from the previous 20 years' count. The purposeful trip, one that moves goods or people from one place to another, had increased fast, but the largest increase was in the category of "transport generated trips": travel in search of a parking space, to the service station for fuel, to the garage for repairs, or to pick up or drop off someone. In the 1980s, trips of this type may exceed business trips.

Even before the energy crisis, some urban observers worried about the social implications of this transportation dynamic. In 1971 somewhat more than a fifth of all families living in metropolitan areas owned no car, and in the central cities nearly a third of the households were carless. What would be the fate of these people as the automobile increasingly became not a convenience but a necessity?

The changing fuel sources underlying our economy and the technologies used to harness them have changed the shape of our urban areas. However, the symbol of America's love affair with the automobile and petroleum, the drive-in, must share this place of honor with the symbol of another technology: the all-electric home. Just as the massive use of automobiles has obliterated political boundaries, the evolving technology of electric generation has submerged the political authority of the city under the scale of the power plants.

CHAPTER **2**

Facing the Grid: From Neighborhood Power Plants to Continental Grid Systems

Scarcely anything of the world before electrification
has remained untouched: how things work, how and
where work gets done, how people are transported, how
food is cooked and served, how people keep in touch,
the kinds of paintings they hang on their walls,
what they see in the manmade world around them.
The very smell of cities has been altered.

"Creating the Electric Age," *EPRI Journal,* March 1979

Gas generated from coal entered the marketplace at
the turn of the nineteenth century. It became the mainstay of a new
lighting system that was cheaper and of higher quality than any of the
previous devices. The embryonic gas utilities tackled the problems of
marketing and distribution, thereby paving the way for the later electric
utilities. The marketing of the revolutionary fuel was not, however, as
easy as one might think. The gas companies had to create a market for
artificial illumination in the face of strong opposition. Some critics worried that extensive artificial lighting would be worldly interference with

the original divine plan that there be night; some were concerned that such lighting would extend the drinking hours and so encourage public drunkenness; and still others worried that the fumes given off by illuminating gas could be harmful to the health.

Gas companies also had to learn how to lay pipelines and how to pump their product over long distances. They developed meters to monitor the consumption of each customer. And they did their job well. By the middle of the nineteenth century, gas lighting for streets had become a virtual necessity, and the industry was raised to the status of a public utility — cities began to grant companies the right to install their pipes and lamps on or under public land. Baltimore awarded the first municipal franchise in 1816, followed by Boston in 1822. By 1845, New Orleans, Pittsburgh, Louisville, Cincinnati, Albany, and Philadelphia had publicly or privately owned gas utilities.

At that time, electricity was still a curiosity. It was in its infancy, the object of intense experimentation by inventors around the world. Ever since Volta developed the first electric battery in 1800, enterprising individuals in backyards and basements and small shops had tried to devise practical ways to use electricity. The first successful application came in 1810, when the arc light was developed. The device forced an electric voltage to leap across a gap between two wire tips, producing a brilliant arc of light five inches long. By the 1860s we had learned to use steam to generate the electricity for arc lighting, and electric light experiments were being conducted in Europe and in the United States. By 1878 a half-mile length of Avenue de l'Opera in Paris was brilliant with arc lights.

But the arc light had several key drawbacks. The tips burned away in less than a night, and the brilliant, glaring light was suitable only for illumination of streets or such very large indoor spaces as theaters and factories. The major limitation of arc-lighting systems, however, lay not in the way light was generated but in the way electricity was distributed. The lights were linked in series. Every part of the circuit had to work for any other part to work; if one bulb burned out, the whole system went dark. Thomas Edison's chief advantage in the marketplace was that he immediately focused on this basic weakness. Edison, fresh from his triumphant innovations with the telegraph and the phonograph, was a pragmatic inventor. His objective was entrepreneurial — to develop technologies that could broaden the market for electricity. And, particularly, he was looking beyond street lighting to the sale of electricity to individual homes. "I saw that what had been done had never been made practically useful. The intense light had not been subdivided so that it could be brought into private homes."[1] After two nights of experimentation, Edison hit on a solution. He designed a circuit "in parallel" that allowed a system's light to continue if one bulb burned out. Having resolved that problem, he turned his attention to the converter of electricity to light — the light bulb. He developed a carbon incandescent light bulb, with a very fine filament of carbon inside an evacuated bulb. The high resistance in the wire generated heat and light when a relatively low current was passed through it. The filament lasted much longer than the tips of the arc lamp.

Edison unveiled his first central electric station in 1882, only four years after his search for a better light bulb began. And electric power captured the fancy of America. Initially there were no electric utilities; electric companies sold complete power systems rather than electricity. Edison owned patents on every aspect of the system, from bulbs and generators to switches and relays. Department stores, local governments, and industries were the first customers. By 1890 a thousand central electric stations were in operation.

The best customer, and the largest generator and consumer of electricity in the first two decades of electric power, was the newly emerging electric streetcar industry. The first streetcar company was established in 1888. By 1890, 51 municipalities had electric streetcars; by 1895, electric trolleys operated in 850 cities on more than 10,000 miles of track.[2]

Streetcar systems were well suited for Edison's dispersed power plants, because the streetcars used electricity in the form of direct current, that is, current that moved in only one direction. The disadvantage of direct current is that the constraint on its voltage limits the area a power plant can serve. (Voltage is a measure of the pressure behind the electric current. One can liken it to the power of the pump in a water system; the lower the voltage, the shorter the distance an amount of current will travel.) The direct current's voltage when it leaves the central generating station is the same voltage at which it enters the customer's premises. Since the voltage usable in residential households is low, with direct current, the central power plant's voltage had to be low. The maximum distance that Edison's first plants could economically transmit electricity was about two miles.

The localist nature of these first utilities can be demonstrated by some contracts power producers had with local governments in the 1880s:

Washington, D.C. — 87 public lamps burning all night every night. Cost, 65 cents per night. Yearly contract.

Wichita, Kansas — 75 lights at street intersections, burning until midnight. Cost, $100 per year.

Chattanooga, Tennessee — 30 lights burning all night. Cost, 33 cents per night. Two year contract.

Sacramento, California — 36 lights at intersections, burning all night except moonlit nights. Cost, $252 per light per year. Two year contract.[3]

By the time electric utilities came into being, the nation had accepted that utilities, like water and transportation, should be regulated by cities. The localist nature of the technology appeared to encourage competition. For example, the Denver Common Council in 1880 granted a city electricity franchise "to all comers" with the sole restriction that "said companies do not obstruct the public thoroughfares."[4] New York City awarded six franchises on a single day in 1887.[5] Chicago had more than 29 electric companies operating in the late nineteenth century.[6] The courts consistently upheld the principle of competition, ruling that, in the absence of statutory authorization, municipal corporations could not grant exclusive franchises for the ownership and operation of public utilities.

In the early 1880s Nikola Tesla, working for George Westinghouse, developed electric generators that produced alternating current. The electric current moved in two opposing directions, and the back-and-forth movement permitted the development of transformers, devices that use the principle of alternating current to raise (step up) or lower (step down) the voltage. Thus power plants were enabled to generate electricity and transmit it at high voltages and then step down the voltage at the customer's premises.

33

Because the electricity could be transmitted longer distances, alternating current allowed power plants to serve larger areas. And this immediately raised the possibility of installing turbines at remote dams and using the power of falling water to generate electricity. In fact, Westinghouse's first major demonstration of alternating current was at Niagara Falls.

The development of parallel circuits and alternating current set the stage for the rapid development of electric utilities that serve large numbers of customers over wide areas; the invention of the steam turbine is what made large power plants possible. The first steam turbine, a 2,000 kilowatt (kW) plant, was installed by the Hartford Electric Company in 1901. In 1903 the Chicago Electric Company installed a 5,000 kW power plant. Eighteen months later the largest power plant generated 10,000 kW. After ten years, the largest plant generated 35,000 kilowatts, and in the mid-1920s the largest plant could generate 175,000 kW, enough to meet the needs of a mid-sized city.

Samuel Insull was a driving force behind the development of ever-larger generators. He also fathered the movement to grant monopoly status to electric utilities. He was a one-man promotional campaign, giving speeches to business organizations and civic groups about the benefits of monopoly franchises. Sixty percent of the nation's electricity was generated on-site, that is, where it was used, in 1900. Insull, the president of Chicago Electric Company, persuaded those who already owned their power plants to abandon them and tie into a central grid system. Insull argued that larger steam turbines were more efficient. And his favorite selling point concerned the "diversity factor" of electric demand. Quite simply, he argued, people tend to use electricity at differing times; therefore, the relationship between increased capacity required and the increase in the number of people who require that capacity will not be direct.

Insull's favorite example concerned a block of northside Chicago homes:

There were 193 apartments on that block, and 189 of them were customers of the Chicago Edison Company. There were no appliances, motors, or other electrical devices to speak of in that block of dingy apartments — just electric lamps. The power demanded by all separate apartments on the block, if totalled, was 68.5 kilowatts.

But ... the different lamps would be lighted at different times, and the actual maximum demand for power from that block of apartments was only 20 kilowatts.
To supply all of these customers from a single source would therefore require generating power of 20 kilowatts. But if each household were to be equipped with a separate generating plant to meet its own needs, an aggregate of 68.5 kilowatts would be needed — more than three times as much.[7]

Insull backed up his rhetoric with a pricing structure geared to attract large customers. In 1915 Chicago's residential customers paid 15 cents

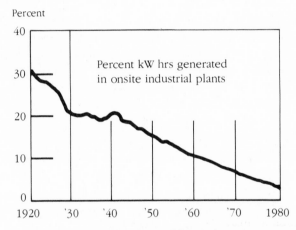

Source: Edwin Vennard "A Study and Forecast
of the Electric Power Business,"
*Report for the Charles T. Main
Engineering Co.,* November 1, 1973.

While most electricity generated in the United States originates in large, centralized facilities owned and operated by electric utilities, the number of onsite generating plants has declined steadily and the average size of utility generating plants has steadily increased. The above figure shows, for example, that onsite generating equipment represented nearly 30 percent of all U.S. generating capacity in 1920 but only 4.2 percent in 1973.

35

per kilowatt hour, while off-peak industrial customers paid only a penny.

Some electric streetcar companies, sensing the potential market for power, transformed themselves into electric utilities. And in 1920, for the first time, the gross revenues of central electric light and power stations exceeded the revenues of the electric railways. On May 1, 1926, *The Commercial and Financial Chronicle* changed the name of its monthly "Electric Railways Section" to "Public Utility Compendium." It justified the change in that issue:

> The development has grown out of the wonderful extension in the use of electricity which is the distinctive feature of recent tihes. Many small undertakings began by furnishing electricity for the running of the local trolley lines and then in order to promote economy of operations and be able to furnish electrical energy at a reduced cost entered the light and power business. The latter grew so fast that the electric railway has now become subordinate to the larger field of work. The next step was to unite the local units so that they might serve larger areas and out of these undertakings have grown in turn the big combinations which, by reason of their splendid achievements in electrical development and in serving the advanced needs of man, are exciting the wonder and the admiration of the world.

By 1920 only one out of five kilowatt hours of electricity was generated on-site. From 1919 to 1927, fifty-two thousand steam engines were scrapped; eighteen thousand internal combustion engines were discarded; and five thousand water wheels were left to rot. To plug into the utility monopoly had become cheaper than to produce your own power.

Public or Private Monopolies?

The nation accepted the monopoly status of the electric utility: the new, large steam turbines and the use of alternating current allowed utilities to serve entire cities, and to duplicate distribution lines was inefficient. But the question remained, who would own and control the electric monopoly? The National Civic Federation, established in the 1890s, undertook a two-year study of municipal owner-ship, and its committee, composed equally of businessmen, organized labor leaders, and politicians, concluded that the issue should be left to each community. "The Committee takes no position on the question of the general expediency of either private or public ownership. The ques-tion must be solved by each municipality in the light of local condi-tions."[8]

Smaller cities typically had no choice. They had fewer potential customers, more widely spaced. As a result, theirs was not a profitable market for investors. According to O. C. Merrill, secretary of the Federal Power Commission, "Municipal development has been resorted to primarily to secure domestic service in communities not reached by the distributing lines of existing private central stations or not having a demand for energy sufficient to justify from a commercial standpoint the construction of a station for such purpose by private capital."[9]

The courts did generally uphold the right of cities to own and operate electric utilities. One Pennsylvania court reasoned that the power of the legislature to authorize municipal corporations to supply gas and water for municipal purposes and for its inhabitants, a power that had "never seriously been questioned" could serve as a precedent for the new age of electricity.

> In view of the fact that electricity is so rapidly coming into gen-eral use for illuminating streets, public and private buildings, dwellings, etc., why should there be any doubt as to the power to authorize such corporations to manufacture and supply it in like manner as artificial gas has been manufactured and supplied? It is a mistake to assume that municipal corporations should not keep abreast with the progress and improvements of the age.[10]

The small cities led the turn-of-the-century move toward munici-pally owned power plants. In 1896 there were four hundred munici-pally owned electric plants in the United States; a decade later there were more than twelve-hundred fifty. More than 80 percent of these were in cities with fewer than five thousand people. Between 1902 and 1907, the rate of increase of municipally owned plants was more than twice as fast as that of privately owned plants.

Small cities were able to finance such systems because of the low cost of money and the extremely favorable market for municipal bonds that followed the demise of the free silver movement. But in the early summer of 1907 the market sagged, and, at the end of June, when New York City failed to sell a 4 percent bond issue, the bond market collapsed. The receivership of one of the major streetcar companies in New York and the financial debacle of October of that year combined to make the market for municipal bonds all but disappear. The market for high-grade municipals did revive after about a year, but the popularity of cities' bond issues went into eclipse. Small and midsized cities then found raising money for major projects difficult. And not until the mid-1920s did small city bonds regain the confidence of investors.

In the larger cities, private ownership of utilities was the dominant organizational form, although in many areas private- and public-power advocates were struggling acrimoniously. In the early twentieth century, Los Angeles, Seattle, and Cleveland were among the large cities that took direct public control of the generation and distribution of power.

Everyone agreed that if private, investor-owned companies were to be given control over a commodity like electricity, which is so essential to the life of the modern community, the public interest would have to be represented in the regulation of the monopoly. Initially, the city, through its city council, set rates and regulated the electric utility, as it regulated the gas utility and transportation utility. But as the utility industries grew more complex, the expertise of city councils to oversee the industries was diminished. The political process of oversight often culminated in political corruption and drawn-out court cases. So a movement arose to have independent state agencies regulate the utilities.

But this was also the time when the municipal home-rule movement, a coalition of urban residents striving for greater political autonomy from their state legislatures, was powerful. And many of its advocates saw the removal of utility regulation from cities to non-elected, remote state agencies as an undemocratic step. Those who supported regulation by the cities — such as Stiles P. Jones, a utility expert with the National Municipal League — considered democratic government, not scientific regulation, to be the goal. Jones cared less about the effect that creating state commissions would have on administrative efficiency than about "its effect on the development of the power of self-government in the people":

> Efficiency gained at the expense of citizenship is a dear purchase. Efficiency is a fine thing but successful self-government is better. Democratic government in a free city by an intelligent and disinterested citizenship is the greater ideal to work to, and democracy plus efficiency is not unattainable.[11]

Indeed, some of the most ardent supporters of municipal regulation, such as Delos Wilcox, were also the most vocal in their demand that active citizenship requires time and homework. For Wilcox, "Municipal franchises are the concrete, definite points of contact between the large public and large private interests. While franchise ordinances and contracts are generally technical, and often elaborate and hard to understand, yet the interest of the people in the terms and conditions of franchises is immediate and supreme."[12] He published a massive two volume study, *Municipal Franchises*, in 1910 and 1911 to give citizens the concepts to govern utilities. This exhaustive survey of existing franchises throughout the country was written so that any intelligent layman could understand it. Wilcox urged municipal officials "to kindle a fire under every sleepy citizen till even the street gamins, the club women, and the great merchants on Broadway know what a franchise signifies."[13]

Some home-rule advocates feared that state regulatory commissions might hamper the ability of urban residents to become utility owners. A city that wanted to buy out an existing, privately owned utility would have to pay a fair price for it. And that price was directly tied to the regulatory procedures of state commissions. Many state commissions felt their primary objective was to provide stable electric service and the best way to do this was to allow investors high profits. Often the utilities were greatly overcapitalized.

> Furthermore, in arriving at property valuations, commissions tended to employ the "reproductive value" theory to set the limit, in addition to allowing generous amounts for "going value" and even for "unusual engineering skill" and "foresight." As a result, if a city wished to purchase a plant it would almost certainly need to increase rates in order to absorb these addi-

tional burdens. The almost sure imposition of increased rates, of course, would eliminate most of the political driving power behind the municipal ownership, since most state laws prohibited cities from establishing their own competing plants.[14]

The technology of electric power plants, too, argued in favor of state regulation. Electric power generation had simply grown too large to be regulated by cities. As early as 1902, electric power was being transmitted 200 miles in the San Francisco area. By 1920, regional interconnections began to occur. Even Delos Wilcox, who best represented those advocating municipal regulation, conceded that "Public utilities, although still comparatively simple industries, have grown far enough beyond merely local bounds to require complex governmental machinery to operate or regulate them."[15]

A majority of states had established regulatory commissions by the 1930s. In some cases, municipally owned utilities, too, came under state commission authority. Municipally owned utilities are subject to the general jurisdiction of public utility commissions in nine states (Maine, Maryland, Nebraska, New York, Oregon, Rhode Island, Vermont, West Virginia, and Wisconsin). In others, such as Colorado, Kansas, Mississippi, Pennsylvania, South Carolina, and Wyoming, the state has jurisdiction over municipalities for which service areas extend beyond city borders. In Illinois, city governments may regulate the local operation of public utilities if the electorate so chooses by referendum. In Kansas, local governments have been authorized to regulate public utilities that operate in single municipalities. In New Mexico and South Carolina, local governments are authorized to establish the rates charged within their borders; upon complaint, any action is subject to review by the state regulatory commission. The regulatory procedures in all states have encouraged the construction of larger power plants and the growth of the electrical industry in general. The states guaranteed the utility investors fair returns on their investments. Power companies were permitted to charge rates sufficient to pay for the physical plants they built regardless of the prudence of the construction; this encouraged companies to build plants larger than needed to serve existing demand. Existing customers paid for the plants even if they were only partially used. And with the surplus capacity, the utility would solicit new customers — larger customers were offered very low rates. Sheldon Novick, author of a major examination of the electric power industry, describes the results of the regulatory process:

> The state would allow a fair return on investment, no matter how large; a company being a monopoly, could charge whatever the state would permit. The more expensive a company's plants, therefore, the more it could charge. Expensive generating plants would expand the profits allowed to a company in absolute terms, ... the company would make more money, but it would not necessarily grow more efficient.[16]

And grow they did. The demand for electricity doubled each decade. The technology underlying the industry continued to evolve, undermining the ability of states to control utilities in the same manner new technologies had once undermined the authority of the municipalities. By 1935, 20 percent of the nation's electrical energy crossed state lines. (By 1925, 17 percent of the nation's natural gas, as well, was in interstate markets.)

The growth in the scale of power plants and in the capability to transmit electricity over long distances was accompanied by a growth in the scale of the organizations owning and operating these systems. Samuel Insull's holding company, Middle West Utilities Company, provided utility services through its operating subsidiaries to more than 5,300 communities in 32 states, mostly in nonmetropolitan areas. In 1932 Samuel Insull was president of 11 power companies, chairman of 65, and director of 85. The actual extent of his control was never absolutely clear, but it seemed to some observers that at the time of the Depression he and J. P. Morgan controlled almost all of the nation's electric power businesses. Senator George Norris, the father of the Tennessee Valley Authority, proclaimed in 1925, "I have been dumbfounded and amazed, and the country will be dumbfounded and amazed when it learns that practically everything in the electric world ... is controlled either directly or indirectly by some part of this gigantic trust."[17]

The federal government reacted to the multistate nature of the utility companies by giving the Federal Power Commission jurisdiction over the interstate transactions of electric utilities, in 1935, and of gas utilities, in 1938. The Public Utility Holding Company Act of 1935 broke up the concentration in the electric utility industry, although, as we shall see, the growth of regional power pools undermined the effectiveness of the act.

The Transmission Age

During the 1950s and 1960s, the process that had begun in the 1920s — the gradual evolution of relatively small, isolated electrical systems into larger and larger interconnected ones — blossomed into nearly continent-wide power pools.

At first, power pools were regional. In 1927 Public Service Electric and Gas Company of New Jersey and the Philadelphia Electric Company established the first power pool. By 1960 there were four power pools, representing 12 percent of the nation's capacity. By 1970 there were 17, representing 50 percent of the nation's capacity. By the late 1960s one utility expert could write, "The United States is already close to being a two-network country, and the process of interconnections across the Rockies to link the two networks has already begun."[18]

A story is told of an Ohio utility that suffered a service interruption during the 1960s. It was connected to a regional power pool. The electrical impulses set up by the failure were felt at progressively greater distances, as each installation down the line had no available power. The first plant to respond to the need was a hydroelectric plant idling in Arkansas: when the demand reached it, the plant began operation automatically. Its gates opened and a large volume of water was released below the plant. At that moment, a man was fishing in a boat too close to the plant — when the sudden rush of water capsized his boat, and he drowned. The story is often cited as evidence of how closely knit the operations of the utility industry have become — a power outage in Ohio can cause a drowning in Arkansas.

The rise of high-voltage transmission systems and interconnected power pools increased the systems' complexity to an unprecedented level. Scientists and engineers began to encounter strange resonances throughout the system, behavior and responses that could not be explained by theory then available. An entirely new science was needed to understand the new electric synergy. The utilities assessed themselves and financed a new research and development organization, the Electric Power Research Institute (EPRI), to investigate the problem. An EPRI publication explains, "The fact is that the electrical systems and the

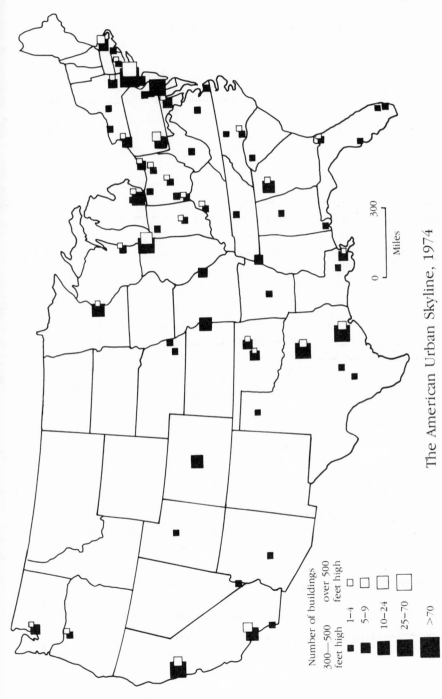

The American Urban Skyline, 1974

Number of buildings

over 500
feet high

300—500
feet high

1–4

5–9

10–24

25–70

>70

Source: Reprinted by permission of the *Journal of Geography*. National Council for Geographic Education.

human systems have become so closely intertwined and so inseparable that they cannot be easily isolated and studied separately. Thus the new science of cybernetics, which deals specifically with man-machine systems . . . began to emerge in the postwar era."[19]

The complexity of the system continued to plague its originators, however. In 1965 a cascading power failure originating in a relay that malfunctioned in Canada interrupted the electrical supply of most of the northeastern United States. Thirty million people lost electric power for as much as 13½ hours. A total of 23 percent of the 1965 U.S. peak electrical demand was unfilled. A decade later, on July 13, 1977, three days after the Chairman of Consolidated Edison Company of New York said he could "guarantee" that a recurrence was remote, nearly nine million people were blacked out, this time for as much as 25 hours. The Assistant Director for Systems Management and Structuring of the United States Department of Energy observed, in 1976,

> It is becoming apparent that the increasing complexities of the nation's electric energy system are rapidly outstripping its capabilities. One interconnected electric energy system seems to be evolving into a new condition wherein "more" is turning out to be "different." As they become more tightly interconnected over larger regions, systems problems are emerging which neither are presaged, predicted or addressed by classical electrical engineering. . . . There does not exist any comprehensive applicable body of theory which can provide guidance to engineers responsible for the design of systems as complex as those which will be required beyond the next generation. . . .[20]

Amory and Hunter Lovins, after an exhaustive analysis of the weaknesses in the electrical transmission systems, concluded, "We may well find, as power systems evolve in the present direction, that they have passed unexpectedly far beyond our ability to foresee and forestall their failures."[21]

Bigness Breeds Dependence

Power plants grew larger, encouraged by the rate-making procedures and the apparent technical economies of scale. The largest steam power plant installed in 1952 was 125 megawatts (Mw);

44

the largest steam power plant installed in 1967 was 1,000 Mw. On the average, unit size increased by more than 700 percent from 1947 to 1967 — from 38 Mw to 267 Mw. There were somewhat more than four thousand power plants in the country in 1977, and fewer than 300 of them, or 7 percent, generated more than half the nation's power. Nuclear power promised even bigger plants. William R. Hughes wrote,

> Most experts believe plant economies of scale in nuclear power are greater than in conventional steam power because of very marked scale economies in the reactor and heat exchange stages. . . . [Yet] the elasticity with respect to unit size for the few engineering functions thus far observed for nuclear units is about 0.7 for all unit sizes up to more than 3,000,000 kilowatts.[22]

As the plants grew bigger, they also grew more expensive, especially when interest rates began to rise after 1965. The high cost made attrac-

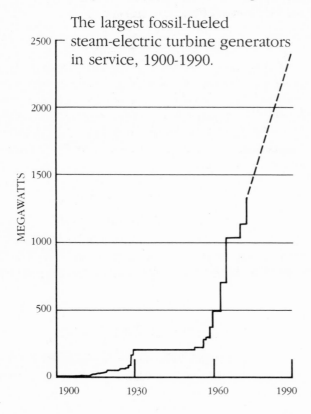

The largest fossil-fueled steam-electric turbine generators in service, 1900-1990.

tive the common ownership of an installation by two or more utilities. The city then had two options. "Centralized power," one study concluded, "makes local communities dependent on large electric utilities or impels them … to purchase a modest share of a larger power plant."[23] Cities that owned their electric systems began to relinquish their power plants, much as industries and transportation utilities had, earlier. In 1935 almost half the municipally owned electric utilities generated all of their own power. In 1975 only one in ten did so. In 1978 the United States electric utility industry nominally consisted of thirty-five hundred systems, but twenty-four hundred of them were involved solely in transmission and distribution of power. Municipalities, public-utility districts, and state power authorities accounted for less than 10 percent of the electricity generated nationally.

Cities dependent on the cooperation of private utilities found such relationships difficult. Private utilities divided up the country. In one case several Ohio cities argued that Ohio Edison (their wholesale supplier) had territorial agreements with neighboring large, private electric utilities making it unlikely that cities could find any source other than Ohio Edison for bulk power, even if they could have arranged its conveyance over Ohio Edison's lines. The Fifth Circuit Court of Appeals found that Florida Power Corporation and Florida Power and Light were part of a conspiracy to divide the state's market.

Private utilities often refused to wheel (transmit) electricity from lower-cost suppliers to cities — especially from federally owned hydroelectric plants. The borough of Grove City, Pennsylvania, contended that the Pennsylvania Power Company refused to sell it wholesale power unless the borough entered into a contract agreeing not to resell the power to industrial and commercial customers. Twelve Michigan cities charged Consumers Power Company with refusal to offer interchange service and power-supply coordination and transmission services. The city of Breese, Illinois, and six other Illinois cities charged that the Illinois Power Company refused to provide steady wholesale power except on restrictive terms and conditions. The cities maintained that, under those conditions and terms, either the cities' generating facilities would be virtually useless or, as a practical matter, the cities would have to purchase all their electricity from Illinois Power.

The United States Supreme Court decided narrowly in favor of four small cities in Minnesota, South Dakota, and North Dakota, in 1972, in their suit against the investor-owned Otter Tail Power Company. These towns had established a municipal distribution system for electricity when the retail franchise of Otter Tail Power expired. Otter Tail had then refused to sell energy at wholesale prices to the new system and also refused to permit use of its wires for delivery of low-cost electricity from a federal reclamation project.

In that case, the Federal Power Commission had decreed that utilities are not required to wheel electricity from another supplier to a customer. The Supreme Court overruled the FPC, however. The court indicated that, since Otter Tail had monopoly control over the distribution system, it had "substantial effective control over potential competition from municipal ownership. By its refusal to sell or wheel power, defendant prevents that competition from surfacing." However, the decision was a close one — four justices to three. The nation still had not decided the responsibilities of electric utility monopolies to those who do not buy electricity directly from the companies. One dissenter in the Otter Tail case was the Chief Justice. He saw no reason that Otter Tail should be forced to sell someone else's electricity. "As a retailer of power Otter Tail asserted a legitimate business interest in keeping its lines free for its own power sales and in refusing to lend a hand in its own demise by wheeling cheaper power from the Bureau of Reclamation to municipal consumers which might otherwise purchase power at retail from Otter Tail itself."[24]

The Supreme Court decision did not end the conflict between municipal utilities that had abandoned their own power plants and the investor-owned utilities they were dependent on for power. The city of Norwood, Massachusetts, for example, brought suit against Boston Edison and the New England Power Company in the mid-1970s. Norwood alleged that Boston Edison refused to provide wheeling services that would permit the city to purchase power at wholesale from the New England Power Company. In Illinois, the city of Batavia alleged that Commonwealth Edison Company had prevented that city from acquiring alternate sources of wholesale power by refusing to provide transmission service at reasonable rates. In another case, Cleveland and a group of Ohio municipalities were allocated inexpensive hydroelectric power by the Power Authority of New York as preference customers. Pennsylvania Power and Light agreed to wheel the power from New York State, but Cleveland Illuminating refused to transmit the power over its lines from the point of intersection with the Pennsylvania utility.

Some municipals have formed cooperative entities. The Missouri Basin Municipal Power Agency consists of 50 municipal electric utilities, in Iowa, Minnesota, North Dakota, and South Dakota. The Arkansas River Power Authority in Colorado includes five Colorado cities and one New Mexico city. More than half the nation's local public power systems have formed 47 joint-action agencies in more than 30 states. "The need for joint action programs — and the response by municipally owned utilities to the need," wrote Madalyn Cafruny in 1979, "is primarily a phenomenon of the 70's."[25] Larry Hobart, assistant executive director of the American Public Power Association, agreed: "Joint action permits an individual system, in effect, to spread its risk by buying pieces of plants constructed over a period of years geared to load rather than sinking its money in a single-shot investment in a plant for its own use over a long period of time."[26]

The Municipal Electric Authority of Georgia has spread its risk by buying 17.7 percent of each of two operating Georgia Power Company nuclear plants and a 15 percent share in each of two Georgia Power Company coal-fired plants. North Carolina's Municipal Agency #1 has purchased a 75 percent interest in a 1,100 Mw nuclear plant operated by Duke Power Company. And the Massachusetts Municipal Wholesale Electric Company, representing 40 municipal utilities in that state, bought a 12 percent interest in the Seabrook nuclear plant, in partnership with the Public Service Company of New Hampshire.

The rise of power pools and joint-action agencies has blurred the lines of accountability in electric distribution. Some believe the growth of regional power pools has been part of a natural historical process. For example, Larry Hobart points to "a general recognition by students of government of the need to apply area-wide solutions to many municipal problems for the purpose of increasing efficiency in the delivery of services. This trend toward regional answers is evident in a variety of local governmental functions including transportation, pollution control, water supply and sewage disposal."[27] Others have worried about power pools' effects on political accountability. The Berkshire County Regional Planning Commission warned, "The size of power pools and the fact that they extend beyond traditional regulatory jurisdictions have created difficulties for representation of local and regional viewpoints."[28]

Some observers have worried that the rise of regional power pools could make the assessment of responsibility in case of breakdowns difficult. An electric utility, as part of its obligations, must supply continuous service on demand. But when utilities are interconnected, a central dispatcher usually schedules the overall generation and transmission with regard for costs, efficiency, revenue needs, and other factors. Once again, the driving force of system-level efficiency blurs the lines of responsibility. In the event of an emergency, the dispatcher would make decisions about where electric reserves would be used and which loads would be curtailed. One attorney notes,

> The central dispatcher following the listed criteria need not call for the most efficient operation of a particular utility if such operation is inconsistent with the most efficient operation of the interconnected system. . . . The dispatcher's emergency procedures may interrupt a utility's service which would not have occurred given independent operation. In other words, the present clear accountability between a utility and its customers is no longer clear. The dispatcher, responsible for major service decisions, is at least one step removed from the consumer and may not have a legally imposed public utility responsibility.[29]

Electricity Über Alles

Overall the electric regulatory system appeared to work. Rate-making procedures favored capital intensive power plants and increased electrical demand; the utilities built larger and larger power plants and more and more powerful transmission systems, and they made higher and higher profits. The cost of electricity kept going down, from about 15 cents in 1915 to about 2 cents in 1968. Given the devaluation of money in that period and the rise in the average worker's wages, it follows that the average factory worker in 1915 would have had to work for 20 minutes to light a light bulb all day, while his 1968 counterpart would have had to work 4 minutes.

By the 1920s electricity had surpassed steam as the major industrial energy source. By 1930 industry was consuming twice as much electricity as the total used by the residential and commercial sectors combined. The only thing the electric utilities had to do was dream up new ways of using electricity. This they did. Utilities moved into the small appliance market. In one case, a utility vice president asked a manufacturer to design a utilitarian electric coffee percolator and guaranteed to purchase eleven thousand. The utility's marketing force consisted of metermen, who took orders on their rounds, and secretaries, who earned a commission by selling door-to-door in the evenings. All eleven thousand percolators were sold in a month. Meanwhile, the same town's 125 percolator dealers sold only four hundred.

There were other, more fertile areas for growth. In 1906 Carter Carrier invented the air conditioner. His equipment was first used in a theater in 1922, and the first fully air-conditioned office building opened in San Antonio, Texas, in 1928. But not until after World War II did mass-produced home air-conditioning units appear on the market. In 1952 dealers sold $250 million of the equipment and had to turn away a hundred thousand customers. There were only 20 companies in the field. By 1954 there were 70, and the original 20 had increased their 1952 output by 400–500 percent. Air conditioning was becoming the norm.

The advent of air conditioning increased electric consumption drastically, and it changed the way we design our buildings. By providing almost total control of the atmospheric variables of temperature, humidity, and purity, air conditioning allowed almost all environmental constraints on design to be overcome. It became possible to live and work in almost any type or form of building in any region of the world.

> With confidence in the capability of mechanical systems to overcome any uneven or unsatisfactory internal conditions caused by too much sun, special programmatic needs, too much heat loss, or inadequate light, architects considered their buildings to be liberated from the local and specific demands that had shaped architecture in the past. . . .[30]

Richard Stein, a well-known New York architect, described the impact of this new technology on the exteriors of buildings:

50

The skin of the building became an abstraction and performed minimally. It derived its form from the symbolic sheathing of the building frame. As curtain-wall technology became more widely developed, the operable window seemed to disappear. Fixed glass became the characteristic light admitting material. Once the concept of the sealed building dominated architectural design, buildings became totally dependent on their mechanical systems.[31]

Electric utilities next moved into the home-heating field. Here they had to compete with independent oil suppliers and the natural gas utilities. John Gilberson, an independent oil jobber from Atlantic City, testified before Congress that in his area in 1960 the electric utility was paying homeowners one hundred fifty dollars a home, and builders as much as a thousand dollars a house, to go all-electric. Another oil jobber from Chester, New Jersey, lamented the decline in his business's growth in the late 1960s when the New Jersey Power and Light Company "took away a subdivision called Old Farm at Tewksbury by literally buying the builder."[32] The developer had originally intended to use fuel oil, but when the power company offered to absorb the entire $28,000 cost of laying in wiring, and to provide free brochures describing the subdivision, and to provide a cash rebate of $200 a home, the developer agreed to go all-electric.

Gas utilities also participated in such promotional practices. However, they simply did not have the kind of money the electric utilities had. People's Gas offered the developer of the John Hancock Center in Chicago $750,000 to use gas. But Commonwealth Edison came up with a package worth $1.5 million, including the following:

> Cash or satisfactory equivalent: $745,000
> Promotional allowance: $105,000
> Thermopane windows, in all apartments: free
> 600 refrigerators: free
> 600 range ovens: free
> 600 range drop-ins: free
> 600 dishwashers: free
> 600 In-Sink-Erator disposals: free[33]

The John Hancock Center went all-electric.

In 1926 the average residential domestic consumption was 430 kilowatt hours. In 1964 it had risen to 4,703 kWh. By 1975 an all-electric home was consuming more than 24,000 kWh. Except during the Depression, electrical demand had doubled every decade from 1910 to 1970. By 1970 residential and commercial demand equalled that of industry.

A growing portion of all fuels were being burned to generate power. One in every ten units of energy consumed in this country in 1930 was used to generate electricity; by 1960 one in five was used in this manner. In 1980 almost one in three was used in power plants, and several studies have predicted that by the year 2000 more than half of primary energy would be used to generate electricity.

Thus, because 70 percent of the energy used to generate electricity radiates away as waste heat, by the 1970s waste heat was the fastest growing component of our energy demand.

The cities, their industries, and our neighborhoods had become by the 1970s no more than bit players in the unfolding energy drama. Large industries that used to generate their own electricity were fearful that the state or federal governments would regulate them as utilities if they attempted to do so again. In New Hampshire, in the 1940s, one small business decided to harness a nearby river to generate electricity. It dropped the idea when the local electric utility said it would impose a $1,200-a-month standby charge. Consumers Power Company of Michigan was formed by buying out a series of small, private companies with operations based on hydroelectric power. Consumers Power later found these dams to be uneconomical, and it abandoned them, transferring ownership of each to some county or city, but with a stipulation: if any was ever refurbished to produce general electricity, its ownership would revert to Consumers Power. (This stipulation was later made voluntary, as part of an antitrust settlement with Consumers Power by several localities.)

And so it happened that by the 1970s there were more than four thousand power plants in the country, but only three hundred were generating about 55 percent of the nation's total electricity. Less than 5 percent was generated on-site by non-utility-owned plants. The utilities were often refusing to interconnect with small power producers, or, if they agreed to do so, they charged extremely high prices for back-up power.

The municipalities that owned electric facilities with any generating capacity were forming consortiums with private utilities.

Energy generation no longer appeared to be practical at the local or even the state level. The projected increase in nuclear power plants from about a dozen existing in 1970 to the perhaps two thousand in the year 2000 could be expected to further undermine the authority of the states. When, for example, Minnesota tried to impose radiation emission standards on nuclear plants that were more rigid than those developed by the federal government, the United States Supreme Court ruled that because of the nature of nuclear power the federal government had preempted local and state authority. Public and private utilities worked to get similar opposition to local authority when it appeared to interfere with the development of new energy facilities. Alex Radin, executive director of the American Public Power Association, best illustrated the attitude adopted by the utilities when he said:

> State and local governments are the basic building blocks of our democracy. But sometimes a national need must take precedence. Energy demands can be such a priority. Only the federal government can act on behalf of all citizens, and if the state and local institutions for their own reasons block or react slowly to proposals for energy for cities where national demands are clearly identified, there should be a mechanism to let the President and the Congress act for the country.[34]

While local needs have been subjugated to those put forward by regional systems, the very scale of new electric projects has pitted one part of the nation against another. Rural areas have fought against the erection of high-voltage transmission lines and the construction of power plants that serve distant urban centers. By the late 1970s, dozens of energy wars were raging around the country. The huge Intermountain Power Project, centered in Utah, is a dramatic example of how one community can bear the costs and another community reap the benefits of electric power production. Building the Intermountain Power Project is the goal of forty municipal utilities, most of them based in California; it would be the largest coal-fired power plant in the nation. If completed, it will serve several million residents. It will also require huge amounts of water — and water is scarce in Utah. The project utilities have purchased water rights from local landowners, and most of them

53

have agreed to sell, because the company can pay as much as four times the going rate for water the landowners used for irrigation. But a significant and vocal minority has held out, challenging the company's right to divert such a precious commodity for the use of people hundreds of miles away. In this instance, for Los Angeles, 500 miles from the plant, to be sufficiently air-conditioned, the area around the small city of Delta, Utah, would have to alter its agricultural base irrevocably.

Such was the situation by the 1970s. Edison's neighborhood power plants had become transcontinental power pools. To meet the voracious electrical demand, communities were pitted against one another; some began to challenge the conventional wisdom that greater electric production was in and of itself a worthwhile social goal. But only after the huge increase in the price of crude oil in the 1970s did the country begin to reexamine seriously the way it generated and consumed electric power.

CHAPTER 3

Governing the City: Municipal Authority and Planning

> When I went to work for the city ... all we
> were expected to do was to sweep the streets and
> pick up the garbage. Now they expect us to
> feed the kids breakfast, rebuild downtown, make
> the air and water clean, train the unemployed
> and who knows what all. And we're supposed
> to do all that without raising taxes.
>
> Local official testifying before Congress

The authority of the American city has been evolving since the birth of the republic. The city is a dynamic organism; it responds to changes in the economic and technologic environment. And, as these changes become more complex, the cities require greater authority to deal with them. In corollary development, the history of America's cities is a progression from passivity to activity, from ignorance to expertise, from impotence to influence. The cities have taken an increasingly active role in controlling and planning their future.

But as cities exercise increasing authority, a fundamental tension arises between individual rights and community power. The more pervasive the power the community collectively wields through its elected government, the greater the conflict between the public and the private sectors. The same fundamental questions have had to be answered by cities and citizens in every era:

> What should be the authority of the community to regulate private development?
>
> How far can the community circumscribe the freedom of action of individual households or businesses to protect or enhance the general welfare? Who defines the "general welfare"?
>
> On what basis should the community allocate scarce resources, such as land?
>
> What size community should determine policy—the neighborhood, the city, the state, or the nation?

This chapter examines how these questions have been answered in each era. The answers vary, in part, according to cultural and economic and even climatic differences among cities. But generally we can isolate a theme. Cities have increased their ability to manage development even as changes in the national political and economic system have removed from their influence many key elements of successful planning.

The city has ceased to be a community enclosed by physical walls, as was the case with the medieval cities — it is now part of an open, dynamic economy. Rather than a self-sufficient village, it has become a stop on a national highway system, a market for global corporations, a ZIP code for intergovernmental transfer payments. Now, the boundaries of local communities are permeable. Residents, stores, factories can all easily relocate outside the city, carrying with them all sorts of resources.

As the city involved itself in the planning process, so did higher levels of government. What has resulted is an overlapping and diluted system of planning and, finally, a process of planning that is so fragmented, society is smothering in an avalanche of regulations and permits.

The citizenry has begun to question the goals of municipal authority. What should the role of the city be? In one view, the city is to actively promote the good life for all citizens, intervening in the private marketplace wherever necessary to protect the poor and the powerless. Others see a more limited role — the city as a provider of restricted services and a facilitator of private goals. By the 1970s both schools of thought had gained a following. A national debate was underway on the role of local government.

The Nineteenth Century City: From Pariah to Protector

The American Constitution does not mention cities. In 1787 America was a rural nation, and its leaders planned to keep it rural. By 1800 only 6 percent of its five million inhabitants lived in communities of more than eight thousand people. Only New York and Philadelphia had as many as twenty-five thousand residents. To the founding fathers, in fact, large cities were threats to political stability. In a letter to James Madison in 1787, Thomas Jefferson observed,

> Our governments will remain virtuous for many centuries as long as they are chiefly agricultural; and this will be as long as there shall be vacant land in any part of America. When they get piled upon one another in large cities, as in Europe, they will become corrupt as in Europe.[1]

Indeed, Jefferson's antipathy to cities was so intense that in a letter to Benjamin Rush, he wondered whether an outbreak of yellow fever might not have some good effects: "The yellow fever will discourage the growth of great cities in our nation, and I view great cities as pestilential to the morals, the health and the liberties of men."[2]

The cities Jefferson and others feared were primarily eastern seaboard cities that served as disembarkation points for the flood of immigrants to this country. These immigrants had strange customs and languages. Cities were the homes for the propertyless; they were often violent, explosive places. Urban population densities encouraged demagoguery and mob action. Alexis de Tocqueville, the French visitor who wrote some of the most insightful essays on the young American republic, warned that

> the size of some American cities and especially the nature of their inhabitants [are] a real danger threatening the future of democratic republics of the New World, and I should not hesitate to predict that it is through them that [the republics] will perish.[3]

He advised the nation's political leaders to establish a federal police force to contain possible urban violence.

57

Yet most political leaders, even as they worried about the effect of large cities in the early nineteenth century, agreed that they were essential for commercial development. "If the city as a place to live was viewed as inherently unhealthy, the desirability of the city as an institution for the promotion of economic activity was seldom questioned," according to Charles Glaab and Theodore Brown, two urban historians.[4] Business development and urban development went hand-in-hand: business located in urban areas to have access to pools of labor and suppliers, and the population followed its lead. By 1860 one in six Americans lived in communities of eight thousand or more. People left the farms to gather in densely populated areas, prompting demands for community-wide services unnecessary in rural communities. Historian Arthur Schlesinger, Jr., comments, "The conditions of living in a circumscribed community forced attention to matters of common concern which could not be ignored even by a people individualistically inclined."[5]

A dense community must provide for lighting, fire protection, the care of streets, crime prevention, sewage disposal, water supply, community health, marketing facilities — such needs as these are immediate and constant. But the American city in the mid-nineteenth century had few such amenities. Its conditions were primitive. Frederika Bremer, the Swedish novelist, visited Chicago in 1850 and called it "one of the most miserable and ugly cities." People had apparently come there, she observed, "to trade, to make money and not to live."[6] Joshua T. Smith, a visitor to Detroit in 1837, commented, "One characteristic of Detroit should have been noticed before — its mud. It is the common topic of conversation and exceeds credibility. After a little rain, the cart wheels sink literally up to the axle-tree in the filth."[7] In New York, hogs roamed the streets as scavengers. The editor of the *New World* commented in 1844, "Our streets have been horrible enough in times past, no one denies, but they are now more abominably filthy than ever; they are too foul to serve as the styes for the hogs which perambulate them.... The offal and filth, of which there are loads thrown from the houses in defiance of an ordinance which is never enforced, is scraped up with the usual deposits of mud and manure into big heaps and left for weeks together on the side of the street."[8] *The Chicago Times* editorialized in 1880, "The river stinks, the air stinks, people's clothing, permeated by the foul atmosphere stinks.... No other word expresses it so well as *stink*. A stench means something finite. Stink reaches the infinite and becomes sublime in the magnitude of odiousness."⁹

The municipal corporation first exercised its authority to protect its citizens from the direct threats to their health. The rapid growth of cities and their primitive living conditions combined to breed disease and spread it in epidemics. Consequently, a public-health reform movement arose. But it met resistance from those who doubted the link between filth and disease and who worried about erosion of private property rights if the municipal government became involved. The demands for public health programs required a delegation of authority to some collective entity. The problem of human waste disposal illustrates the point; sewers were in use in American cities, but using them to carry human wastes away from the city was a new concept. Until the mid-nineteenth century, the sewer was simply an elongated cesspool with an overflow at one end. It collected filth and had to be dug out periodically. Reformers wanted to build narrow sewers made out of smooth ceramic pipes that would allow a flow of water sufficient to flush waste matter away from populated areas. Such a system would require, however, the installation of completely new water and sewer pipes and the development of more powerful pumps. These projects would involve substantial capital outlays. The system also required the water and sewer mains to be laid out in straight lines, so the wastes would move through. And this meant the city would have to intrude on private property.

The argument between those who defended private property rights and those who supported municipal involvement continued for several decades. The controversy was resolved only with the outbreaks of epidemics and the discovery by science that epidemics are caused by bacteria. In the 1880s, for example, typhoid epidemics swept through city after city along the Merrimac River in Massachusetts, prompting the city of Lawrence to adopt the first plumbing code and later to install a new type of sand filter for water purification. In 1888 Providence established the first municipal bacteriological laboratory, and in 1893 New York City introduced chlorination. By 1910 ten million Americans received filtered water; some observers credit to this improvement the dramatic reductions of the death rates in New York, Philadelphia, Boston, and New Orleans.

Cities also began to enact regulations on the quality of foods sold within their jurisdictions. In 1907 Chicago became the first major city to require that all milk be pasteurized. By World War I, most major cities had enacted similar requirements. Even though such regulations affected dairy farms outside city limits, the courts upheld the municipality's authority, because of the direct connection to public health.

The City as Servant to the State

As the giant industrial cities arose, the municipal corporations gained increased authority over their citizens but became less autonomous within their states. Ironically, the new size of cities, even as it prompted the need for greater authority, attracted growing state interference. In the early 1800s Alexis de Tocqueville had noted the lack of interest among state legislators for the "petty housekeeping of a few small communities which in the aggregate composed but an insignificant part of the entire population."[10] But urban populations grew three times as fast as that of the nation as a whole in the period 1810–1860. In 1840 only New York City's inhabitants numbered two hundred fifty thousand; by 1890, 11 cities had that many, and three had more than a million residents.

State legislatures reacted to this dramatic growth in two ways. They began to intervene strongly in local affairs, and they changed representational formulas of the legislatures to reduce the potential influence of urban areas. The representational change they justified by the need to preserve rural values in the national political system. James Kent, New York State's Chancellor, argued against a proposed amendment to the 1820 state constitution that would permit non-property owners to vote. He claimed that if their vote were permitted, given the rapid growth rate of New York City, within a century the city would "govern the state." Kent, and many others, believed agriculture not only was the leading interest of the state but that it should be the governing interest. As long as the electorate was confined to "the owners and actual cultivators of the soil," the state was assured of a government of "moderation, frugality, order, honesty and a due sense of independence, liberty and justice." But there would be no security against "fraud and violence," Kent claimed, if the vote were given to "men of no property together with crowds of dependents connected with great manufacturing and commercial establishments, and the motley and undefinable population of crowded ports."[11]

In 1819 the delegates to Maine's constitutional convention established a ceiling on the number of representatives any one town could have in the state legislature. New Orleans was given reduced status in the Louisiana legislature by an 1845 state constitutional provision that restricted the city, which contained 20 percent of the state's population at the time, to 12.5 percent of the state's senators and 10 percent of the state assemblymen. In 1894 the New York state constitution gave perpetual control over the state legislature to rural areas. One delegate from agricultural Oneida County claimed, "The average citizen in the rural district is superior in intelligence, superior in morality, superior in self-government to the average citizen of the great cities."[12]

The rural-dominated legislatures repeatedly intervened in the affairs of their largest cities. In 1857 New York's legislators enacted the Metropolitan Police Act, depriving the city of New York of control over its own police forces. Legislators in Michigan, Massachusetts, Maryland, and Missouri followed suit and assumed control of the police departments in Detroit, Boston, Baltimore, St. Louis, and Kansas City — nearly all the large cities in the nation.

State legislatures regularly created new city positions, ordered salary increases, and hiked pensions. They passed bills relating to such minutiae of city life as the naming of streets and the closing of alleys. Between 1885 and 1907 Massachusetts' state legislature enacted 400 special laws dealing solely with Boston; between 1880 and 1890 New York's legislature enacted 390 statutes dealing solely with New York City. Indeed, one could argue that the extent of municipal debt after the Civil War was due in part to state intervention. *The Report of the Commission to Devise a Plan of Government for the Cities of New York*, issued in 1877, showed the breadth of New York State's interventions:

> Cities were compelled by the legislature to buy lands for parks and places because the owner wished to sell them; compelled to grade, pave and sewer streets without inhabitants, and for no other purpose than to award corrupt contracts for the work. Cities were compelled to purchase at the public expense and at extravagant prices the property necessary for streets and avenues, useless for any other purpose than to make a market for the adjoining property then improved.[13]

61

The courts upheld all interventions. Judge John Foster Dillon formulated the judicial doctrine that still reigns:

> It is a general and undisputed proposition of law that a municipal corporation possesses and can exercise the following powers, and no others: first, those granted in express words; second, those necessarily or fairly implied or incident to the powers expressly granted; third, those essential to the declared objects and purposes of the corporation — not simply convenient but indispensable. Any fair, reasonable doubt concerning the existence of power is resolved by the courts against the corporation, and the power is denied.... All acts beyond the scope of the powers granted are void.[14]

Two decades later the U.S. Supreme Court affirmed this doctrine:

> The State ... at its pleasure may modify or withdraw all [city] powers, may take without compensation [city] property, hold it itself, or vest it in other agencies, expand or contract the territorial area, unite the whole or a part of it with another municipality, repeal the charter, and destroy the corporation. All this may be done, conditionally or unconditionally, with or without the consent of the citizens, or even against their protests.[15]

The City as Servant to Business Corporations

Fossil fuels, combined with new production technologies, created the giant industrial city. They also created the giant industrial trust. While commentators could justifiably point to the period 1870 to 1900 as the era in which America became an urban nation, it was also the era during which it became a corporate nation. A majority of the population lived within the jurisdictional limits of municipal corporations while a majority of the workers were employed by private corporations.

The fossil fueled corporation was radically different from its animal powered or renewable resource powered predecessors. In the early days of the republic private business corporations were chartered by state governments to operate specific enterprises. State and local governments often purchased stock in such enterprises. Corporate books

62

were available for inspection by state agencies. Normally the corporation was chartered to perform a function that served a public purpose. Of the 335 corporate charters issued for the entire nation up to 1800, for example, more than two-thirds were for transportation-related enterprises. Only 13 were awarded for what might be deemed private business activities.[16]

But the maturing economy prompted businesses to demand permission to operate in several fields under the same charter, and demands were forthcoming for relaxed incorporation rules so that more people could take advantage of the privileges accorded corporations. In the 1840s and 1850s states began to permit businesses to write broad charters that gave them the ability to carry on many economic activities. They also made it much easier to gain these charters. The effect was dramatic. As one Illinois judge wrote in 1857, "It is probably true that more corporations were created by the legislature in Illinois at its last session than existed in the whole civilized world at the commencement of the present century."[17] In 1850 Michigan had only 75 corporations. By 1894 it had more than 8,000.

The use of concentrated fuels in new production processes expanded the output of factories enormously. New production advances also brought new products. The economy was unprepared for the avalanche of products, new and old, that poured into the embryonic marketplace after 1880. When production outstripped demand prices fell. Falling prices and falling corporate profits were a central feature of this time. The existing retailers were incapable of demonstrating, servicing, or providing credit for the new array of expensive durable products industry offered, products like sewing machines, bicycles, cash registers, and electrical machinery and equipment.

Industries responded to the new dynamics of production by coalescing hundreds of firms into a few dominant companies, called trusts, that could divide up markets and control supply and price. In 1882 Standard Oil devised the trust as a means of acquiring legal control of an industry. Others quickly adopted the device. In 1889 New Jersey enacted a general incorporation law that allowed one company to hold the stock of many others. The holding company rapidly superseded the trust as a "more effective and inexpensive way of controlling price and production."[18]

A wave of mergers swept the country. Between 1895 and 1905 more than 3,000 industrial firms were swallowed up. In 1899 alone more than 1,000 firms were absorbed into mergers.[19] The companies formed at that time remain some of the largest in the world. International Harvester. Swift. Anaconda Copper. Du Pont. American Smelting and Refining. United States Steel.

During the 1870s and 1880s the tradition of rigidly regulating private corporations through specific terms of individual charters was abandoned. The true function of the law of private corporations came to be to provide for businessmen the maximum freedom and utility in pursuing production and commerce. Willard Hurst describes this new attitude of state governments and state courts:

> The new style of corporation statutes in effect judged that corporate status had no social relevance save as a device legitimized by its utility to promote business. . . . The function of corporation law was to enable businessmen to act, not to police their action.[20]

Cities were mostly helpless before the combined might of state legislatures and corporate holding companies. It is interesting that the key judicial decisions ruling on the authority of municipal corporations vis-a-vis the state and the business corporation concerned disputes with railroad companies. Fueled by coal, driven by the steam engine, travelling over steel rails, the railroads were the commercial lifeline of the country.

When Illinois gave railroads the right to seize unlimited amounts of city land without compensation the city of Clinton went to court to stop what it considered to be an illegal and unwarranted intrusion into local affairs. Judge Dillon's ruling is still cited as precedent for the subordinate status of cities in our political system:

> Municipal corporations owe their origin to, and derive their rights wholly from the legislature. It breathes into them the breath of life, without which they cannot exist. As it creates . . . so may it destroy. If it may destroy, it may abridge and control . . . They are . . . mere tenants at the will of the legislature. Unless there is some constitutional limitation . . . the Legislature might, by a single act, if we suppose it capable of so great a folly, and so great a wrong, sweep from existence all municipal corporations of the State, and the corporations could not prevent it.[21]

In another instance Santa Clara County tried to improve the working conditions of railroad employees working within its jurisdiction. The Supreme Court struck the ordinance down. The "liberty of contract" it declared, "cannot be unreasonably interfered with."[22]

A nation imbued with the belief that it was God's will for it to spread from shore to shore, a nation that was pouring much of its national wealth into the construction of a national transportation system, worried that city or state regulation of commerce could balkanize the nation. Cities and states acting only in their own self-interest could divide the country into tiny trading zones, hampering innovation and the efficiencies that come from large scale production. The courts gave the transportation of goods and people across the country a constitutional standing. Article 1, paragraph 8, clause 2 of the United States Constitution gives sole authority to "regulate commerce ... among the several states" to Congress. The commerce clause, as this has come to be known, elevates free trade from a philosophical argument to a national objective. The right to ship a ton of steel or a pound of tomatoes or a human body from one end of the nation to the other was, according to the Supreme Court, in an 1886 case that once again involved a railroad corporation, "essential in modern times to that freedom of commerce from the restraints which the state might choose to impose upon it, that the commerce clause was intended to secure."[23]

By the early 1900s the distinction between the public and the private corporation was complete. The nation, through its courts and state legislatures, had relegated the municipal corporation to a subordinate role, restricting it to the regulation of activities that directly affected public health. The private business corporation, however, was given broad and almost unquestioned authority to operate in many communities, to become involved in diverse economic activities, to own subsidiary companies, and to freely transport its products across political boundaries.

Corruption and Reform

The courts may have decided that cities were mere tenants at the will of the legislature, but the growing needs of the cities swelled their budgets and their debts. Much of the physical infrastructure of a city — its roads, water lines, docks, wharves, sewers — was

65

built with public money. Cities used their borrowing authority to finance massive construction projects. Municipal debt increased from $28 million in 1843 to $516 million in 1870 to $1.5 billion in 1900. At the beginning of this century, the cities' expenditures for capital improvements were six times more than the states' and 50 percent more than the federal government's. In some instances, the projects were engineering marvels, such as the Brooklyn Bridge. The course of the Chicago River was changed, so that it emptied into the Mississippi rather than Lake Michigan. Chicago residents could then drink Lake Michigan's water without worrying about its contamination by urban sewage. Cincinnati, bypassed by the regional railroad track, built at public expense a long section of track that linked the city to the south, thus allowing it to survive as a major trading center.

But much of the money was misspent. Cities did not have the administrative ability to handle such large projects. Boss-run political machines arose in the larger cities, bolstered by the patronage generated from public works programs. Cities invested in speculative enterprises. They borrowed money to pay ordinary expenses, and they borrowed money to pay off previous debts. "Much of the borrowed money found its way into the pockets of grafting officials and contractors with the result that the cities had often little to show for it," said one urban historian.[24]

The public-works programs were not the only disgraceful operations in turn-of-the-century cities. The real estate development practices were equally scandalous. In city after city, regardless of local climatic or topographic constraints, the standard rectangular plot became the norm. It had been developed in Philadelphia to encourage real estate speculation and make future development easier; it successfully accomplished this objective, but at the expense of destroying the quality of neighborhoods. The essential unit was no longer the European-like quarter, with its integration of residence, workplace, and recreation. "The functional unit was now the block. The street was a traffic artery." In Brooklyn, according to Mumford,

> The indifference to geographic contours, in the application of the formal gridiron to the land surface, was nothing short of sublime: the engineers' streets often swept through swamps, embraced dump-heaps, accepted piles of slag and waste,

climbed cliffs, and ended up a quarter of a mile beyond the low
water mark of the waterfront. . . .
On steep hilly sites, like that of San Francisco, the rectangular
plan, by failing to respect the contour levels of the hillside,
placed a constant tax on the time and energy of its inhabitants,
and inflicted on them and their heirs a daily economic loss,
measured in tons of coal and gallons of gasoline wasted, to say
nothing of undoing the major esthetic possibilities of a hill-site
that is intelligently planned.
In the layout no thought was given either to the direction of the
prevailing winds, the placing of industrial districts, the salubrity
of the underlying foundations, or any of the other vital factors
involved in proper utilization of a site.[25]

The situation had become intolerable. The existing political authority and administrative structure of the city were simply inadequate to
cope with the tidal wave of humanity. But the situation was not un-
noticed. Between 1882 and 1892 *Poole's Index*, the basic reference
source for articles on political science, listed more articles discussing
the conditions of city government than during the preceding eight decades! The National Municipal League was formed in the early 1890s and
quickly gained more than 150 members. The central problem of urban
political development at this time, according to one urban specialist,
"became a matter of providing cities with a form of government that
would enable them to confront and ameliorate the effects of the national industrialization, urbanization and modernization process."[26]
The municipal reform movement arose, with three objectives: autonomy, efficiency, and expertise. To achieve autonomy for cities, the
members of the movement developed a political theory to support their
contention that large cities deserve more power than the average rural
community, that such cities have an inherent right to self-government.
As Leo S. Rowe, one of the leaders in the movement for municipal
autonomy, explained, "when a considerable population is massed
within a limited area, a community life is developed whose needs and
circumstances are very different both in degree and kind from the
isolated individual lives of dwellers of agricultural and grazing regions."
New York City's lower east side, for example, had a population density
in the 1890s of more than five hundred thousand people per square

mile. That type of congestion demanded new political structures, these reformers believed. Rowe proclaimed to the first Good City Government Conference, in 1894: "the doctrine that a municipal government is but a subordinate branch of the general governmental power of the State" is "as false in principle as it is detrimental to progress in its operation."[27]

The movement for municipal autonomy, which was popularly known as the municipal home-rule movement, tried to write provisions for city independence into state constitutions. The Missouri Convention of 1875 was the first to grant local governments the right to frame and adopt charters with governmental structures tailored to their own needs and with at least some authority to act without specific legislative directive. St. Louis quickly established itself as the nation's first home-rule city. By the mid-1890s California, Washington, and Minnesota joined Missouri in adding home-rule provisions to their constitutions. By 1925 such provisions were made in the statutes or constitutions of 14 states.

These home-rule provisions often reversed the traditional state-local relationship. Ultimate power would still reside in the state. But whereas before home rule cities could act only when specifically authorized by the state legislature, with home rule cities could act unless specifically prohibited by the state. In other words, the city no longer had to ask permission to act, as long as the activity was not specifically prohibited by the state.

The home-rule movement developed unevenly during the next century. Overall, it has provided cities with new authority over matters previously considered out of their scope.

The home-rule movement encouraged an expanded municipal authority, but that was only one goal of the municipal reformers. Home rule without competence would matter little. Municipal reformers wanted to transform the corrupt and administratively weak municipal corporation into a model of businesslike efficiency. The reform movement imposed debt ceilings. It promoted uniform accounting systems so that cities could compare the efficiency with which they delivered services to that of other cities. Lord Bryce observed in the 1891 edition of *American Commonwealth* that American cities were beginning to see themselves as "not so much little states as large corporations." Another contemporary reformer agreed that the "government of cities is business and not politics."[28] In place of democracy, reformers wanted expertise.

Many reformers believed that the control of the city by a city council representing individual neighborhoods introduced politics into the day-to-day operations of the municipal corporation. City councillors were not elected on the basis of administrative skills, and the cities suffered from a lack of competent management. The inefficiency of the then-current city-council system of municipal government was underlined by happenings in Galveston, Texas. In 1900, a hurricane and tidal wave struck the city. Within 24 hours a sixth of the population drowned and one-third of the property was destroyed. The regular city government was incapable of managing the crisis. It appointed five local businessmen to govern the city, each taking charge of one section of the city. One person acted as coordinator.

Galveston's successful administration led other cities to establish city governments managed by full-time professionals, with commissioners overseeing specific departments of the city. By 1911, a hundred cities had established like systems. Today half of all American cities have such commissions or city-manager forms of government.

The reforms instituted in this period isolated the elected government from community-based organizations, however. Mayors, elected by the whole city, were given increasing authority in place of the ward-based city councils. City councillors were elected by the entire city; they no longer represented specific wards or neighborhoods. City elections became nonpartisan. People did not run on national political-party platforms or tickets. To further divorce local elections from national politics, the elections at the local level were held at times different from the state and national elections.

Although the movement for municipal efficiency at the expense of community-based politics represented the major thrust of local reform efforts during this era, a significant movement also arose to allow citizens more direct participation in decision-making. Several states, and many cities, most of them in the western part of the country, enacted statutes or constitutional amendments permitting citizens to recall legislators, to initiate legislation directly through petition, and to vote on legislation through the referendum process.

The municipal reformers wanted the city to emulate the private business corporation. But they also wanted the municipal corporation to expand its authority over private corporations operating within its jurisdiction. The major private economic activity in cities has traditionally been in real estate development; so in the debate about the city's authority to interfere with private enterprise, the control of land development became a central issue.

Controlling Real Estate Development: The Rise of Urban Planning

When, in the 1877 case of *Munn* v. *Illinois*, the Supreme Court ruled that state governments had the right to regulate private industry when it is endowed with "a public interest," cities immediately construed that right to extend to the regulation of land and buildings in their jurisdictions. The question of what involved the public interest, and how far the municipal corporation could go to protect that interest, would involve city councils, private businesses, the courts, and state and federal governments from that time onward.

Initially cities intervened only after a problem became so apparent that popular dissatisfaction forced action. New York City enacted the Tenement House Law in 1879, and after the turn of the century hired more than 150 housing inspectors to see that tenement structures met minimum standards. In 1867 San Francisco prohibited the establishment of slaughterhouses, hog storage facilities, and hide-curing plants in certain districts of the city.

Gradually a movement arose for the city to become more involved in anticipatory planning. Hartford established the first city-planning commission in 1907; Milwaukee followed in 1908, and Chicago in 1909. That same year Harvard offered the first formal course in city planning, followed shortly thereafter by the University of Illinois. The first national conference on city planning took place in Washington, D.C., that year. And four years later Massachusetts required all cities with populations greater than ten thousand to create official planning boards.

Approximately two thousand people attended the ninth national planning conference, held at Kansas City, Missouri, in 1917. At that meeting, the American City Planning Institute was established.

Although a handful of cities engaged in comprehensive planning, the vast majority planned in a fragmented manner. The major tool of planning was land-use zoning. New York City became the first to adopt a comprehensive zoning ordinance, in 1916. The United States Supreme Court in 1926 upheld New York's right to do so, thus giving constitutional validity to the more than five hundred cities that had, by then, already adopted land-use ordinances. On the eve of the Depression, eight hundred cities had them.

The initial planners were preoccupied with designing communities to encourage the automobile. In 1920 there were six million automobiles on the road in America. In 1930 there were 26 million, one for every five people. Many cities required subdivision developers to submit plans that conformed to regulations concerning the width and location of major streets and the maximum block length.

Since the zoning process was not a part of a more comprehensive plan, the cumulative result of hundreds of individual decisions by zoning boards was fragmentation of the cities into haphazard sections. Because a city has a fixed measure of land, the land's value is directly tied to the kind of uses to which it can be put. To Samuel Kaplan, an urban planner, zoning has the effect of a printing press:

> An acre of land for farming purposes might be worth, depending on one's crop $500 to $1,000. If you could put one house on the acre its worth can be increased to, say $10,000. If you can put two houses on it, the value could be $18,000. But if there is a market for a high density use and the land is zoned appropriately, its value could be increased to $100,000 an acre. The power to zone, therefore, is the power to make money.[29]

Planning was still constrained by the American attitudes toward government regulation. A contemporary English writer commented, "In America it is the fear of restricting or injuring free and open competition that has made it so difficult for cities to exercise proper and efficient control over their development." The tendency, therefore, has been "to promote those forms of civic improvement which can be carried out without interfering with vested interests."[30] Thus codes such as would limit the height and density of dwellings or prevent the destruction of certain amenities on privately owned land, because they would reduce the profits of the speculator, were usually avoided. In

1929 only 46 cities had planning budgets greater than $5,000. On the other hand, the purchase of large public parks and the development of civic centers was a form of public investment that added to the value of privately owned land and buildings in the city. Therefore the "city beautiful" movement was encouraged, and thrived.

The rapidly growing suburban cities often used their zoning power to keep low-income groups or racial minorities from following their white, middle-class predecessors out of the central cities. In 1953 a New Jersey township, Bedminster, enacted a zoning ordinance that required a minimum plot of five acres. The New Jersey Supreme Court upheld Bedminster's right to pass the ordinance as a way of "preserving the character of the community" and "maintaining the value of property."[31] But the International City Management Association says,

> Armed with such legal support, and using the neighborhood unit with its focus on single-family, detached, owner-occupied homes as a basic structuring system, community after community enacted similar regulations, usually with standards far beyond the minimal protective needs. The ability to zone was beginning to be used to support private financial interests and for social goals that were incompatible with the society's objective of equality and mobility.[32]

The concept of urban planning changed along with the changes at all levels of government that were precipitated by the Great Depression. Immediately after Franklin Roosevelt established the National Resources Committee to recommend solutions to the nation's problems, it set up a subcommittee on urbanism. That subcommittee's report, *Our Cities: Their Role in the National Economy*, was issued in June 1937. It concluded that "the entire scope and conception of local urban planning need broadening." It expressed the opinion that planners had not given "proper emphasis to the social and economic objectives and aspects of planning and zoning." The study also recommended that planners study "the economic base of the community, its soundness, deficiencies and its prospects, and the need for a selective program of industrial development," and that they pay more attention to the "pressing problems of housing."[33]

In 1940, for the first time, the census examined the housing stock of the nation, giving urban planners their first comprehensive data on their buildings. In 1949 the federal government established programs to aid central cities directly. Huge areas of central cities were cleared by local redevelopment authorities and reconstructed by and for private enterprise with federal assistance. Cities had to submit general plans before the projects could proceed, stimulating a considerable amount of planning activity and resulting in growing numbers of professional planners.

Many of these urban renewal programs were little more than clearance programs. Although in 1954 the federal government expanded the concept of redevelopment to include rehabilitation as well as removal, cities continued to demolish neighborhoods to make way for commercial districts or high-rise, high-income apartment complexes. Walk through neighborhoods in central cities today and see the results of that era: some neighborhoods are cut in half by freeways; others are only half the size they were before urban renewal took place. Still other neighborhoods have completely disappeared, replaced by barren parking lots and high-rise office buildings.

Neighborhoods fought back. In 1966, when the Department of Housing and Urban Development was established, the Model Cities Program specifically targeted low-income areas for reconstruction. It also required that low-income residents and neighborhood people be included in the planning process. In the 1970s the federal government emphasized rehabilitation with the community-development block-grant program, which distributed billions of dollars and in 1977 issued regulations that require local planners to furnish comprehensive, three-year plans for revitalizing neighborhoods.

Cities began to expand their concerns from the housing sector to the job sector. They began actively intervening to encourage the expansion of their local economies. The state-of-the-art of urban economic development programs advanced rapidly in the 1960s and 1970s. Two urban economists writing in the late 1970s concluded, "Programs have moved from simple business promotion to targeted intervention in the local economy based on economic research and planning and using more sophisticated tools and techniques." The public development efforts began to extend beyond the traditional revenue functions to more "entrepreneurial investments in business development and financial leveraging."[34]

The expansion of municipal authority was justified on the basis of the increased responsibilities of government at all levels of society and the increasing complexities of the modern economy. The judiciary largely supported this extension of city power.

One Minnesota high court upheld the extension of municipal authority by noting, "The need for local power grows with the complexity of modern life and the population."[35] A federal court of appeals agreed that "as a commonwealth develops politically, economically, and socially, the police power likewise develops within reason to meet the changed and changing conditions."[36] A third court found that "economic and industrial conditions are not stable. Times change. Many municipal activities, the propriety of which are not now questioned, were at one time thought, and rightly so, [to be] of a private character.[37]

Municipalities were not, however, given carte blanche in undertaking economic projects. They were still governed by state constitutions or statutes. Often what constituted a public function differed from state to state. A California court held and an Iowa court denied, for example, that a municipal opera house was a public function. The municipal manufacture and sale of ice was ruled a public purpose in Georgia; when a Louisiana court held otherwise, the state constitution was amended to authorize such plants. A recent study by two municipal finance experts concluded that, on the whole, low-rent housing, airports, and off-street parking garages have gained acceptance as public functions, while commercial undertakings such as hotels, restaurants, and liquor stores generally are considered not to constitute public functions.

The involvement by the municipal corporation in matters of land development and economic development was applauded by some, but was angrily opposed by others. Many developers and private businesses considered such authority to be an excuse to delay development more often than to channel it. Some of the most vocal opposition, however, came from neighborhood organizations that wondered for whose interest the city was exercising these powers. Neighborhoods worried that the cities were primarily interested in increasing tax revenue, and that the way to do that was to attract industry and reduce its residential base, especially to reduce that part of the population that had little money and large families — for that portion of the population required large public investments in services but contributed little tax revenue.

Long-time residents of the cities wondered how much consideration city governments were giving to stability, compared to revenue generation. When zoning and land-use regulations affected the communities, neighborhoods fought with varying degrees of success for major roles in their cities' planning processes.

The Eroding Municipal Authority: The Private Sector

By the 1970s cities had become involved in overseeing development. But overseeing it did not mean they controlled development, nor that they exercised significant influence over their economies. As far back as World War I, Delos Wilcox, conceding that municipalities could no longer regulate their electric utilities, explained, "the day of walled cities is past and now an urban community is primarily a congested spot on the state map, a center of population and of industrial activity intimately related to the personal and property interests of all the citizens within its sphere of influence, which often extends to and beyond the boundaries of the commonwealth itself." For Wilcox, the "fact [is] that the incorporated city or village was no longer the natural unit of control as it ceased proportionally to be the natural economic unit of supply."[38]

By the 1970s regional and even national economies had given way to global corporations. "For business purposes," said the president of the IBM World Trade Corporation, "the boundaries that separate one nation from another are no more real than the equator. They are merely convenient demarcations of ethnic, linguistic and cultural entities. They do not define business requirements or consumer trends. Once management understands and accepts this world economy, its view of the marketplace — and its planning — necessarily expand. The world outside the home country is no longer viewed as [a] series of disconnected customers and prospects for its products but as an extension of a single market.[39] An assistant vice president of the Texas Commerce Bank in Dallas added, "The concept of the local bank really makes no sense when once isolated cities are linked together by population corridors and when banking technology permits instantaneous transfer of money from city to city and around the world."[40]

75

The city, once proudly the birthplace of businesses, became a company town dependent on far-flung corporate empires. The cities competed against one another to attract branches of these large industries. Atlanta advertised its wares on Cleveland television programs and opened an industry-recruitment office in New York. In the small city of Bossier City, Louisiana, the chamber of commerce got school children to write more than nine hundred letters to corporate executives to tell them of the city's need for jobs and of such assets as clean air.

Their self-promotional activities constituted the benign side of the competition between cities for corporate investment. When the stakes were high, a growing number of local officials were willing to exercise the full authority of the municipal corporation to attract large plants, even at the cost of destroying existing communities. One of the best examples occurred when General Motors announced it would build plants in cities in Kansas, Oklahoma, and Michigan only if the local governments met its demands. Cities that failed to accommodate GM, the third largest private corporation in the world, were informed they would not be considered. Several cities, including Detroit, agreed to all conditions. According to GM, its plant there would generate six thousand jobs; in return, GM wanted the city to clear a 465-acre site. Unfortunately, the 465-acre site was home to many people — Poletown, as it was called, was predominantly Polish and had strong social cohesion. When 90 percent of the neighborhood owners refused to sell, Detroit used a recently enacted Michigan statute called the "quick take" law that allowed a city to condemn private property for public purposes and take title within 90 days, whether or not the value of the property for compensation purposes had been agreed on. In March 1981 the Michigan Supreme Court ruled in favor of the city and its Economic Development Corporation. The court ruled that the city was exercising its powers of eminent domain for a public purpose, the creation of "programs to alleviate and prevent conditions of unemployment." However, in this instance, in order to create a maximum of six thousand jobs the city of Detroit would raze 1,300 homes, 16 churches, and 143 businesses, destroying an entire community that had existed there for several generations.

Even after a large company is enticed to set up shop within a city's jurisdiction, the impact is not always beneficial. A firm with highly specialized labor requirements might bring along its best-paid workers, hiring local residents only for menial jobs. The imported population increases the demand for new schools, roads, police and fire protection, raising local taxes. According to Neil Peirce, a columnist specializing in state and local governmental affairs, "Capital investments to attract new firms have virtually bankrupted some communities."[41] Yet eventually the big multinational firms lured to the communities may decide that better prospects exist somewhere else and close down the operation. Absentee owners are certainly less concerned about the local community; they don't move within commuting distance. In fact, according to one economist, the firms owned by the largest companies tend to move longer distances when relocating.[42]

Branch plants are not closed only when they lose money. As Joseph Danzansky, formerly president of the Giant Foods, a Washington, D.C.–area supermarket chain, candidly concedes, "Let's face it. Many stores are closed not because they operate at a loss, but because they are marginal and the capital can be more advantageously invested elsewhere."[43]

Cities are discovering that reliance on one or two very large employers leaves them vulnerable to cyclical instabilities in the local economy. To rely on a more diversified base, composed of smaller enterprises, tends to make a more stable economy. Most jobs are created not by large plants but by the millions of tiny businesses. David Birch, of MIT, tracked 5.6 million firms that provide 82 percent of the nation's private-sector jobs, between 1970 and 1978. He found that small firms were the country's biggest job producers; two-thirds of all new jobs were in companies employing fewer than 20 people. The top 1,000 firms on *Fortune* magazine's list contributed just 75,000 new jobs in the 1970–1976 period, during which the overall economy added 6.2 million jobs, or 82 times as many.

Rather than creating jobs, in fact, large absentee-owned businesses may actually drain capital from their communities. One neighborhood in Washington, D.C., determined that a fast-food store collected $750,000 a year in revenue from local customers and exported from the community more than $500,000. An older, ethnic neighborhood in Chicago found that of the $33 million it had deposited in one local savings and loan association, only $120,000 had been returned in loans. The rest was being lent outside the neighborhood, in many cases outside the city itself.

Eroding Municipal Authority:
The Public Sector

During the past generation, cities have lost control over the physical development of their territory to entities called public benefit corporations, or, more commonly, public authorities. They came into use in the 1930s; Franklin Roosevelt made them the principal tools for implementing his massive nationwide public-works programs. In 1932 FDR distributed to each state sample enabling legislation for state and local governments to use in creating public authorities. By personal letter, in 1934 he encouraged governors to endorse this legislation and to modify debt laws. The RFC and the Public Works Administration (PWA) were funded to purchase the revenue bonds of these authorities.

Nearly half of the first 50 municipal authorities in Pennsylvania were created with federal assistance. In 1935 the Pennsylvania legislature passed the Municipal Authorities Act, which exempted government-owned corporations from municipal debt restrictions. In 1945 the legislature amended the original act to make it the most permissive authorization in the nation. By 1959 Pennsylvania had twelve hundred municipal authorities, one for every four local governments.

The Federal Reserve Bank of Philadelphia described "Pennsylvania's Billion Dollar Babies" in 1958, as "not quite governments and not private businesses. Paradoxically they are born of government, yet not directly controlled by the electorate. Nourished by business methods they are nonprofit, have no stockholders, and are immune from anti-trust laws. They build public projects using private money. They operate public utilities yet they are not regulated by Public Utilities Commissions."[44] They are, in the words of one urban analyst, "corporations without stockholders, political jurisdictions without voters or tax-payers."[45]

Public authorities are not tiny parts of the political system. They are central to it. The biography of Robert Moses, the former director of various public authorities in New York, tells us much more about how and why New York City developed as it did than the biographies of Robert Wagner or John Lindsay, two long-term mayors of New York. Public authorities are the largest category of borrowers in the tax-exempt bond market, raising more money for capital investment than either all state or all municipal governments. Ann Marie Haucks Walsh, an expert on these unelected governments, expresses the fear that they wield "a massive influence on the patterns of development in the nation," an influence "that is largely insulated from public debate."[46] The operation of these quasi-governmental entities has undercut the ability of the elected political unit, the city, to comprehensively manage current development in accordance with an overall comprehensive plan.

A final piece of the planning jigsaw puzzle has been the proliferation of overlapping planning districts since 1960. Many metropolitan areas have councils of governments, regional transportation agencies, or regional environmental planning organizations with jurisdictions that overlap with those of the local governments. And almost all states have substate planning agencies for regions that overlap the planning areas of local governments. Sometimes these various agencies coordinate their efforts; more commonly they operate in complete isolation, and often their plans interact in ways that undermine each agency's original objective.

The New City Planning: A Sense of Place

Citizens and city officials of the 1970s, armed with data showing the loss of resources through their borders, attempted to reduce the ease with which locally generated resources could leave the area. Peter Libassi and Victor Hausner, two urban economists, wrote in 1977 about the need for cities to have both a "foreign" and a "domestic" policy.[47] Neighborhood activists convinced the United States Congress to enact legislation that requires a depository institution to recycle into the community part of the money generated locally.[48] The Home Mortgage Disclosure Act, enacted in 1976, requires depository institutions to divulge where they lend their money. And the Community Reinvestment Act of 1978 requires depository institutions to reinvest a portion of locally generated deposits in the local area.

When older central cities discovered that many high-paying government jobs were being held by people who live outside the cities, they enacted new regulations. By 1969, 15 of the 47 cities with populations greater than two hundred fifty thousand had ordered their firemen to live within city boundaries. Philadelphia, San Francisco, Detroit, Los Angeles, Milwaukee, and Pittsburgh have required most of their employees to live within the city limits.

Cities also began to limit commercial developments outside their territories that would draw away business from existing downtown commercial sections. Vermont amended its environmental-impact-statement regulations to include consideration of the economic impact of developments; its planning board denied a building permit for a regional shopping mall after concluding that the mall would draw away business from a nearby city, reducing the city's tax revenue substantially. Michigan enacted legislation to prohibit one Michigan city from taking away an industry from another one without that city's approval. In the Twin Cities metropolitan area of St. Paul and Minneapolis, a number of cities entered into a tax-sharing agreement under which, if a business moves into one city, a portion of the increased property tax is apportioned by a formula to all the metropolitan cities. This lessens the incentive for cities to compete for the relocation of existing industry.

Alexandria, Virginia, enacted a neighborhood parking ban. Commuters may no longer park their cars on neighborhood streets for longer than two hours. The United States Supreme Court upheld the ordinance, noting, "The Constitution does not outlaw the social and environmental objectives, nor does it presume distinctions between residents and non-residents of a local neighborhood to be invidious."[49] In Berkeley, California, residents were given permission to bar street access at one end of each block. In effect, this has turned cross-town thoroughfares back into quiet, residential streets. The need for neighborhood stability was viewed by the city council as a greater priority than the need for through traffic — and the courts agreed.

Intervention by cities has perhaps been most controversial when they have attempted to limit population growth. Cities have often used zoning techniques to limit the influx of certain races or income classes, as has been discussed. However, after 1965 and the enactment of civil rights legislation, the courts became reluctant to uphold ordinances that exclude certain populations unless there were "a balancing of the local desire to maintain the status quo within the community and the greater public interest that regional needs be met."[50] One court, overturning a growth-limiting ordinance, ruled, "Towns may not refuse to confront the future by building a moat around themselves and pulling up the drawbridge."[51] The Supreme Court of New Jersey held that the township of Mount Laurel had a legal obligation to provide its "fair share" of the housing needs of the region around it, especially its share of low-cost and moderate-cost housing.[52]

In the South and West, cities are newer, and they have faced different problems. They are growing fast and discovering the costs as well as benefits of population growth. Fairfield, a San Francisco suburb long progrowth in attitude, discovered through a computer study by the Association of Bay Area Governments that total tax revenues from a proposed new subdivision would pay for only half the new police services required for the subdivision and would pay for no other services to it at all. A study of the Colorado Springs area determined that, at current growth rates, by the turn of the next century the population will exhaust its water supply.[53]

Eventually, the courts began to uphold the right of cities to curb population growth — that is, the cities' right to limit the freedom to migrate. The landmark case involved the city of Petaluma, California, which had grown from fourteen thousand residents in 1960 to twenty-five thousand in 1970 and thirty thousand in 1971 because of suburbanization in the San Francisco Bay Area. The town's public-works department predicted that the sewer system could handle only one more year of growth at the current rate. In addition, the town's consumption of water had caught up with its availability, the schools were already on double sessions, and the use of land set aside for parks was being threatened. In August 1972 Petaluma instituted a "rationing" growth ordinance, allowing no more than five hundred new residential units during the next five years. By a four-to-one vote, the residents approved the ordinance in June 1973. After hearing an appeal of the ordinance, the United States District Court in 1974 ruled that the constitutional right to travel takes precedence over the right of a city to reduce future burdens on its resource base. However, the appeals court in August 1975 unanimously overturned the lower court's decision, stating, "We conclude ... that the concept of public welfare is sufficiently broad to uphold Petaluma's desire to preserve its small-town character, its open spaces and low density of population to grow at an orderly and deliberate pace."[54]

One of the traditional benefits of population growth is that it raises property-tax income. But in California, after Proposition 13 reduced property taxes in June 1978, growth no longer engenders great benefits. Since its passage, at least 32 growth-controlling propositions have been initiated by the people of California's cities and counties, and 19 have passed. A Santa Barbara initiative limits population growth to 0.9 percent per year. The city of Santa Cruz limits growth to 1.4 percent per year. Belmont's initiative allows only 56 additional housing units per year, and Redlands allows 450. Stockton's and Modesto's growth measures effectively require a popular vote before those cities can expand beyond their present limits. When Stockton's city council asked the voters to restore the council's authority over growth management, the referendum was defeated by a two-to-one margin.

While some cities begin to control their maximum populations, others have tried to protect the rights of their citizens to remain in their homes. Two hundred communities, mainly in New Jersey and some northeastern cities, had imposed rent control as an outgrowth of controls instituted during World War II. When the postwar baby crop matured and began to seek housing in the early 1970s, many cities in other parts of the nation also instituted some form of control on housing. To stem speculative property purchases that were driving up the property prices, Davis, California, enacted an ordinance requiring any person who bought a house to occupy the unit as his or her principal personal residence within six months of the completion of the purchase and to live there for a minimum of 12 consecutive months. A Milwaukee ordinance allows tenants to withhold rents, depositing them in escrow accounts, until building and zoning code violations are corrected. Madison, Wisconsin, has established the Rental Relations Board to certify tenant organizations, which then become collective bargaining entities. A Madison ordinance mandates collective bargaining for all rental property with more than four units and also requires landlords to develop economic impact statements concerning the effects of proposed sales on current tenants. The District of Columbia has implemented a freeze on condominium conversions and allows tenants the first right to purchase buildings; the same law also protects the rights of residents 65 years and older in buildings to be sold.

Clearly, society has been "in the midst of . . . one of the most radical changes in our concept of private property that we have ever seen in this country," as expressed by James Rouse, a developer of new towns and central cities, in 1977.[55] Two land-use attorneys, after an exhaustive study of changes in land-use law during recent years, concluded that the most important change is in the traditional idea that "a developer has a right to develop because he owns a piece of land and the public must let him."[56] The territory of a city is finite; increasingly, society allows communities to allocate their scarce land resources in ways designed to enhance their current residents' quality of life.

By the 1980s cities had the desire, the mandate, and the ability to plan with sophistication unimagined a century before. Newly emerging computer graphics techniques allow city officials and, increasingly, average citizens, to develop such tools as color-coded maps that illustrate changes over time, and computer models that estimate the impacts of various development strategies.

In many parts of the country, cities — and often counties, which themselves gained a great deal of planning authority in the 1960s and 1970s — have moved toward the development of comprehensive plans. Many of these have entailed considerable citizen involvement and addressed a great many factors; they map water tables, soil consistency, and vacant land, and they target various tracts for development. In some places — Oregon and New Jersey, for example — comprehensive plans have had to take into account such factors as energy efficiency. In parts of California, local governments have inserted the requirement that the potential for small-scale sewage treatment systems be included in master plans.

But a reaction has also been setting in. Many citizens still wonder whether the authority of the local government is being used in the community's interest or merely in the interest of some private interests. And citizens are growing wary and skeptical of the planning process itself. The development industry has witnessed a permit explosion. One sympathetic environmental attorney declared in 1976, "A project that required one permit a decade ago could easily require half a dozen or more today." Each permit, he believed, "represents a response to serious public concern about a particular issue." But their "proliferation may indeed provide grounds for serious public concern. The processes of negotiating a disconnected jumble of procedures may have become so complex as to impede achievement of both the protective objectives of permitting programs and necessary planned growth. The current political reaction against 'big government' may be a demonstration of politicians' recognition of the impatience felt by a large proportion of the electorate with the complexities of government regulation."[57]

Even as cities entered new areas, such as noise control, and air- and water-quality control, their citizens and planners have lost faith in their own abilities to plan effectively. Some urban planners look with envy at the handful of cities, such as Houston, where no zoning process operates at all, yet diverse and stable neighborhoods seemed to have evolved. Some economists have proposed "enterprise zones" in older cities, areas where there would be no regulations. Stuart M. Butler, the chief theorist behind this concept, advised in *Planning* magazine that the primary feature of such zones would be their unplanned nature. "We have tried several decades of bureaucratic planning," he said, "and that has not solved our inner city problem. Now we may get a chance to see what unplanning can do."[58]

The debate about the role of planning at the local level constitutes only a part of a much broader discussion — on the role of government in society. What right does the community have, through its elected government, to supervise the physical development of its land? Who should allocate scarce resources, such as land and water? What level of government, if any, should have the responsibilities for oversight?

A critical aspect of this debate concerns money. Cities were given increased responsibilities, but their ability to raise money from their own populations has eroded. Increasingly, they have become dependent on higher levels of government for financing. The power of the purse largely determines political authority. We turn now to the examination of this power.

CHAPTER 4

Financing the City:
The Power of the Purse

He who pays the piper calls the tune.

In 1900, the cities received five times as much tax revenue as the states, and about half again as much as the federal government received. Federal grant programs provided less than 1 percent of all state and local revenues, and federal grants-in-aid constituted only about 1 percent of federal expenditures. Compare 1900's funding arrangement to that of 1980, when the federal government received 60 percent of all tax revenues, three times as much as the states received — and the cities received about 20 percent less tax revenue than the states. Most local governments received more money from state legislatures than they raised from their own resources, and the bigger cities received 50 cents of federal aid for every dollar they generated themselves.

This astonishing change in fiscal autonomy illustrates the changing nature of American federalism. The cities' budgets have mushroomed, and their responsibilities have been extended significantly. But the cities no longer have the power of the purse. Rarely do they develop their own programs or their own procedures.

The change in intergovernmental relations started when the sixteenth amendment to the Constitution gave the federal government the right to impose an income tax. In total funds generated, this tax quickly surpassed all other sources of revenue. By 1932 half of all governmental tax revenues were collected by the federal government. The federal government, its income tax increasingly productive, was pressed more

85

and more to finance state programs. And in the 1920s it did so, moving into the field of highway construction — its first major involvement with lower levels of government.

The income tax gave the federal government the means; the Depression gave it the motivation. Harassed by the twin problems of rising relief expenditures and growing tax delinquencies, urban leaders were exposed earlier than the nation's governors to the need for massive action. City halls around the country were targets for protests by the unemployed. Initially, city officials turned to state capitols for assistance, but rural-dominated legislatures and budget-minded governors opposed loosening the purse strings to assist "profligate" cities.

Rebuffed at the state level, municipal officials turned to Washington for help. A new organization, the United States Conference of Mayors, was established to lobby for federal aid for localities. Historian Mark Gelfand notes,

> The New Deal marked a new epoch in American urban history. . . . The cities finally gained some recognition from Washington. . . . Each successive relief and recovery measure opened up new lines of communication between two levels of government that had not previously acknowledged the other's existence.[1]

Roosevelt's National Resources Committee's 1937 report *"Our Cities: Their Role in the National Economy"* concluded that cities had assumed a "preponderant role in our national existence" and therefore it was "imperative that [they] acquire a central position in the formulation of national policy."[2]

Local revenues from the federal government jumped from $10 million in 1932 to $229 million in 1936, becoming nearly equal to that given the states. But the relationship between Washington and the country's cities was an ambivalent one. The New Dealers wanted more social-welfare money channeled directly to cities. They wanted cities to have more planning responsibility and, in that planning, to take into account social and economic factors. But at the same time they viewed large cities with suspicion, believing that concentrations of population had unbalanced the country. To right the balance they envisioned establishing greenbelt areas around central cities. Rexford Tugwell, the head of the Federal Resettlement Administration, aimed to achieve (in

Ebenezer Howard's words) "a union of city and country life in which every foot of land was planned to eliminate waste and to provide its inhabitants with pleasant and spacious living."[3]

Harold L. Ickes, as head of the federal Public Works Administration, was placed in charge of the federal public-housing program. He proceeded to buy sites for that purpose, to draw up project plans and to build houses. By 1937 the Public Works Administration had undertaken 51 projects in 36 cities, constructing 21,770 dwelling units for about 87,000 people.

When landowners refused to sell their land, the federal government boldly acquired it under the power of eminent domain. However, at the time the program began, the courts had not ruled on the constitutionality of any New Deal programs. The Supreme Court had ruled that the federal government could spend money for almost any purpose, or at least that was the effect of its denying taxpayers or local governments the ability to sue because of such programs; but the taking of land was another thing entirely. When Mr. Ickes used the power of eminent domain to acquire a site for later construction, several landowners were given the right to sue in court. A lower federal court issued an injunction against Ickes, and an appeals court upheld the injunction.

Ickes was prepared to appeal this decision to the Supreme Court, but other political advisers were worried about the effect an adverse ruling would have on the whole New Deal. Fortunately, another case arose that established the precedent. The New York City Housing Authority had proposed a project of its own on the lower east side, entailing the remodelling of some tenements. When one of the tenement owners refused to sell, the housing authority filed eminent domain proceedings, and the state's highest court sustained the local authority's right to acquire land as a proper exercise of the state's police power.

For the federal government, the course of least judicial resistance was to adopt a hybrid program. The federal government would do what it was constitutionally enabled to do — that is, provide funds. The local housing authority would do what it was legally permitted to do — that is, acquire land and build housing.

However, the local housing authorities chafed under the aggressive and intimate supervision by Ickes and pressed for a law to set up a separate United States housing authority. The law passed Congress in

1937. Reluctantly, the federal government became only the financier and subsidizer of housing projects, and the local housing authorities, already the acquirers of land and the builders, became also the managers of all future projects. Essentially, that remains the formula today.

During the Depression, federal aid to cities went primarily for welfare. After World War II, much of the federal money went directly into building the interstate highway networks. The federal grants to state and local governments were used for objectives these lower levels of government had developed. This aid was typically a fifty-fifty match; one dollar of federal money matched one dollar of local money. Federal administrative controls were loose, because the recipients were defining the programs and raising significant portions of their own money through local taxes.

Aid as Policy Maker

The situation changed radically in the 1960s, a decade that was a watershed for the federalist system. The riots in black central cities exemplified the dissatisfaction of minority organizations and poor people with the unresponsiveness of state and local officials to their needs. The federal government responded by establishing the War on Poverty, sending money directly to cities and subcity units for social purposes and creating the Department of Housing and Urban Development to give cities a Cabinet status comparable to that given agriculture a century before.

Between 1962 and 1975, the aid to cities increased from $2.5 to $19.6 billion, or almost 800 percent, including the money passed through the states. The direct aid to local governments increased 5,000 percent between 1957 and 1977. Primarily, the direct aid was targeted to large cities. The aid to the 47 largest, excluding New York, grew from $406 million in 1967 to $5.4 billion in 1978. Whereas federal aid in 1967 amounted to only 9 cents for every dollar of locally generated revenue, in 1978 federal aid had increased to 50 cents for every dollar these larger cities raised.

Unlike the period before 1960, the federal government set policy and developed programs. State and local governments carried them out. To encourage participation, cities that agreed were given 100 percent grants. But they had to compete for the grants and their performance was closely monitored. Applications were approved on a project-by-project basis. By 1970, there were more than 500 categorical programs — a management maze for local governments. The proliferation of programs naturally raised the value of grantsmanship to a premium. To "get its share" of federal funds, the city or county had to keep track of what programs existed and to submit applications and proposals most likely to please the federal reviewers. Planning departments became grant-writing offices. James Gleason, chief executive of Montgomery County, Maryland, commenting on the increasing concern that local governments were being preempted, remarked in 1978, "The federal government has absorbed so much of the government jurisdiction that [it] has become the decider of all programs, and state and local officials have become implementers of those programs. It's not what you think is good for your community as an elected official. It's what they [the federal bureaucrats] think. It makes a mockery of the elected franchise."

Once the federal government began to view itself as a vehicle for imposing national policy, whether programs were administered by lower levels of government or by nongovernmental entities no longer mattered. School districts, regional bodies, special districts, local public authorities, nonprofit organizations, neighborhoods — all shared in the federal largesse. The antipoverty program channeled funds to nine hundred community-based agencies.

By the late 1970s no sector of the economy was untouched by federal funds. Neal Peirce could note, with considerable justification, "Today, virtually no town, village, township, county or Indian tribe in America is without direct ties to Washington, D.C. And there is virtually no function of local government, from police to community arts promotion, for which there isn't a counterpart federal aid program."[4]

In the early 1970s the federal government tried to simplify its funding programs by combining many related categorical grants into fewer, lump-sum block grants. These programs had their own dynamics. The community-development block-grant program, for example, had a lower population limit for entitlement. Those cities with more than fifty thousand people, or situated in a metropolitan area with seventy-five thousand people, were guaranteed funding. The rest had to compete for portions of the remainder. A complicated formula was the basis for distributing the income, taking into account need, local efforts at raising revenue, and population; battles over the composition and weighting of the distribution formula were common. The northern states, for example, managed in the late 1970s to get the age of housing included as a factor. Those cities with housing stock that was aging and deteriorating would be given more funds than those with an equal amount of housing stock that was newer and more structurally sound.

General revenue sharing, another lump-sum program, simply allocates funds according to population. This minimizes administrative procedure but has enormously expanded the number of recipients of federal aid. And the money often goes to places that have little need for it and few governmental operations. Thirty-nine thousand local governments receive general revenue-sharing funds; nearly twenty-eight thousand have populations of fewer than twenty-five hundred people, and fourteen thousand have fewer than five hundred inhabitants. Political scientist G. Ross Stephens criticized this homogeneous approach to revenue programs: "Making nomenclature [names the federal government applies to municipal units with some specified characteristics] the criteria [sic] for eligibility for direct federal aid is an extremely questionable practice. The United States has a surplus of 'toy governments.'"

General revenue sharing is an excellent example of how a program can be made administratively simple at the expense of effectiveness. Uniform rules gloss over the significant variations in state-local relations. Congress acted on the assumption that all units of general-purpose local government in the United States possess the same responsibilities and authority. This is not true. Revenue sharing is distributed one-third to state governments, two-thirds to local governments; yet in Hawaii 80 percent of the revenue and service delivery is done by the state government, and in New York State local governments account for more than 70 percent of all state and local expenditures. Some states administer the welfare programs themselves; in other states they are administered by counties; in still others, by the cities. In some areas fire protection, water supply, and sewerage are municipal functions. Elsewhere they are the responsibility of a regional authority or a special district.

The block-grant programs did help local and state government officials, who knew how much they would be receiving, to plan their budgets more effectively. But only 25 percent of federal aid to local and state governments came from those programs. The rest issued from categorical programs. Indeed, during the 1970s Congress added 150 more categorical aid programs and began to attach strings even to revenue sharing and other block-grant programs. Apparently the federal government could not restrict itself to being a banker, to simply collecting and redistributing revenue on the basis of need and population.

The relationship of cities to the federal government changed during the seventies and so did their relationship with their state governments. In part this was a result of the mid-1960s Supreme Court rulings that required states to allocate legislative representation based on the one-man-one-vote rule. Rarely have Supreme Court rulings so directly affected local governments.

Before these rulings each state had at least a two-to-one disparity in voter representation between the least- and most-heavily populated districts, and in some cases the disproportion was much greater. Within five years of the 1964 *Reynolds* v. *Sims* decision, all but one state had carried out — or promised to carry out — some form of reapportionment. The cities gained power in their previously rural-dominated state legislatures — not only the large central cities, but also the growing suburban population centers. State municipal leagues proliferated to lobby the state legislatures for local governments and to provide information and technical assistance to their members.

States responded by modernizing the machinery of government. For example:

In 1960, 31 legislatures met only every other year; in 1980 only 14 met so infrequently.

Only three state legislatures in 1960 had more than five professional staff members in their reference services, and only three had a comparable number in their legal-services units; by 1980 these and other units in practically all the states provided an array of central staff services.

No state staffed its standing committees in both houses in 1960; by 1980, 36 did so.

More than half the state constitutions in 1960 restricted the regular legislative sessions to 60 legislative or calendar days, or fewer; in 1980 only 19 did so.

The development of government at the state level had other characteristics as well:

The number of state employees grew at a rate twice as fast as that of
municipal employees between 1970 and 1980.

The share of state-local taxes going to the states surpassed that going
to the local governments in the early 1960s. By 1980, almost 60
percent of state-local tax revenues were generated by the states.

In 1979, 41 states had broad-based income taxes, and 45 had corporation income taxes; a like number imposed general sales taxes.

Thirty-seven states used all three as a revenue source in 1979, almost
twice the 19 that did so in 1960.

The state dominance in the state-local relationship was further
strengthened by the fact that federal aid was primarily funneled through
states. In 1980, for example, more than 70 percent of all federal aid to
lower levels of government went through the states. Part stayed at the
state level, and part passed through to local governments.

Originally, the pass-through money was thought to add leverage to
other state money. In 1972 each dollar of per capita federal aid that was
passed through the state was matched by $1.07 of state aid generated
from its own tax revenues. But by 1977 the pass-through money generated a 47-cent reduction in the state's own aid. Two political scientists,
writing in 1979, wondered whether the process of passing this money
through the states was not counterproductive. "It is possible," they
wrote, that

states have adopted an attitude of allowing the federal government to supplant a portion of their aid to local governments
which the states would normally supply. In other words, one
price to the local governments of increased federal direct pass-
through is a reduced rate of state own-source aid. The net result,
when coupled with increasing direct federal to local aid, is increasing reliance of local governments on federal dollars and
attendant standardized national priorities.[5]

By the late 1970s the capacity of cities to generate their own funds
had declined considerably, but their budgets had continued to expand
— it was a classic case of the responsibility and the money being at two
different levels. Cities have to rely primarily on taxes from property.

Four dollars of every five they raise in taxes come from this type of tax. State governments generate a third of their income from taxes on personal income, and a significant amount from sales taxes. The federal government, however, collects 60 percent of its revenue from the income tax, both personal and corporate. Thus the federal government uses a tax that raises more revenue as inflation increases and salaries escalate into higher tax brackets, while the municipal governments are forced to rely on one of the most unpopular taxes. And raising property-tax rates, or the valuation of property, elicits immediate and hostile reactions from voters.

Unfortunately, as the cities' sources of revenue have decreased, their responsibilities have increased. This is partly a result of mandates from state or federal governments. One report concluded that there are almost a thousand mandates per jurisdiction. Most of these are procedural, such as guaranteeing citizen participation, requiring public hearings and requiring affirmative-action hiring programs. But in many cases the mandates require expenditures of local funds, and there is no accompanying money. In the past few years, some cities have refused federal funds that have contingent conditions making acceptance more costly than rejecting the aid. Suburban communities surrounding Hartford, Connecticut, for example, refused community-development block-grant money because they would have been required to develop a housing-assistance plan that included low- and moderate-income housing. Several cities refused money for new sewage treatment plants, believing the requirements for plant construction to be so onerous that, even with 80 percent federal money, in the long run to build the plants would be too costly.

The Pie Stops Growing

Shortly after the 1973 oil embargo, the federal largesse to state and local governments stopped growing, and in 1978 per capita federal aid to state and local governments declined for the first time in the post-World War II era. Rates of growth in spending and employment, too, dropped considerably after 1975. As one report indicated, "There is accumulating evidence that the growth period in local government is coming to an end, or at least peaking."[6] Another report

93

concluded, "We appear to be entering a period when federal aid to state and local government will cease becoming an ever-larger share of state and local finance."[7]

Grants to state and local governments peaked in fiscal year 1978 at 17.3 percent of the federal budget. Local aid dropped to 15.8 percent in 1980, and some predict that by the mid-1980s it will drop further, to about 10 percent of federal outlays. Intergovernmental aid is divided into two parts. One is grants to states and localities and is intended primarily for welfare or income-maintenance programs to benefit individuals. The second consists of grants for activities directly under state and local government control, such as community development, public-service employment, mass transit, and public works. The most significant reductions are in this second category.

In a number of states, tax revolts have contributed to the problem of cities' finances. Proposition 13 in California and Proposition 2 1/2 in Massachusetts slashed property taxes — the most important source of funds for cities. This led inevitably to a major increase of state involvement in local affairs. Given the states' key position in the federal system and their more varied revenue sources, they will probably assume an even larger role in financing state and local public services as federal aid declines. And the state legislatures will also assume a larger role in public-policy making and service delivery.

The new conservative Republican administration in Washington, D.C., has indicated its objective of devolving responsibilities to state and local governments. However, there remains the question of where the financing will come from for these essential public programs. President Reagan has conceded, "We cannot balance the federal budget by asking other governments to do the work, while the national government continues to preempt so much of the nation's tax base."

The slowdown in intergovernmental transfers of money has come at a time of increasing regional disparity in revenue needs. The older industrial cities, built at the turn of the century, are discovering that their physical structure has deteriorated. Leaks in Boston's ancient water mains, some dating back to the 1840s, causes loss of half the 150 million gallons of water the system moves daily. New York City's two massive water tunnels are crumbling. Most of New Orleans' sewers need replacing; some were purchased — secondhand — from Philadelphia in 1896. When it rains in Chicago, the sewers back up into basements in about one fourth of the homes. Forty-nine of Cleveland's 163 city-maintained bridges examined by federal inspectors in 1978 were "intolerable" or "unsatisfactory."[8]

Compare the dramatic deterioration of the roads and utilities of our older cities to the circumstances in the states in a position to benefit from the rapidly rising energy prices that result from the federal decontrol of oil and gas prices. In the next decade, four states — Texas, Alaska, California, and Louisiana — will collect 83 percent of United States revenues from oil sales, taxes, and development rights. In the same period, benefits stemming from oil-price decontrol will net the state of Alaska a budget surplus of $37 billion. Its 1979 budget surplus of $1 billion allowed the state to abolish its state income tax; Alaska was about to give every resident a $400 grant, but that was ruled illegal.

State-owned oil fields in Texas will bring in more than $33 billion in the 1980s, according to the estimates by the U.S. Treasury Department. Texas has no state income tax and will probably do away with its sales tax. The state's $3 billion surplus in 1979 matched the size of its state budget. California expects to receive $22 billion; and Louisiana, a net of $14 billion.

Ironically, more federal aid might be given to these energy-rich states because of peculiarities in current distribution formulas. A state's efforts to collect taxes is one of the criteria for apportioning federal aid, and the windfall taxes from oil and gas make state governments appear to be making greater efforts. Thus, adding to the vast disparity in economic circumstances among the states, the ones with the least need for federal money will receive the most.

Recent experience suggests that both the political and the economic strains on the federal structure will be more pronounced in the years ahead than they have been in years past. "Our past muddling-through," one constitutional lawyer believes, "has been heavily dependent upon rapid average rates of economic growth, relatively cheap energy, ample capacity for capital formation, and the capacity of the states to offset, however disparately and inadequately, the chronic fiscal mismatch in the core cities. None of these factors appear as favorable now as in earlier years." The crucial question, he believes, is "whether a federation formed to protect diversity among states can deal with increasing concentration of its have-nots in a small minority of state and local jurisdictions of steadily weakening political influence."[9]

The Collapse of Federalism

By the time the Republicans came to power in Washington, D.C., in 1981, calls were increasing for some national debate on the role of the different levels of government — indeed, on the role of government itself. As some officials were pointing out, the federal system had become in a short period bewilderingly complex and overloaded. The annual meeting of the National League of Cities, held in Atlanta in 1980, went so far as to hold a workshop entitled "Are Cities Obsolete?" The Advisory Commission on Intergovernmental Relations called for a national convocation on federalism to meet in 1981. The Republican governors and the National Municipal League approved resolutions supporting that convocation. Governor Thornburgh of Pennsylvania declared, "It's time we took a hard look at our state houses, our courthouses and our city halls and asked ourselves: 'Are we ready, willing and able to carry out the awesome responsibilities of a resurgent federalism?' I believe that in far too many cases, the answer may be no."[10] William Gorham, president of the Urban Institute, and sociologist Nathan Glazer, both men enthusiastic architects of the new system of federal-state-local relationships, expressed the discouragement of many when they said in 1976, "There is less consensus on the ultimate causes of many serious urban problems, and even less consensus on the measures that would ameliorate them, than there was in 1966 or in 1956." They concluded, "It is clear that something beyond the complex structure of federal aid that has been built and rebuilt since the early 1960s is going to be necessary."[11]

The solutions that experts have offered vary considerably. Some want to rearrange political jurisdictions to match population concentrations. They want to create metropolitan-area-wide governments or to consolidate cities and counties into one government — as Indianapolis, Jacksonville, and Nashville did in the 1970s.

Others believe that the fragmentation of governments in metropolitan areas is fine, that the literally hundreds of different municipalities, townships, special districts, and public authorities within each area provide people with a choice. Elinor Ostrom has commented, "In a metropolitan area with many governments, the act of moving is voting with one's feet."[12] Sometimes the debate about the proper scale of government confuses the different functions of government. It is primarily a mechanism for generating and imposing a rule of conduct on its population. When government is defined as a decision-making process then politicians and ordinary citizens alike tend to advocate a scale of government that provides for face-to-face decision making. For example, Senator Mark Hatfield offered the following as a plank for the Republican Party's 1972 national platform: "It is clear today that the great experiment of our cities is a failure. We must return to a scale of government which is comprehensible to our citizens. By developing neighborhood government — not by fiat, but by an organic evolution from community organization — we can develop a sense of community through the state and a sense of individualism and neighborhood throughout the nation. To date, the centralization of government has destroyed community self-management and citizen participation. We must reverse this trend and develop our cities along the lines of neighborhood government and inter-neighborhood cooperation."[13]

Government is not only a governing entity but also a taxing authority and a provider of services. These functions have engendered a great deal of debate. Some believe the government should take care of the needy and provide public services and that the level of government best prepared to accomplish this is found at the community level. The Advisory Commission on Intergovernmental Relations has called for cities to grant limited power of taxation to neighborhoods. For example, to grant "a fractional millage on the property tax to be collected by the city or county as a part of the property tax bill and returned to the neighborhood for use as its governing body determines."[14]

Other political analysts prefer to reduce taxing authority at any level of government. One method to accomplish this is to have government provide fewer services. Robert Poole, a political analyst who argues for cutting back city hall, has said, "Much of what cities and counties do is essentially the operation of service business. But they very seldom operate these services like businesses."[15] He has favored increasing "privatization" of the economy.

As the 1980s beckoned, cities had to look, for the first time in a generation, to more austere times. The era of expanded, even bloated, budgets and of increasing employment by the local government is over. The new debates focused on the boundary lines between the private

97

and public sectors, the definition of the public welfare and the extent to which the community could intervene to restrict individual freedom. Yet even as the nation undertook a reexamination of its political bases, the natural resource shortages and rapidly rising energy prices broadened the responsibilities of cities. How would these governments closest to the people cope with the new era?

PART II

Gaining
Autonomy

Is there to be a greater and greater
centralization of energy planning and
production in this country, or is there a
chance that individuals, communities, and
local government will reject such centralization
by choosing their own energy alternatives,
and therefore, their own energy future?

Energy in Arkansas: Moving Toward Self-Reliance,
Arkansas Department of Energy, 1980

CHAPTER 5

A Critical Juncture

When the Mexican boll weevil ravaged the 1915
cotton crop around Enterprise, Alabama, where cotton
was king and farmers knew little about growing
anything else, the economic impact was devastating.
The impoverished cotton farmers soon agreed that
diversification was best and the next year planted
their first fields of corn, potatoes, sugar cane,
peanuts, and hay. The new crops prospered and soon
brought the average area income to three times its
former level. On December 11, 1919, the citizens of
Enterprise dedicated Boll Weevil Monument, the only
monument in the world glorifying a pest:
IN PROFOUND APPRECIATION OF THE BOLL WEEVIL AND
WHAT IT HAS DONE AS THE HERALD OF PROSPERITY BY
THE CITIZENS OF ENTERPRISE, COFFEE COUNTY, ALABAMA.

History is neither linear nor cyclical. Its dynamic may
have been best captured by writer Jon Berger, who likened it to the
motion of a corkscrew. From a distance we can make out its overall
course. But the closer we get the narrower our perspective becomes.
We can no longer distinguish the overall drift but only the mini-trends
represented by sections of the spinning blades. At any given moment
segments of the corkscrew are moving in almost any direction.
    This book has so far explored history. It has examined the period
1870 to 1970, the era of cheap fossil fuels. Future historians may determine that the age of low-priced fuels lasted longer than the latter date.
But then, they will have the luxury of a more distant perspective of the
corkscrew's motion.

The second part of this book describes contemporary affairs. And it focuses more narrowly on energy. Since the process it describes is still building, the tone is more discursive, and more anecdotal. The process of change is the cumulative effect of many events and many dynamics. By selecting certain events the author presents the book's theme: rising energy prices encourage us to link production and consumption more closely, and if cities pursue a policy of energy self-reliance they may find that it carries with it the much broader search for self-reliant cities.

Most observers who disagree on the future of our energy supplies agree on the dynamics that took place over the last century. From 1870 to 1970 America became as dependent on petroleum as the Enterprise farmers did on cotton. Petroleum in the early 1970s generated 50 percent of our total energy and was the basis for industries as diverse as clothing and pharmaceuticals.

OPEC is our generation's boll weevil. Its actions have brought home the dangers of dependence on a one crop economy. During the era of falling energy prices we built a society indifferent to the amount of energy it used to accomplish its tasks.

It did not matter that power plants were less than 30 percent efficient, that more than 70 percent of the fuel consumed was given off as waste heat.

It did not matter that we consumed the equivalent of several gallons of oil to make each aluminum can from virgin bauxite, only to throw it away after one use.

It did not matter that we built houses with little or no insulation or that we used twice as much energy getting food from the farm to our table as we did in growing it.

During this period our cities developed a parasitical relationship with their natural resource base. "How can cities survive even though their human populations vastly exceed the carrying capacity of their land areas?" A. Wolman asked in an article written in 1965. "The answer, in a word, is energy. A city is a gigantic living organism with a voracious appetite. The metabolism of this organism demands an uninterrupted flow of inputs from external sources."[1] The average city of fifty thousand imports 100 tons of food, 475 tons of fuel, and 31,250 tons of fresh water each day.

OPEC reminded us that our fossil fuel reserves were limited. Its actions touched every sense and fiber of our system, forcing us to reexamine our ways, to rebuild our energy system and make it more diversified, more resilient, more flexible in the face of changing resource realities. In the process the question was raised — how much can cities reduce their imports and rely on indigenous resources?

Our transition to energy efficiency will be more tortuous than that accomplished by the intrepid Alabama cotton farmers. They restructured their planting patterns. We will have to restructure society, discarding many cherished institutions, technologies, and legal concepts evolved during a period of abundant and cheap fossil fuels.

After the Distribution Age

During that century of falling energy prices, progress became synonymous with separation. We separated our homes from our places of work, our factories from their customers, our fuel supplies from our furnaces. The neighborhood bakeries, ubiquitous in 1900, were replaced with regional automated plants that baked bread for communities several hundred miles away. The 400 local breweries in existence in 1910 had dwindled to 60 by 1980, and most industry observers predicted no more than a handful of national companies in existence by the year 2000. It was, as Ralph Borsodi noted, "the Distribution Age."[2]

This was an age during which we became more and more dependent on institutions farther and farther away. Big government and big business took over the functions traditionally reserved for the family, the neighborhood, the homestead, and the crafts shop.

And it was an age that ended abruptly when, between 1970 and 1980, world crude-oil prices increased 2,000 percent. The continuing political instability in the Persian Gulf has demonstrated to America and the rest of the world the vulnerability of industrial societies dependent on one commodity. The rules of the game have changed — dramatically. But institutions, technologies, laws, and habits evolved over a century do not adapt so rapidly.

The national instinct has been to look to the federal government and the larger energy corporations for leadership. Yet these two entities, rather than trying to resolve the problems, spent most of the seventies criticizing each other. Their bulk providing an enormous inertia, these institutions lumbered like dinosaurs toward extinction. Years would

103

pass before they could change their course. They became objects of ridicule. During the 1970s many of our central institutions, both public and private, suffered a crisis of credibility and legitimacy.

The soaring prices of conventional fuels in the seventies called into question the structure of our energy-generation and delivery system; the issue of scale crept into energy planning. For example, a proposed large nuclear power plant cannot provide electricity for 10 to 15 years, and this makes us vulnerable to changes in demand. Smaller power plants, however, can be built more quickly and therefore lessen our vulnerability to unpredictable demand swings. Blackouts, we now realize, are not caused by problems in power plants but by breakdowns in the distribution systems. If we were to increase the number of generators and situate them nearer their final customers, the overall reliability of the electric distribution system would increase significantly.

For other reasons, as well, scale should be a major consideration in designing future power-generation facilities. In an age of scarce fuels, to use the heat generated in the process of electricity production makes good sense. And that heat can be distributed most economically if the generation of power is scaled to local need.

Initially, the new, smaller power plants still will rely on fuels imported from remote areas of the country and the globe. Increasingly the fuels themselves can be gathered locally. Solar energy in its many forms — wind power, hydroelectricity, alcohol, or methane from plant matter, or direct solar conversion into heat or electricity by the use of solar collectors and solar cells — is most efficiently harvested in decentralized locations.

In short, the basic lessons of the new age of energy are that the efficiency, economy, and technical stability of our energy system will be greatly enhanced if we depend on millions of power plants rather than thousands, and we use fuels generated locally.

The Sociology of Energy

Resolution of the energy crisis appears to be an issue as sociological as it is technical — or even political. People who live in identical houses use widely varying amounts of energy for the same functions. So education and peer pressure will be as important in accelerating energy conservation as the development of new technologies or even the use of creative financing mechanisms.

This lesson in the sociology of conservation complements the lesson in scale of energy generation. The experiences of people in western Massachusetts and in Colorado show that, although conservation is much more cost effective than investments in solar technology, those who invest in solar technologies are spurred to conserve, as well — but conserving does not as often spur use of solar technologies. One sociological difference between conservation and the use of solar technologies is that the latter gives people a source of supply; the consumer becomes a partial producer. And by combining that production ability with aggressive conservation efforts, the consumer can move closer to energy independence. In America, independence and self-reliance are powerful motivating factors.

Like the Alabama cotton farmers, we must diversify our economic foundations. Economic diversification in our energy system appears difficult, if not impossible, however, when planned by national entities. The federal government and huge corporations tend to favor homogeneous solutions. But the nation's energy needs are anything but homogeneous: Santa Monica, California, uses most of its energy for residential hot-water heating; Portland, Maine, uses most of its energy for space heating; and Miami, Florida, uses its for air conditioning. Neither are our resources homogeneous: In January, Yuma, Arizona, has only 10 percent cloud coverage, while Buffalo, New York, and Portland, Oregon, have almost 80 percent cloud coverage. A solar collector suited for Arizona may not be suited for Buffalo. Similarly, which plants are best as fuel sources depends on local climates and soils. The eucalyptus tree might be best for Hawaii, the tumbleweed for southern Texas, the hybrid poplar for upper Michigan.

The 1970s also taught us that energy is only the first in a series of shortages the world will confront. Already shortages of water plague the southwestern and mid-Atlantic states. As the rest of the world attempts to imitate America's wasteful industrial development patterns, the competition for materials will increase greatly, despite our ability to map and mine the earth and the oceans in a way unimaginable only 20 years ago. If the age of abundant fossil fuels was characterized by separation, the age of energy efficiency will be characterized by integration. The wastes of one process will become the raw materials of another. Pro-

105

duction will take place close to consumption. Distribution lines will be considerably shortened.

A Nation of Cities

The new resource realities force us to look to our local governments, our small businesses, our neighborhoods and households for leadership. Where, after all, do we turn in moments of crisis? The mayor of Hartford, Connecticut, answers, "When there were gas lines, do you think people complained to Sheik Yamani? No. Did they call President Carter? No. They came to me." When energy supplies are disrupted, as has been the case in parts of the country every year since 1973, the community structure becomes the only effective means of mobilizing people.

America is a nation of cities. Half the population lives under the direct authority of municipal governments; more than 90 percent of the population lives on 2 percent of the land area. These dense areas have been the centers of commerce, knowledge, technical invention, and social innovation during much of our history.

Cities have power. Their governments directly control, or significantly influence, the way we use our land, the way we design and construct our buildings, and the way we transport ourselves and our goods. Cities build and maintain roads. They own and operate waterworks, and more than two thousand cities own and operate their electric utilities. They collect solid waste, operate sewage treatment plants, and supervise large capital-improvement programs. They often own large areas of land and large numbers of structures.

And, the city governments are those closest to the people. As a result, they lend themselves to active participation in decision-making by the greatest number of citizens. Cities are the means for responding to what Hannah Arendt calls the need for "public freedom," the need to participate actively in making basic societal decisions. We are forced by the energy crisis to grapple with truly complex issues; many of these, because they deal with building codes and land-use plans, will have to be decided by local governments. What, for example, should be the relationship between private-property rights and society's need to reduce fossil-fuel dependence? When we encourage solar technologies at the household level, how can we guarantee that homeowners' access to sunlight will be uninterrupted? Should my neighbor's freedom to build be restricted so that I can achieve energy independence? Is a contract between me and my neighbor for a "solar easement" legally binding?

A majority of the housing stock that will be standing in the year 2000 already has been built. How do we accelerate the conversion of these buildings to energy-efficiency by, say, landlords who do not pay the energy bills, or by tenants who have no interest in improving the value of property they do not own? Whatever the solutions, cities are the logical level of government to oversee the debate. And when the decisions have been reached, the city residents can, through their city charters, develop the rules to govern the progress of enactment.

Humanly scaled energy systems mesh well with the potentially democratic nature of decision-making. Amory Lovins observes that such humanly scaled systems "automatically allocate the energy and the social costs or the side effects of getting it to the same people at the same time, thus enabling those people to integrate costs and benefits with their own senses and decide how much is enough."[3]

We cannot expect transition to a more stable, diversified society without the normal complement of failures, both technical and institutional. One of the major benefits of experimentation at the local level is that the damage done by failures is minimized and the lessons of successful projects can be disseminated to other areas of the country. More than a thousand cities in our nation have significant populations. Each one can become a laboratory of the new age.

One of the ironies of history is that the energy crisis should occur just as the American federal system begins to collapse. Cities have had to fight for a place in a political system governed by a federal Constitution that makes no mention of municipal corporations. Cities that once did nothing more than provide police and fire protection are now actively involved in comprehensive planning, economic development ventures, and population growth ordinances. Many cities are monitoring the quality of their air, the composition of their solid-waste streams, the flow of capital through their borders, the amount of ground water beneath their feet — all with unprecedented sophistication.

Yet cities also have become more dependent on state and federal governments. City governments have been converted into administrative entities for government at higher levels; the cities may provide the services, but they do not generate the money. Nor do they decide on the level of services they will provide. And, because revolts aimed at reducing taxes have focused on the easiest target — the property tax — and property tax is the major source of local governmental revenue, cities are forced to rely more on state and federal grants. The proliferation of special districts and regional planning authorities has fragmented authority and responsibility to the point that few really know who is in charge.

A growing body of political observers believe the American federalist system needs a major restructuring. Some would like to consolidate many of the local governments into county-wide or metropolitan-area-wide authorities. Others take the opposite view. They believe the city is already too remote from its citizens and that the neighborhood should become the basic governing and service-delivery unit, because the neighborhood is where face-to-face decision making can take place and services can be tailored best to local needs. (These observers like to note that many big-city neighborhoods were themselves once independent cities.)

There are those, too, who believe that government itself is the problem. They want to minimize the role of government and "privatize" the economy. Under such a scheme, governments would develop guidelines for contracting with private companies to provide services and would establish free-enterprise zones in inner cities where private companies would have carte blanche to invest.

That a problem as global as the energy crisis can be solved by local actions is hard to believe. Yet about half of the total energy we use is consumed in urban areas. It is on the local level that systems can be fashioned to use our natural resources most efficiently; only on this level can the goals of self-reliance and independence be compatible with the new energy systems.

Those American communities and small businesses that were most actively involved in developing new, energy-efficient designs in the 1970s were also those most optimistic about the future and most self-confident about their ability to make the transition. Maybe, like the residents of Enterprise, Alabama, with the boll weevil, we will look back on the energy crisis as the catalyst that forced us to a better way of living.

CHAPTER 6

First Steps

We cannot any longer look to foreign
nations, oil companies or the federal
government to explain or solve our energy
crisis. We must recognize that the crisis
is real and immediate, and we must look
to ourselves to find the answers.

George Latimer, Mayor of St. Paul

When OPEC cut back our oil supply in late 1973, and then raised the price 400 percent, it ushered in a crash program in energy education. Americans were almost illiterate in energy matters, but to begin coping with the new energy situation we quickly tried to piece together a picture of how we use energy.

It proved embarrassingly difficult to do. One of the major problems was the energy vocabulary itself. An individual who wants to trim his or her waistline can gauge how to do it relatively easily. All food energy is measured in the same units; whatever we might purchase, bread or milk, canned goods or cookies, the energy content is measured in calories. Compact booklets at the checkout counter contain lists of popular foods and the number of calories each contains. We know how many calories we need to maintain specific body weights and how many calories we consume in various activities.

For an individual or a nation to calculate an energy diet is more difficult. Various fuels are measured with a bewildering variety of terms: natural gas is measured in therms or cubic feet; electricity is measured in kilowatt hours; fuel oil and gasoline are measured in gallons. To develop a coherent energy policy when each fuel carries its own peculiar vocabulary is troublesome.

Another problem is that almost all of the initial data gathering was done by the federal government, adding more strange terms to our energy dictionary, such as quads (quadrillion Btus) and gigawatts (one billion watts). The terms were not only unfamiliar, they were so large as to be meaningless for communities. Hearing that the nation uses 75 quadrillion Btus a year is like hearing that the national debt is a trillion dollars. The numbers are too large to be related to individuals' actions.

Even more difficult is to gather information on specific communities. The regions that electric and gas utilities serve rarely coincide with political jurisdictions. Fuel oil dealers and gasoline-station operators tend not to maintain accurate records, and even when they do keep good files, they are reluctant to divulge sales data because of the highly competitive nature of their business. Highway departments collect transportation data on a regional basis.

Sometimes, as in the study of Columbus, Ohio, the statewide data are used and are prorated for the locality. Some cities have used unorthodox methods to assemble data. When Carbondale, Illinois, population thirty thousand, learned that its gross receipts tax revenue on natural gas and electric consumption had declined in 1979, it demanded that the utilities verify the figures by providing an exact breakdown of consumption within its borders. The utilities complied. When Carbondale found gasoline-station operators reluctant to divulge their sales data, university students read gas pump meters late at night to find out how the transportation-related energy dollar was spent, persevering despite complaints by retailers of trespassing. Despite the obstacles, a growing number of communities have compiled enough data to illuminate their dependence on various fuels.

When the data came in, we learned that although the rising cost of energy affects all sections of the country, the energy crisis has different meanings in different cities. Los Angeles, like Miami and Burlington, Vermont, relies on oil-fired electricity; Chicago relies on coal and uranium to generate electricity; and Seattle and Nashville rely on water power. The vast majority of the residents in Dayton, Ohio, heat their homes with natural gas, while in New York City the majority use oil. In Eugene, Oregon, space heating is done electrically, while in Missoula,

Montana, about half of the residential space heating is done with wood. The primary energy consumer in Santa Monica is the hot water heater; in St. Paul, the furnace; and in Jacksonville and Phoenix, the air conditioner. In Los Angeles it is the automobile.

Changing the Rules for Buildings

The first step was data collection. The second was to identify those areas where the city could encourage conservation. Cities have little control over appliance or automobile efficiency, but they directly control the design of buildings and the way we use land. About a quarter of the nation's energy is used to light, heat, and cool our buildings. Building-related energy comprises about half of all energy consumed within our cities.

Americans dislike regulations. Applying building codes and zoning have become acceptable governmental activities because they have been viewed as a means of protecting the health and safety of urban dwellers. In densely populated areas, a building that represents a fire hazard, for example, is a threat to surrounding buildings. The first use of zoning was to separate industrial functions that generated noise and odors from residential sections of the city.

The use of building codes and land-use-planning regulations to reduce energy consumption has been a controversial extension of traditional local government authority. For the first time, local regulations are being used not to protect the health and safety of the population directly, but indirectly to protect the welfare of the entire community — and the nation. The extent to which municipalities are allowed to use energy efficiency as a factor in developing building codes or zoning ordinances varies significantly from state to state. Montana's cities can adopt only the state building code. Washington's cities can develop a code that differs from that of the state but cannot be more rigorous. Illinois's localities can develop codes that are more stringent than the state's. In most states, only home-rule cities have the right even to include energy efficiency as an element in the planning process without express authorization from the state legislature. Yet Oregon, New Jersey, and other states require localities to consider the efficient use of energy as part of their comprehensive land-use plans.

111

The federal government has encouraged uniformity by requiring each state to adopt a building energy-conservation standard for new construction as a prerequisite to receiving federal energy-related planning and demonstration funds. The states, in turn, required their localities to adopt such codes. But in some areas of the country, especially the Midwest, earlier court decisions that prohibited states from imposing building codes on localities left the enforcement of such requirements in limbo.

To make easier the building industry's compliance with the new standards, the federal government made them nominal. The standards were developed by builders, engineers, and architects. The entire group had to agree before a standard was adopted. The codes are very simple. They prescribe specific amounts of insulation in walls and attics, a specific number of air changes per hour, and specific levels of efficiency for mechanized equipment. The organization that oversaw the development of the standards — the American Society of Heating, Refrigeration, and Air Conditioning Engineers — advises those thinking of adopting the code in clear terms: "The intent of this section is to provide minimum requirements for building envelope construction in the interest of energy conservation. *These requirements are not intended nor should they be construed as the optimization of energy-conserving practices*"[1] (emphasis in the original).

Some architects have complained that the code's specificity hampers innovation. They have designed buildings that surpass the code in overall performance but do not comply with the energy-specific section of the code. Most architects prefer performance standards. These establish a level of energy consumption per square foot of floor space; as long as a building meets the overall standard it is approved, even if it does not meet each of the prescribed standards on individual parts of the building.

The problem with performance codes is that they make the job of the builder and the building inspector much more difficult. Instead of looking to see whether a wall has three inches of insulation to gauge energy consumption, one has to use a computer model. Unfortunately the accumulated knowledge about heat loss is still embryonic, and computer models can differ dramatically in their assumptions and conclusions.

Computer models are particularly difficult to develop because weather can vary even within very small areas. Rainfall in Portland, Oregon, for example, varies from 27 inches to 64 inches annually in different parts of the city. "Persons living in the east part of the city," writes Steven Johnson, a local historian, "are much more under the stupendous effects of the Columbia Gorge, which can bring in gusty hot and dry winds in the summer and frigid dry air in the winter."[2] People living in San Francisco are intimately aware of the variation in cloud cover and fog depending on which side of and how far up on a hill one's house is situated.

In St. Louis, a six-year exhaustive study of the climate called MET-ROMEX found that the eastern part of the city has heavier summer precipitation, 10 percent more cloud cover, 30 percent more rain, 50 percent more heavy rainstorms, and 100 percent more hail than nearby rural areas. A study of four buildings in Helena, Montana, determined that wind speed and direction vary greatly even in that city on the flat plains. Santa Cruz designers isolated at least four major microclimatic regions in that California county.

Despite these complications, builders found they could construct houses, and even apartment houses, that reduce energy consumption dramatically without looking like space-age capsules. Wayne Shick, a professor from Illinois, developed "low-cal" homes. The homes are oriented to take advantage of the sun's heat in the winter. Shick discovered that with conventional stud wall construction, because the insulation has to be placed between the studs, the stud itself became a major source of heat loss. So he designed staggered studs, giving not only twice as much room for insulation, but allowing insulation to be placed in back of the wood studs, reducing heat loss substantially.

Eugene Leger built a house in East Pepperell, New York. He too used a double stud wall, along with double or triple glazing on all the windows, and he added some new wrinkles. The front and rear doors not only are heavily insulated, they open into vestibules, to limit heat losses. And other than for doors and windows, there is only one break in the plastic membrane (vapor barrier) of the walls and ceiling: a vent pipe within a partition wall of the bathroom. The house Leger built is so efficient that it has no furnace. Only appliance waste heat, lights, and body heat are necessary.

113

A 95-unit complex in Davis, California, consisting of townhouses and apartment houses built by Tandem Associates is oriented to make the best use of the local climate, and it includes solar hot-water systems. These houses use less than 20 percent of conventional homes' yearly demand for energy for space heating, cooling, and hot water. Their total energy costs per unit were estimated in 1979 to be less than $20 a year.

The building codes in the United States are among the most precise and cumbersome of all governmental regulations. And they impose specific burdens on such new technologies as solar energy systems. Three basic building codes apply in this country, each with separate codes for plumbing, electrical, and mechanical systems. The Uniform Building Code, developed by the International Conference of Building Officials, is in force mainly in the western half; the National Building Code, issued by the National Board of Fire Underwriters, is in force primarily in the eastern states. The Basic Building Code, promoted by the Building Officials Conference of America, is used in the central states, and it may be the most widely used of all. Thus if a solar energy system, for example, were to be approved under one building code, it would be approved only for those jurisdictions using that code as their standard.

Amending a code can be a tedious process. There are more than six thousand local building codes. When no specific language in a code covers a new technology, as has been the case for solar power, a great deal of discretionary authority rests with local officials. This has led to problems.

Travis Price, an architect hired by the Tennessee Valley Authority in 1977 to design and implement a program to install a thousand solar hot-water heaters in Memphis, Tennessee, found himself trying to cope with new technologies and evolving codes simultaneously. "During the first three or four years that solar hot water systems became competitive the technical requirements for installing them kept getting more strict,"[3] he recalls. A solar hot-water system usually consists of collectors that heat air or liquid. Tubes carry to a storage tank the hot air or liquid. Water is a cheap liquid for this purpose, but it can freeze and crack the collector. Designers who use an antifreeze solution have to keep the antifreeze separate from the drinking-water system by installing heat exchangers; a heat exchanger in this instance is a series of tubes through which hot water flows and transfers its heat to the water in the tank. When solar technology became more widespread, state and local governments worried that the heat exchanger containing antifreeze could develop a leak and mix the harmful antifreeze with the potable water. They required double-walled exchangers for extra protection.

The Memphis solar systems had double-walled heat exchangers. A hundred such exchangers were already installed, and several hundred others were on order, when Los Angeles came up with another precautionary measure. It required that the heat exchanger be vented. If a leak in the inner wall of the heat exchanger developed, the gas would spill through the vent, warning the residents. "It was a good idea," Price concedes, "even though the chances of a double leak are infinitesimal."[4] The cost of installing the vent on a new system was about $20. But it would cost $200 to go back and redo each system already installed in Memphis. Even so, the local building inspector was adamant that the residents of his city should have protection equal to the Los Angelenos'. He ordered all the systems already installed to be refitted with the early warning systems.

Zoning and Land-Use Regulations

Many communities have private, as well as public, rules requiring homes to be designed in harmony with the community standards. The accoutrements of solar technologies tend not to conform. An historic district commission in Connecticut refused to allow a rooftop solar system because it was not "aesthetically compatible."[5] The chairman of the planning board in Coral Gables, Florida, proposed an ordinance that would ban solar water heaters from any rooftop that was visible from the street because they were "unsightly."[6] Three of the five members of the zoning board of appeals in Madison, Wisconsin, denied a homeowner permission to install a solar system because, the chairman of the commission said, it was "hideous."[7]

The courts rarely intervened in such cases. But as the energy crisis worsened and supply disruptions became more common, the courts had to balance the right of the community to regulate its own affairs with the right of the individual to follow a policy that serves national

115

goals. When the town of Mamaroneck, New York, denied the application of attorney Arthur Katz to install three solar panels that would cause his house to be above the height limit, 26 of his neighbors signed a statement of support. The zoning appeals board denied his appeal, but in a precedent-setting case, New York State Supreme Court Justice Harold Wood accused the town of an "ostrich head-in-the-sand" approach and suggested that the zoning authorities reexamine their attitudes in light of "changing scientific advances and national and state interests in energy conservation."[8]

No matter what the outcome, those experimenting with new technologies in urban areas could count on one thing — that the process of gaining building permits, zoning variances, and authorization from historic preservation groups would try their patience. Eric Peterson, an engineer and Department of Energy employee, has tried to help others who might attempt to crack the "solar barrier" in their cities by writing a detailed account of his own tortuous experience in getting approval for a solar system. The account is appropriately entitled "Urban Pathfinder Retrofit."[9]

Many innovators grew restless with the time required for local codes to change. For example, many localities, to protect residents from having to live in dark basements, had developed regulations that require a certain amount of one's living space to be above ground. These have been a problem for the architects and builders who discovered that earth-sheltered homes could be light and airy, and remain warm during the winter and cool during the summer. One builder of earth-sheltered homes in Roone, Iowa, expressed the frustration felt by many innovators: "It's a matter of dealing with uneducated people who are set in their ways. People don't know anything about earth shelters. Bankers don't. Code inspectors don't. Nobody does."[10]

Jay Compon ran out of patience after waiting more than two years for his town — Hanover, New Hampshire — to develop a windmill ordinance. "I can't flimflam with this any longer," he declared. "I'm going to build my windmill without a building permit and let them take me to court." Mel Moench, an engineer in Waverly, Minnesota, didn't even try to go through official channels. Believing he could not obtain a permit to build his "autonomous" house — complete with solar and wind technologies, a composting toilet, and a fish pond — he went ahead without one. The local authorities, though conceding he might have been turned down if he had asked for a permit, went to court and succeeded in having Moench cited for contempt. He spent several days in jail.

Despite such frustrations, the number of citizens and small businesses willing to sacrifice time and money to revamp urban regulations that prohibit energy self-reliance continued to increase. Robert Crawford owns a mobile home in Thornton, Colorado. In 1979 he installed a wood-burning stove, but when he tried to install solar panels the owner of the mobile home park threatened to evict him. The objection was later dropped. In early 1981 the Architectural Review Board of Thornton rejected Crawford's proposal to install a 200-watt windmill on the roof of his home. The Board said the windmill would be "incompatible" with other dwellings in the mobile home park. Crawford was in the process of getting a variance to allow him to build a separate structure for the windmill as this book went to press. Such have been the trials and tribulations of the pioneers willing to experiment with new technologies.

Technologies that are decentralized are inherently a matter of neighborly concern. So the pioneers often need to educate their neighbors as well as city planners. When Patrick McLoughlin tried to get a permit to install a four-kilowatt wind turbine in Mechanicsburg, Pennsylvania, his neighbors opposed the request. The zoning board denied the permit, citing violations of rear- and side-yard setback provisions as well as height regulations. In Jefferson County, Colorado, Wayne Dingerson planned to build a structure 60 to 80 feet high but was faced with a 35-foot county height restriction in his subdivision, southwest of Denver. When he applied for a height variance, neighbors protested and threatened a lawsuit because a subdivision covenant further limited structures to six feet above the roof line. Dingerson said he could have found a legal way to break the covenant, but he decided against it and withdrew his variance request just before it was to go to the county Board of Adjustments. "I felt [being granted a variance] was a very feasible thing," Dingerson said. "We all have obligations to pursue alternative energy sources. The hurdle is not the government; the obstacle is that you still have to educate the people. . . . You've got to live with these people," he added.[11]

117

Sometimes neighborhood disputes have threatened to erupt into full-scale war. In July 1980 Charles Olmsted and Jeanine Lanier, botanists at the University of Northern Colorado, were granted a variance to build a greenhouse onto their house despite the vigorous objections of Shalto and Alma Davis, neighbors to the south. The Davises objected that the greenhouse would create glare and that melting snow would slide from the greenhouse roof and ice up their driveway. Initially the zoning board of appeals told the neighbors to work out an agreement. When they could not, the board gave the botanists a variance so that they could build to within two feet of the property line on the condition that they construct a curb and a four foot fence the entire length of the 22-foot greenhouse. The Davises appealed the variance to the city council, but the council not only upheld the board's decision, it removed all the conditions of the variance. The greenhouse was built and, according to Olmsted, supplies much of the home's heat. The Davises, however, claimed that their original objection had in fact been well founded. The greenhouse reflected sunlight onto and into their house. They claimed the glare harmed Mrs. Davis's eyesight, killed or harmed houseplants, and even peeled the paint on the house. Olmsted conceded that the greenhouse created some glare, but zoning regulations prohibited his changing the slope of the outer greenhouse wall by making it vertical and thus eliminating the winter glare. He offered to buy reflective window shading material for the Davises, but they refused. Instead, they built a six-foot fence on their lot line. It partially shades the greenhouse, and they are seeking a variance to erect a covered carport for a recreational vehicle. This would shade a much larger portion of the greenhouse. It was Olmsted's turn to object. As this book went to press, he was threatening to sue the Davises for the amount of fossil fuels he would have to purchase as a result of decreased heat from the greenhouse.

A Right to Sunlight?

Solar energy will never play a significant role in urban energy systems if continued access to sunlight is not guaranteed. As Gail Boyer Hayes, environmental lawyer and author of *Solar Access Law*, states, "The power of the sun is awesome, but it can be blocked by something as seemingly fragile as an aspen leaf. If we are to harness solar energy, barriers between the sun and solar collectors must be prevented."[12] This, however, has not proved easy to do. In England the right to light is accepted. Japanese courts regularly award monetary damages to homeowners whose access to sunlight is obstructed. But no such right exists in the United States. When Miami's Fountainbleau Hotel planned to build a 14-story addition that would cast a shadow over the Eden Roc's cabanas, swimming pool, and sunbathing terrace, the Eden Roc's directors went to court, claiming that the lack of sunshine would reduce the hotel's revenues. The United States Supreme Court refused to stop the construction.

The problem is a knotty one. A locality that guarantees solar access for one piece of property may reduce the value of adjoining property. Should a solar energy system that saves the owner of one lot $100 a year in fuel be allowed to prevent the construction of a $5 million building on an adjacent lot?

The homeowner or apartment developer can negotiate a private contract with the neighbor by agreeing to pay him or her for the right to continued access to the sun. Such solar easements are already specifically permitted in 20 states. Most lawyers believe they would be legally acceptable in every state. This may work in residential sections, but in areas zoned for high-density commercial buildings, can a prospective solar installation pay its way? Arnold Wallenstein, lawyer for the Northeast Solar Energy Center in Boston, gives the example of a New York City apartment house that faced an empty lot to the south and wanted to install a vertical solar collector along its south wall. The lot was owned by a company with the resources to develop a 30- to 50-story office building, tall enough to block the apartment house's access to sunlight. "Let's say that the existing building is a ten-story apartment house," explains Wallenstein, "and the other company would have built a 25-story luxury hotel. The property rights for their lot are worth millions. The apartment building's energy savings might amount to $100,000 over five or ten years, which is substantial but can't compare to the other lot's potential value. The strict economics are that the solar easement would cost as much as, or more than, the developed value of the southern site. That's a very neat case. The solar wall doesn't get built."[13]

If solar access is to be guaranteed, how much of the building site should be accessible? During what periods? Should a building be allowed access to sufficient sunlight to heat 60 square feet of solar collector, enough for a family's hot water needs? Or should the entire south side of a building be accessible to sunlight so that the winter sun can warm the interior? The winter sun hangs low in the sky. Therefore, to guarantee access, buildings and trees on the south side of a house must be very far away. The city of Los Alamos, New Mexico, requires solar access for structures from 9 A.M. to 4 P.M. Can traditional urban densities be maintained under such provisions? To provide adequate access to sunlight, urban planners might be requiring such low building densities that the increased transportation-energy consumption would more than offset energy saved through use of sunlight.

In an increasing number of instances, developers are using private covenants to establish a right to sunlight in new housing subdivisions. Because covenants often have been used to thwart the installation in existing subdivisions of solar equipment that was considered aesthetically incompatible with the existing homes, these new agreements represent a turnabout. Village Homes, in Davis, adopted such a covenant. It reads, in part:

> All south-facing glass and solar space heating collectors in each house shall remain unshaded from December 21 to February 21 between the hours of 10 am and 2 pm (solar time) except as provided herein.
>
> All roof-top solar hot water collectors on each house shall remain unshaded each day of the year between the hours of 10 am and 2 pm (solar time), except as provided herein.
>
> Shading caused by the branches of deciduous trees shall be exempt from this restriction.
>
> Shading caused by original house construction or fences built within six (6) months of occupancy shall be exempted from this restriction only upon special approval of the Village Homes Design Review Board.
>
> Homeowners may encroach upon their own solar rights. The Board of Directors of the Village Homeowners' Association shall have the authority to enforce this restriction.

Cities have been slow to develop comprehensive energy conservation ordinances. A survey of fourteen hundred local, regional, and state planning agencies conducted by the American Planning Association in 1979 found only 13 communities that had enacted land-use regulations specifically designed to save energy. One of these pioneers was Davis.

Davis—A Pioneer

Davis is a university town with a total population of thirty-six thousand. More than half the adults living in Davis are either students, faculty, or staff at the Davis campus of the University of California. Following the late 1950s, when the university expanded its agricultural school into a liberal arts campus, its enrollment expanded so dramatically that automobiles and bicycles competed for the right-of-way on streets. When the city council refused to construct bike lanes, probicycle candidates ran for political office, and they won. During the decade following their election in 1966, Davis constructed more than 28 miles of bikepaths. Today there are twenty-eight thousand bicycles in Davis. They are an important part of the transportation system. One traffic count taken during the summer (when few university students are in town) showed that bicycles constitute 40 percent of all traffic on a heavily traveled street. The emblem of the city is a gay nineties two-wheeler.

In 1972 hundreds of citizens developed a comprehensive plan for Davis, placing a limit on future growth and calling for resource conservation. Jonathan Hammond, then a lecturer at the university, proposed an energy conservation code that took account of the unique climate in Davis. He established a consulting group called the Energy Conservation Ordinance Project and spent a year measuring temperatures and comparing utility bills in homes and apartments. The study's conclusion was that the most important energy variable in Davis is a building's orientation to the sun. Buildings that take advantage of the sun can use as little as one-seventh of the energy required by buildings not so oriented.

When the oil embargo hit, Davis was prepared. In January 1976 it became the first city to implement a comprehensive energy conservation code. Among other requirements, the code regulates the amount of a building's window area in relation to the floor area. If more glass is desired, the architects must arrange it on the south-facing portions of the building or employ thermal glass. The amount of unshaded glass is strictly limited. The code specifies the shading of south-facing windows in the summer, heavily insulated attics and walls, cross-ventilation for cooling, and light-colored roofs to reflect the summer sun.

Plans for new buildings are carefully checked by city officials; and

121

they put scale models of proposed buildings under a solar simulator. The simulator is a gadget with light bulbs canted at different angles to represent the rays of the sun on different days of the year. It can provide a quick indication of whether the proposed building is properly positioned on a lot, whether it has too much glass, and whether the glass is properly shaded.

Davis's code concerns matters beyond buildings, in other energy-consuming aspects of the city's terrain. It allows builders to narrow streets, thus reducing the amount of asphalt used, and requires roadways to be shaded, thus reducing the amount of waste heat given off by steaming asphalt during the torrid Davis summers. To reduce energy spent for transportation, Davis encourages home businesses. In 1979 the city issued 130 permits for home crafts and art studios, haircutting salons, and realty offices. To reduce gas and electric demand for clothes dryers, Davis lifted a ban on clotheslines (there they are called "solar clothes dryers") and even requires apartment landlords to install them for tenants.

At first the local builders were vehemently opposed to the new ordinances. Ronald Broward, president of Broward Construction, Inc. felt that "after having built several hundred homes during the past 18 years, I knew how to build an energy-efficient home better than the young men who proposed the ordinance." He monitored indoor temperatures in several unoccupied new duplexes for 15 days and discovered, to his surprise, that the indoor temperatures never rose above 75 degrees even though the outdoor temperature soared above 100. Broward, like most other builders, also feared that the new code would increase house construction costs substantially, but the added cost for the first 46 homes built to code specifications was just $35.10. A year after the code went into effect, six of nine local builders supported it, and only one continued to oppose it. When Broward testified before Congress in 1978, he admitted, "I was wrong and now believe the Davis Energy Ordinance should be a model for all new homes and apartments being built."[14]

Documents on Davis's experience were compiled in a pamphlet and published by the city and a private organization. Several thousand copies were distributed, educating other communities to the intricacies and benefits of energy conservation planning.

Davis's comprehensive code has not yet been equalled by any other American city. But a number of cities have taken significant steps to make their populations more energy self-reliant. Cities that have implemented population growth controls are often able to integrate energy efficiency considerations relatively easily because of the intense competition for the limited number of building permits awarded each year.

Boulder, Colorado, is using incentives for conservation and solar energy in its Growth Management System. In an effort to limit its growth to 2 percent a year, the city has limited building permits to 450 a year. Developers compete for the permits by earning points under a merit system. Projects are rated on a scale from minus 30 points to 105 points. One to 20 points can be awarded for energy conservation proposals that include documented savings.

The point system is not the only carrot available to cities to encourage builders to comply with energy efficiency standards. Fort Collins enacted an addendum to its Land Use Development Guidance System to award density bonuses for energy efficiency improvements beyond code requirements. For example, if a developer can demonstrate that a project will result in 10 percent energy savings by exceeding code requirements, the builder is awarded a 10 percent increase in the building density allowance. Port Arthur, Texas, requires all houses in subdivisions to be oriented for maximum use of the sun during the winter and to be shaded during the summer. In return, builders are rewarded with the right to reduce street width from 60 feet to 50, allowing them to build more houses per acre. Lincoln, Nebraska, authorizes developers complying with a set of conservation standards to increase the number of dwellings per acre by 20 percent.

Municipal Government Looks Inward

While a handful of cities try to promote energy efficiency through redesign, hundreds of city governments have taken modest steps to reduce their own energy consumption. In a 1980 survey of more than a thousand cities with populations greater than ten thousand done by the International City Management Association (ICMA), 60 percent of city officials said that energy expenditures constituted the second largest element in their operating costs, trailing only personnel costs. Cities began to do the simple housekeeping tasks necessary to lower their energy costs. Unfortunately, they found that even the simplest measures were hard to implement.

Many cities had never taken a full inventory of their building stock. Bill Clement, energy coordinator of Lawrence, Massachusetts, admits that he uncovered two additional city-owned buildings a year and a half after the survey began. "Last year we spent $45,000 to heat and light a building we didn't use," he ruefully remembers. "It was unoccupied."[15] Portland, Maine, required three weeks to compile data on 58 individual buildings. Deputy City Manager Tom Valleau explained, "The oil truck comes, makes three drops at three separate buildings and gives us one bill. We don't know what each building is using."[16]

For many, automobile use would be the single most difficult place to achieve energy conservation. Law enforcement vehicles usually get six miles per gallon. But police view their vehicles as a symbol of authority. When city officials recommended reducing the size of police vehicles, many police believed they would be unable to catch fleeing criminals. One Massachusetts municipal energy coordinator remembers the reaction to his attempt to get police to drive smaller cars, turn off their engines for 15 minutes an hour, and walk their beats. "I received four tickets the next morning," he says.[17] An order from President Jimmy Carter eliminating free parking spaces for federal employees in Washington, D.C., brought cries of anguish. Los Angeles city councillor Joy Picus tried for more than four years to stop the city from providing city employees parking spaces for $5 a month, less than the cost of mass transit. In fact, the automobile has proved to be an albatross to most energy plans. When Los Angeles Mayor Tom Bradley instituted car-pool lanes on the freeways, there was an actual uprising of the local citizenry. Several enterprising commuters even purchased life-sized dummies to look like passengers. The special lanes were quickly scrapped.

One of the major expenditures of city governments is for street lighting. Worcester, Massachusetts, population a hundred seventy thousand, and Portland, Maine, population fifty-six thousand, among others, spend more than $10 per person per year for street lighting.

Advances in lighting in the 1970s allowed the mercury vapor street lights to be replaced with high-pressure sodium lamps that use 50 percent less electricity to generate about the same amount of light. However, some cities receive free street lighting as a part of their utility franchise agreements. Thus they have little economic interest in reducing consumption. Other cities do not own their street lights. They rent the poles from the local utility company, which again has no interest in energy conservation. Sometimes the city owns some and the utility owns some. Oakland, for example, owned 10,500 street lights in 1979, and the utility owned 13,200. To benefit from conservation, Oakland would have to purchase the lighting system from the utility.

Sometimes the public opposes changes in street lighting. When Oakland installed 70-watt high-pressure sodium bulbs in residential districts, the lighting became more uniform but the level of lighting decreased by 10 percent. Citizens in residential communities complained vociferously. The installations were delayed so the city could develop a solution.

A unique problem occurred in San Jose, California. The city has thirty-seven thousand mercury vapor street lights, and when it decided to replace these with more efficient high-pressure sodium lights, astronomers at nearby Lick Observatory were reported to be "in a dither." Mercury vapor shines in only four narrow channels of the electromagnetic spectrum and is easy to filter out of the sky, but high-pressure sodium pollutes the entire red-orange-yellow half of the spectrum; filtering would be hopeless. The reduced viewing ability would render the 120-inch telescope about as useful as a 50-inch scope. Its value would drop from $15 million to $1.5 million, and its reduced capacity would force many of the staff astronomers to work on less significant projects. Some might leave.

Then one astronomer discovered that low-pressure sodium lamps, used widely in Europe, use 13 percent less electricity than even the high-pressure sodium lights. Since the amber light produced by the low-pressure lamps is squeezed into a single channel of the spectrum, the sky could be filtered to make it darker than it had been in years, making the Lick telescope even more valuable. Test installations of low-pressure sodium showed it equally as acceptable to residents as the high-pressure sodium lamps. The city finally agreed to install low-pressure sodium bulbs within nine miles of the observatory even if they cost more and to install them outside this perimeter on a cost-effective basis.

Given the importance of energy expenditures on municipal budgets, that only a few city governments have full-time energy officers is surprising. Many cities are reluctant to hire additional staff for energy matters while faced with budget reductions and staff layoffs. Only 38 of 1,295 cities surveyed by the ICMA in 1980 had created positions for full-time energy coordinators. Most part-time energy coordinators spent less than one day per week on energy matters. Even in cities with more than five-hundred thousand people, only 11 hours a week were devoted to energy-related activities.

But as energy prices continue to soar, more and more city officials recognize the cost effectiveness of spending money for staff. City Manager Anthony Shoemaker of Clearwater, Florida, population ninety thousand, argued this case before four hundred local energy officials in Denver in 1980. The average city spends between 8 and 10 percent of its operating budget for energy, Shoemaker argued, and 20 to 30 percent of the city's energy consumption could be saved with little or no capital investment. Thus, if the operating budget were, as was the case with Clearwater, about $40 million, the energy expenditures would be $3 to $4 million, and the city could save about a quarter, or $1 million, with inexpensive energy conservation measures. So it pays to spend $100,000 to staff a full-time energy office. This argument convinced Clearwater's city council. Shoemaker has three full-time staff members to handle energy matters.

Mobilizing the Citizenry

Looking back, we can discern two periods of local involvement in energy matters. The first, catalyzed by the oil embargo, took place from 1973 to 1979. This was the period of education, demonstration, and preparation. The federal and state governments slowly enacted and implemented tax incentives and regulatory legislation. A few cities — for example, Davis, Seattle, and Portland — began to develop an understanding of the role that communities could play in energy planning. But overall, when oil supplies were reestablished after the embargo and, between 1974 and 1978, the price of oil actually fell, relative to the consumer price index, the country lapsed into complacency.

That complacency was ended forever in 1979 when the Shah of Iran was toppled, OPEC doubled the world oil prices, American hostages were seized by revolutionary Iranians, and a nuclear reactor near Harrisburg, Pennsylvania, nearly melted down. Communities, spurred by fear, rage, and renewed conviction, moved into action.

To save gasoline, the citizens of Grand Junction, Colorado, put together a bus system where none had existed since 1940. In one blazing nine-week period in the fall of 1979, a third of the forty thousand residents of Fitchburg, Massachusetts, installed caulking, weatherstripping, and insulation in more than half the homes, reducing their space-heating needs by 14 percent. In neighboring Northampton boy scouts trudged through the snow dropping fliers in the doorways and mailboxes of the thirty thousand residents. They followed up with phone calls, urging residents to attend a Button Up Northampton workshop. If the resident had a baby, a babysitter was provided. If he or she needed a car, a carpool was established. The workshops, held in January 1980, taught residents how to conserve energy and cut fuel costs, and in conjunction local hardware stores offered a 25 percent discount on the cost of weatherization materials. More than four out of every five people who attended the workshops purchased and installed energy conservation materials.

Perhaps the most impressive mobilization, however, took place in St. Paul, Minnesota, a city characterized by long, cold winters and reliance on oil for space heating. Mayor George Latimer had established a citizens committee in August 1979 to investigate the energy problem. Its original name, Committee of 100, had to be changed to the Committee of 100+ when more than three hundred people showed up to participate in the five task forces. Their draft reports, submitted in January 1980, urged active conservation. Meanwhile Alice Murphy, the "ombudsman" for St. Paul, was receiving an increased number of calls from frightened and cold residents.

Urged by Murphy and David Broeker, the city's chief administrative officer, Latimer announced a city-wide mobilization for Valentine's Day.

127

Using funds from local foundations and the mailing privileges of a local congressman, the city sent out a hundred thousand questionnaires to residents asking three basic questions — What would you like to do to save energy? What is stopping you from doing it? How much energy are you using?

Muriel Humphrey went on television to urge St. Paul residents to return their questionnaires. Latimer gave all nonessential municipal employees three days off to take part in the largest citizen mobilization in the country. More than three thousand people, mostly non-city-employees, showed up at a local auditorium in response to the mayor's plea for volunteers, and every one of the hundred thirteen thousand homes and small businesses in St. Paul was visited. "Everyone in town knew about it," one neighborhood resident said, "which was sort of amazing. That was what the city was thinking about for a few days."[18]

To encourage participation, St. Paul awarded prizes to volunteers and to those who returned questionnaires. The information on the questionnaires was fed into a complex computer program devised by a local foundation to break down energy-use figures by neighborhood. By the end of the three-day period, 25 to 30 percent of the forms had been returned.

St. Paul's one thousand city employees were not at first "overly excited about the project," Alice Murphy remembers. "Walking the streets of St. Paul in mid-February is not exactly a piece of cake."[19] The grand prize for volunteers was a week for two in Mexico. ("Not the most energy conserving prize," Murphy admits.) Appropriately, when the prize was announced for the winner, who is a truck driver for the city public-works program, he was in bed with a cold he claimed to have gotten while walking the streets of St. Paul distributing questionnaires.

The Municipal Balance of Payments

St. Paul and Fitchburg focused their residents' attention on what they could accomplish with community-wide campaigns: the events of 1979 catalyzed the whole country. In the long run, however, another factor in local energy planning would have an influence greater than did these — the discovery that rising energy prices seriously weaken the local economy.

The dollar we spend on energy stays in the local economy much more briefly than do other expenditures. Purchase a loaf of bread from the corner grocery store. The clerk might live in the neighborhood. The manager could live upstairs. The bread might be baked in town, and perhaps the wheat in the bread even comes from nearby agricultural areas. However, when you fill up at the gasoline pump the money quickly leaves the community. The gasoline may come from halfway across the nation, or possibly from halfway around the globe; the links to the local economy are few.

In Franklin County, Massachusetts, thirty-seven thousand citizens spent $43 million for energy. This equalled the total payroll of the ten largest employers in the county. In comparison, a single OPEC price hike in 1979 caused the expenditure of an additional sum by Franklin County's residents greater than the payroll of the county's largest employer. "We would have to clone the largest employer in the county every year just to attract sufficient payroll dollars to make up for the loss of local dollars to pay for energy," said Fran Koster, one of the people gathering data from the local economy on the impact of rising energy prices.[20]

Studies of the District of Columbia, population six hundred twenty thousand, and Carbondale, Illinois, population thirty thousand, traced the paths of dollars spent for energy and concluded that only 15 cents of the energy dollar returns to benefit the local economy in any manner. That is, only 13 cents are respent in the form of salaries and wages to local residents, as profits and dividends to local businesses, or as tax revenues to the local government. Communities get back between 60 cents and $1.20 for each dollar of federal taxes they pay. But they benefit from only 15 cents for any dollar of energy they purchase.

Investments in conservation and such indigenous fuel sources as solar energy benefit the local economy in several ways; a dollar spent locally tends to multiply its benefits. The grocer who sells you the loaf of bread then buys supplies from another local business. That business might deposit the money in a bank account, and the bank might lend it locally. The District of Columbia study concluded that a dollar spent locally could generate as much as 2.5 times its value in total economic activity. Investments that reduce the outflow of energy dollars generate more jobs, and they involve more local businesses than money spent on new power plants or new oil wells. Storm window companies, insulation contractors, and solar-equipment installers are often local businesses. Thus programs that encourage energy self-reliance reduce the city's cash hemorrhage and, recycling money in the local economy, create jobs.

Time and again, community energy studies emphasize economic concerns. As Cambridge, Massachusetts, reported in 1980, that city of a hundred thousand was spending more than $360,000 a day on energy. "This bleak economic future provides the motivation and justification for this study," the Cambridge energy report notes.[21] Northampton, Massachusetts, a city of thirty thousand, justified its emphasis on reducing imported energy and substituting energy generated from indigenous resources by stating, "It is simply a fact that the vast majority of the energy used in Northampton is not used productively (in the economic sense) and that money which leaves the city's economy to pay for this nonproductive energy is not available for productive uses within the city."[22]

Richard Archer, dean of the department of design at Southern Illinois University, supervised a study in 1980 concluding that Carbondale, population thirty thousand, was paying an energy bill of $30 million. About $1,000 per person was "directly exported," Archer concluded. "While the exportation of $90 billion for foreign oil — or $400 for every man, woman and child — may not bother people at the national level, the exportation of more than $1,000 per capita from the city of Carbondale is very much the concern of the city government."[23] Mayor Paul Lattimore, of Auburn, New York, speaking before the Northeast Governors' Association meeting in early 1981, repeated the theme: "Economically there is no difference between sending energy dollars to the Arabs or shipping them to Texas. The balance of payments of the local economy suffers just as much."[24]

Most of such studies' results have been translated into reports or slide shows. The residents of Salem, Oregon, population one hundred thousand, have developed a unique method of illustrating the local import of energy expenditures. A clock in the middle of town ticks off the energy-related dollars leaving the local economy each minute.

A Matter of Compulsion

Change has come — slowly. For those who believed
the energy crisis was an immediate problem of resource exhaustion, the
leisurely pace of federal action they perceived was frustrating. The increased price of energy did spur its conservation, but some believed the
marketplace moved too slowly and did not maximize the energy-saving
investments. For builders to learn how to construct energy-efficient
homes and office buildings has taken years. Consumers still rarely have
taken into account energy operating costs when purchasing appliances.
And bankers still have ignored the energy costs of a home in evaluating
the ability of the potential buyer to carry the mortgage.

The rental sector has been targeted for particular concern. Landlords have little incentive to invest in energy conservation or solar
energy, even though such investments might repay themselves quickly.
Urban housing often is rental housing. Eight of every ten units in Santa
Monica is rented, about the same as in Eugene and the District of
Columbia. In fact, urban areas have more than 80 percent of all the
rental housing in the nation. Rental units tend, too, to be in older
buildings. Most have little or no insulation. Moreover, average renters
have smaller incomes than owners and, therefore, less ability to invest
in energy conservation even if they have the incentive to do so. The
family income of the average renter in 1980 was about $8,000, com-
pared to $12,000 for the average homeowner or condominium buyer.

As the 1980s dawned, increasing numbers of people felt that only by
mandating energy-saving investments could communities quickly move
toward energy self-reliance. Mandatory ordinances are the most controversial energy measures. Less controversy accompanies ordinances
that mandate energy-efficiency levels for new construction, but the opposition to mandating energy-efficiency standards for existing buildings
is strong. What right does the community have to regulate individuals in
this way? Some officials, like San Diego county supervisor and real
estate developer Roger Hedgecock, believe "We must begin to look at
mandating solar in the same way we have mandated health and safety in
building codes."[25] San Diego County, in fact, became the first locality in
the nation to require solar hot-water systems in all new construction in
1980. Half a dozen California cities and counties followed its lead in the

next 18 months, and some predicted that by 1982 one quarter of the state's population would be covered by these ordinances.

A small indication of the changing times occurred in Soldier's Grove, Wisconsin, population 524. Built on the flood plain of the volatile Kickapoo River, Soldier's Grove had frequently watched the river's waters spill over the banks and cover large portions of downtown. So after a major flood in July 1978, the village decided to relocate on high ground. The village selected a Chicago architectural firm, Hawkweed, to help design their new town with energy efficiency in mind, and among their measures is a building code with a section entitled "Renewable Resources." It requires that "all buildings must be at least 50 percent solar heated."[26] A local bank was constructing a $250,000 building, which originally was to feature a solar hot-water system that would provide 70 percent of the building's heating. But when the bank management priced the system and concluded it would add $27,200 to the cost, it was quietly dropped. When residents of the village saw the south-facing roof being shingled over, they went to Zoning Administrator Ron Swiggum, who issued a citation. Rodney Wright of the Hawkweed group observed that it was the "first time in the history of the country that someone was given a citation for trying to build a structure without solar heating."[27] Local architects showed bank officials how they could install a skylight and achieve the desired heat-system savings for about $4,000, and everyone was satisfied with the outcome.

Opposition to mandatory solar requirements has come from a number of sources. When Sacramento enacted a measure that required all heated swimming pools to use solar energy, John O'Lear, president of one of the largest manufacturers of solar heating systems for swimming pools, expressed the concern that such ordinances might make the field "*too* attractive . . . resulting in a new rush of suppliers who are not qualified or competent."[28] One outspoken opponent to mandatory solar-energy use in Santa Clara, California, worried about its compulsory nature, when the overall energy savings to be gained by solar hot-water systems were so small. Still others worried that, by mandating a specific technology, the community could dampen innovation. Some wondered whether the use of solar collectors for hot-water heating, for example, might not be overshadowed by other technologies at some future date. This fear was reinforced when electric hot-water heat pumps were introduced in late 1980. The manufacturers claimed to save almost as much energy as solar hot-water systems, at one-third the cost. Some communities, Santa Clara County for one, have dealt with the prospect of evolving technologies by framing their ordinances to permit the owner or builder to substitute a technology that might be more cost effective than is solar equipment.

The primary battle, however, is being fought over ordinances that force existing buildings to become more energy efficient. Supporters have argued that existing buildings still will be standing 50 years from now and will become an increasingly heavy burden on the homeowner and society in general if they are not brought up to maximum efficiency levels. They have doubts that the rising energy prices will stimulate building owners to invest in cost-effective energy efficiency measures. In Portland, a vice president of the local investor-owned utility company was one of the last to testify in favor of the mandatory provisions of the city's energy conservation ordinance. He argued that people were not acting like rational economic beings. "Although the company has promoted and explained the benefits of conservation, . . . the cost-effective conservation which could and should have materialized has not occurred."

Some people have supported mandatory measures out of a conviction that the finiteness of our energy sources has made individual waste a community issue. When Portland enacted its mandatory conservation ordinances in August 1979, it distributed seventy-five thousand fliers throughout the city to explain its rationale. "If we each had our own supply of energy, it wouldn't matter that you conserved, and I didn't. But we share a common supply. When I waste energy, you pay too because we both bear the cost of new supplies. Put simply, my failure to conserve causes your rates to go up. It costs the whole community. That's not fair."

The *Eugene Register-Guard* sensed the popular response to compulsion: "Tell some people that the city of Eugene is considering making it mandatory for them to button up their homes to save energy and you set off a chorus ranging from 'A man's home is his castle' to 'That's a violation of my property rights'. . . . Such responses overlook a simple fact: without mandatory weatherization, they may not have electricity in a few years to light the castle or heat the property."

The fervent desire of Americans to be left alone has made cities that want conservation requirements to enact them slowly. Portland's ordinance, for example, will not take effect for five years. After 1984, commercial and residential structures have to meet energy-efficiency standards at the time of sale, when a tenant moves, or when a business applies for a permit. Seattle proposed a requirement that would take effect in three years only if voluntary compliance was deemed inadequate during that period. Eugene enacted an ordinance in 1981 that will not take effect for four years. At that time the city council will review the progress residents have made, and, if it decides voluntarism has not worked, it will implement the mandatory procedures.

Even with these palliatives, communities have been sharply divided. For example, Davis, California, passed an ordinance requiring energy conservation investments of as much as $500 for existing homes at the time of sale. Then residents circulated a petition and gathered signatures sufficient to put the ordinance to the question on the city-wide ballot. The ordinance was upheld — by the relatively close margin of 53 to 47 percent. The Portland City Council voted four to one in favor of its entire energy conservation policy, but the lone dissenter specifically opposed the mandatory provisions. And in 1980, after Portland's mayor left to become the nation's secretary of transportation, the dissenter, Frank Ivancie, was elected mayor. Part of his campaign was a promise to eliminate the mandatory aspect of the energy plan. In late 1980, the citizens of Portland approved a ballot initiative that requires a special referendum before the mandatory requirements can be put into effect.

In Seattle's case, according to Sam Sperry, director of the Seattle energy office, the city failed to have adequate citizen participation in drawing up its plan. The result was such bitter opposition that the plan was shelved. "People called us Nazis, or the Ayatolla," Sperry remembers. "Dixie Lee Ray [then Washington's governor] criticized us for intruding on other people's affairs. The Washington League of Cities said this type of thing conjured up visions of energy auditors checking up on their neighbors."[29]

In spite of the controversy engendered by the mandatory energy conservation requirements, cities continue to enact them. Indeed, some officials favor such measures specifically on account of their controversial nature. When the state realtors' association in California tried to have the state legislature enact a measure that would have made energy conservation for existing buildings mandatory after 1987, but which would also prohibit local governments from enacting their own mandatory provisions, the Local Government Commission of the SolarCal Council opposed the measure. "Mandatory requirements are a sure fire way to attract people's attention," said one city councillor. "It brings people to public hearings. That type of citizen involvement is our goal because only with the active involvement and support of the local population will these measures work effectively."[30]

The Movement Expands

By the early 1980s city officials had begun to understand the relationship between rising energy prices and weakening local economies. More than half a dozen state-wide coalitions of local energy officials were sharing information and technical expertise. Meanwhile, an entire industry in conservation and solar technologies has developed. Conservation was a $9 billion industry in 1980; the same year, solar energy revenues reached more than $250 million. More than a hundred fifty thousand homes had solar energy systems. In Memphis, Tennessee, alone there were a thousand systems, and Nashville had more than two thousand.

Several hundred communities were involved in developing their own energy plans. Energy futures conferences attracted hundreds of local residents in Salem, Oregon; Boulder, Colorado; and in Missoula, Montana. Indeed, friendly rivalry between communities that conserve began to take shape. In more and more localities, citizens espoused the belief that innovations in energy would "put us on the map." Billings, Montana, approved a resolution to establish the goal of making it Montana's most energy-efficient city by 1982. Five New England cities and five Canadian cities took part in a three-day competition to see which could reduce electrical demand the most. When Portland, Oregon, enacted its energy conservation policy, neighboring Eugene was miffed. Its daily newspaper ran three consecutive editorials admonishing the city for having been upstaged. An energy advisory board was immediately established, and within a year it was implementing far-reaching measures.

135

Self-interest is always a highly motivating factor. When Secretary of the Interior James Watt declared he would issue leases to oil companies to drill off the coast of California, many local governments published statements opposing the drilling for fear of oil spills. The county of Santa Cruz went further. By a unanimous vote of its supervisors, Santa Cruz issued a challenge to the federal government. The county, through aggressive energy conservation and solar-energy activities, would save or generate an amount of energy equivalent to an amount estimated to be Santa Cruz's prorated share of the oil that could be tapped offshore — in exchange for a reprieve from the drilling. There was no reaction from the White House.

The first decade after the oil embargo was one of experimentation and education — the country learned how it used energy. Much of the emphasis was on conservation and the use of solar energy for hot-water heating. But as energy prices continued to rise and new energy technologies evolved, cities began to grapple with the most exciting question — could they actually generate a significant portion of their energy needs internally? Can our urban areas move toward energy self-reliance?

CHAPTER 7

Humanly Scaled Energy Systems

Self-reliance does not mean isolation, nor
is it equivalent to self-sufficiency. Self-
reliance is development which stimulates
the ability to satisfy basic needs locally:
the capacity for self-sufficiency, but not
self-sufficiency itself. Self-reliance represents
a new balance, not a new absolute.

Russell E. Anderson

The 2,000 percent increase in crude oil prices in the
1970s forces us to reconstruct our energy generation and distribution
system. No longer is it efficient to build massive power plants that
require ten years to come on-line, because we can no longer predict
future demand with any accuracy. No longer does it make sense to rely
on fuels imported from halfway around the globe, because the stability
of the supply lines has become tenuous. Nor is it economical any longer
to support an energy system whose fastest growing component is waste
heat. The response to these changes, from both the private and public
sectors, is activity as unprecedented as the price increases in fossil fuels:
new energy systems are being developed that emphasize efficiency,
decentralization, and integration.

The energy conservation industry was nearly nonexistent in 1973.
But in 1980 total sales reached $9 billion, about as much as Americans
paid for Japanese automobiles. And photovoltaic devices, popularly

known as solar cells, have decreased in price by a factor of 50 from 1973 to 1981. In 1973, the electricity produced from solar cells was 500 times more expensive than that of conventional power plants; in 1981 it is ten times more expensive, and industry and government alike predict that parity will be achieved by the mid-1980s.

The upside-down world of energy economics is perhaps best illustrated by the changing comparative prices of alcohol and gasoline. In 1978 to produce a gallon of alcohol from corn cost about $2.00: a gallon of gasoline at that time cost 65 cents. In 1981 to produce a gallon of alcohol from corn cost $1.20: a gallon of gasoline cost $1.40. Alcohol fuel prices had gone from having a three-to-one disadvantage to a 20 percent advantage in three years.

As we change our technologies, our ways of doing things, we also change the institutions built up around the obsolescent technologies. We may add new functions to old institutions, such as having energy utilities finance the installation of storm windows. And we may create new institutions, such as the cooperative apartment utility companies mentioned below. The only certainty is that our changing fuel base will have far-reaching structural and administrative ramifications.

What follows is a snapshot of an ongoing process. Some of the projects discussed in this chapter are taking place now. Some have already taken place. Many are tentative, slippery. It is a wonderfully exciting time, a heady era of possibilities and pitfalls.

Energy Efficiency

The key characteristics of the new energy systems, regardless of their fuel sources and technologies, are efficiency and integration. Systems that are efficient extract the greatest amount of useful work from an amount of energy, whether it is a cubic foot of natural gas, a pound of coal, or an hour of sunlight.

A narrow application of this principle of efficiency occurs when we make use of the waste heat given off during manufacturing processes or conventional electric power generation. If we capture the waste heat of a power plant, we can triple the overall efficiency of the fuel cycle. And we can use the waste heat not once but many times, extracting every last calorie of usable heat. The technical term for this process is *cascading*—the successive use of progressively cooler fluids. Cascading could begin, for example, with steam at 400° F., which can generate electricity; the waste heat from that generation may be 300° F. and could be used for crop drying. At 200° the heat is sufficient to supply hot water, and at 50° sufficient heat energy remains to warm a pond, so that fish can grow more rapidly. Or, by a similar process, heat energy of a temperature too low to be used directly and so traditionally ignored can be used indirectly. For example, the temperature of ground water stays at a relatively constant 50° F. year round. Though this is not warm enough to use directly, the heat within it can be extracted and amplified by using a small amount of electricity, or other energy source, in heat pumps.

This new era of energy efficiency is a distinct departure from normal practice. Ours has been a civilization based on combustion. Boil water to produce steam. Use the steam to turn turbines that generate electricity. To heat our homes to 70°, we boil water at several thousand degrees Fahrenheit in our power plants. In the future, however, we will more closely match the energy source to the need. We will extract heat from the earth, the air, or the water around our buildings and will use heat pumps to boost the temperature slightly. Instead of downgrading temperatures of thousands of degrees to those needed inside buildings, we will upgrade 55° ground water by the 20 or 30 degrees necessary for use in space heating.

Systems that are efficient also use the wastes of one process as the raw materials of another. And efficient systems reduce the need for transportation by linking production and consumption in close proximity. So waste heat becomes the fuel source for another, nearby process. Human wastes become a source of nutrients for neighboring agricultural land. And solid wastes become a treasure chest of raw materials for area factories that run on scrap. In each case, the uses of the resources are integrated.

Emphasis on integration is a recurring theme in community energy planning. Portland, Oregon, concluded that the city could reduce future energy consumption by 5 percent if it revived neighborhood grocery stores. Urban planners had zoned such stores out of existence by segregating the functions of the city into commercial, residential, and industrial sections. As a result, to buy a bottle of milk, a loaf of bread, or a pack of cigarettes, one had to drive to a shopping center.

In decentralized systems, the localist nature inherently produces an

139

integrated system design; the production facilities are situated close to the customers.

Decentralized systems also have attractions politically. Conventional energy systems impose the costs and benefits of energy generation unequally on the communities at different ends of the oil pipeline or the electrical-system grid. Several dozen energy wars are now taking place across this country, the products of centralized energy generation and long distribution lines.

Two types of decentralization are discussed in this chapter. One is the decentralization of the power plants, that is, moving the generation of electricity back into the community. The other is the decentralization of fuel sources, that is, relying on indigenous fuel sources. The interaction of the two is complementary.

Already rising energy prices make it economical to tap the smaller gas and oil deposits located in many parts of the country; eventually renewable energy sources instead will provide a very large part of our needs. Unlike the concentrated deposits of coal, oil, gas, and uranium that are unequally distributed around the globe, such renewable resources as wind, water, plant matter, and especially direct sunlight are ubiquitous. Just as the former lend themselves to ownership by global corporations or nation states, the latter lend themselves to distributed ownership. And as power generation is moved back into the community, reliance on indigenous fuel sources follows naturally.

The exploration for new fuels, their harnessing, and the introduction of new technologies is not confined to urban areas—indeed, for such fuels as wind and plant matter, rural and suburban areas will likely host the industries. Yet cities do have a particular relationship to these new technologies. They are spatial communities. They have the ability consciously to design their land for energy generation and efficiency.

Cities also tend to have access to water power; many are situated along our faster-flowing rivers because, when most cities were founded, rivers were the major freight routes and power sources. In addition to water power, cities have "waste power." The densely congregated households and businesses of urban areas generate a huge stream of solid and human wastes. It is now technically feasible and economical to convert the garbage into alcohol and to generate methane—sewer gas—from the human waste. And cogeneration systems that produce heat and electricity in the same process are most economical for larger buildings and more densely populated areas.

Humanly scaled energy systems may seem inevitable. But they will not happen by themselves. Some of the stories in the next section suggest the institutional warfare that has broken out as we develop new energy sources. We should not expect that the transition to a scale of energy systems several orders of magnitude below those now in operation will be smooth or painless.

No one can predict the level of energy self-reliance cities might achieve. Nor can we set a timetable. Self-reliance is a process as well as a goal; what follows are some of the stories of the beginnings of that process.

Reducing the Demand

We're largely concerned here with the supply side of the energy equation. But self-reliance really begins with conservation. Only by making the physical stock of the society—its buildings, vehicles, appliances, and machinery—efficient will significant self-reliance be possible. A typical community that consumes the equivalent of a thousand barrels of oil per day, for example, currently imports all of it. The energy self-reliant community may generate the equivalent of only 50 barrels of oil internally—but it will consume only 100 barrels. Efficiency makes the difference between humanly scaled energy systems contributing a minor fraction of communities' energy needs or the major share.

The very profligacy with which America has used energy provides us the opportunity for dramatic energy savings. Harvard Business School's classic study, *Energy Future,* cites conservation as the cheapest and most productive energy alternative. A serious commitment to conservation could reduce by 30 to 40 percent our consumption of energy, the equivalent of eliminating our need for imported oil while maintaining or even raising our standard of living.

Energy efficiency is big business. Investments in improving the way we consume energy increased from $100 million in 1974 to $9 billion in 1980, an increase of 9,000 percent, and most industry observers predict that by 1990 investments will soar to $50 billion.

Pioneering builders have already demonstrated that new homes and office buildings can be constructed that for relatively minor additional costs consume only 10 percent of the energy consumed by their 1970 counterparts. Existing buildings can cut their energy use by half with investments that repay themselves in less than ten years. In office buildings, the rapidly growing innovation is in computer-controlled energy management. Such a system has sensors situated throughout the building, connected to a central computer; the computer automatically adjusts the heating and cooling sources to take into account heat generated by machines, lights, and people. Lights are now available that adjust themselves according to the light coming in from windows. Other lights have devices that can detect motion or body heat and can turn themselves off when people leave the room.

Industry is heavily involved in energy-efficiency improvements. The Department of Energy reported in early 1981 that the most energy-intensive industries—including steel, aluminum, and chemicals—had improved energy consumption by 15.4 percent since 1972. The Department of Energy has estimated, however, that United States industry as a whole could reduce its energy demand by 50 percent and still manufacture the same quantity. Union Carbide developed a process for producing polyethylene with only one quarter of the energy used by existing manufacturing plants, in effect rendering obsolete all existing polyethylene capacity. The Tennessee Valley Authority's National Fertilizer Development Center in Muscle Shoals, Alabama, developed a process that cuts energy consumption used in turning out granulated nitrogen fertilizer by 60 percent. By 1981, 27 plants had been outfitted with the process at a cost of $20,000 each, and each was already saving $150,000 worth of natural gas annually.

The transportation sector is witnessing one of the most radical transformations in energy efficiency. The average car in 1975 achieved a fuel efficiency of 14 miles per gallon. By 1985, under federal legislation, automobile manufacturers must meet a new-car fleet-average standard of 28.5 miles per gallon, and General Motors predicts that by 2000 its fleet average will be 40 miles per gallon. Meanwhile, in 1981 Americans already can choose among several vehicle models achieving fuel efficiencies of 40 miles per gallon, and Volkswagen is working on a 60-miles-per-gallon car. Instead of consuming 800 gallons of fuel yearly, as was typical in 1980, the car in 2000 will probably be consuming only 200 gallons.

No one knows what the technical capacity for conservation is. Roger Sant, the author of a study on energy efficiency done by the Mellon Institute Energy Productivity Center, predicts that "even the most optimistic projections we're making today may be understating conservation's real potential."[1] We have been a fat society. The most cost-effective objective is to become lean and hard. For our existing cities, this probably means reducing building energy consumption by 50 percent and transportation energy consumption by 75 percent.

The Proliferation of Power Plants

For more than three-quarters of a century, the gods smiled on electric utilities. The price of electricity fell each year. The demand for electricity increased in clockwork fashion, doubling every ten years. It was a pleasure to build new power plants; one could predict future demand a plant should meet simply by extrapolating from the past. Power plants were constructed in three to five years, and the money borrowed to finance them carried an interest rate of 1 percent. To meet that predictable future demand, utilities built larger and larger power plants—by 1975 the average power plant was five times the size of its 1950 predecessor, and the largest power plant generated enough electricity to meet the needs of a region of several million people.

In the 1970s this confluence of favorable factors vanished. Interest rates moved into double digits as energy prices fueled inflation. Massive power plants, once attractive because of their engineering economies, began to impose burdens; especially this was true of those fired by nuclear reactors. Power plants took longer to build in part because, increasingly, they were one of a kind. Each plant completed was a new engineering marvel. The environmental impact of the nuclear power plants had begun to concern the nation, and by the late 1970s to build one would take more than ten years.

These long lead times, coupled with the rising costs of money and materials, created a serious financial burden on electric utilities. They had to raise billions each year, yet that investment would not yield a return for many years. Unfortunately, but not coincidentally, just as the financial penalty for a wrong projection rose drastically, the demand for electricity became erratic, unpredictable. To estimate future demand accurately became impossible. The rate at which the demand for electricity rose in the late 1970s was less than a third of its historical rate. In fact, in 1979, for the first time in its history, giant Commonwealth Edison, serving Chicago and vicinity, successor to Samuel Insull's Chicago Electric Company, sold less electricity than it did the year before. Utilities that guessed wrong on future demand found themselves saddled with billions of dollars worth of idle plants. In 1980 New York's utilities had 50 percent more power than they ever would use, even to meet peak demand. Northeast Utilities—which serves part of New England—the Tennessee Valley Authority, and Commonwealth Edison suffered similar problems.

In light of the new unpredictability of demand, medium-sized power plants have become more attractive. They can come on-line more rapidly, and one important result is that money does not have to be borrowed for so long, a significant consideration when today's investor is reluctant to lend his or her money over a long term because of the instability in the world economy. Smaller plants have other advantages, as well; their designs can be standardized, allowing mass production economies. And there is evidence from studies done by Los Alamos National Laboratory, among others, that several small power plants can effectively substitute for one large power plant that has a greater total generating capacity. This is possible because the overall reliability of the generation and distribution system improves when it is decentralized and because a huge power plant also requires an equally huge reserve power plant. Smaller plants require proportionately smaller standby capacities.

Actually, the recent records on very large power plants show operating levels that are disappointingly low. Not only do the plants malfunction regularly, but, in the case of nuclear plants, when problems arise they tend to remain inactive for hundreds of hours. Robert Mauro of the American Public Power Association remarks that the vaunted promise of efficiencies that led many municipally owned utilities to abandon their small units in favor of large ones has proved hollow. The fault is in the large plants' disappointing unreliability, which has "diminished, if not entirely dissipated, the theoretical savings expected from bigness." Ironically, he concludes, the small utilities that "have been jeered at for operating 'obsolete' plants with 'tea-kettles,' have had fewer problems in maintaining adequate power supply than some larger systems with modern large-scale units."[2]

Utilities officials consider plants producing 300 megawatts to be small. A plant this size, only about a third the size of a typical new plant, is still big enough to supply a city of a hundred thousand—and the applicable advantages of reduced financial risk and increased reliability apply to even smaller power plants. An additional advantage of small power plants is that they can be situated nearer their final customers; thus their waste heat can be more economically distributed to surrounding buildings.

Cogeneration equipment (which recovers waste heat, and so generates both electricity and heat during the same process) is not new, but heretofore it had been commercially practical only for large industrial users. With cogeneration, too, the rapid price increases in oil and gas and attractive federal tax incentives have spurred the development of plants for apartments and small businesses—even households. In 1980 the Italian automobile giant FIAT introduced its Total Energy Module (TOTEM). A converted auto engine, TOTEM has heat-recovery equipment and a noise-reducing housing. It is about the size of a gas furnace and can run on natural gas, oil, or methane. In 1981 it cost about $15,000 and could generate heat and power sufficient for a half-dozen or so homes.

Although the increases in energy prices have made cogeneration and other decentralized electric generation technologies economical, their use has often been blocked because our contemporary energy system is dominated by monopolies. The gas and electric utilities in this country produce or distribute about 40 percent of the nation's energy. And the electric utilities traditionally have refused to allow independent power producers to interconnect with the grid or have charged these producers extremely high backup prices. They strongly oppose the entry of small businesses, office buildings, apartment houses, and individual homes into the power business, fearing losses of revenue and reduced system reliability.

Some of the most dramatic confrontations have occurred in New

York City, home of Consolidated Edison, the privately owned utility that serves more than 15 million people in the New York metropolitan area. Ironically Con Ed evolved directly from Thomas Edison's first central power plant in downtown Manhattan. That plant served only a few buildings. Now, as a matter of corporate policy Con Ed opposes the revival of such small plants.

Seal-Kap Company, a small manufacturer of yogurt lids, was one of the first to test Con Ed. Business was booming in 1980, but high electricity prices forced Seal-Kap to consider leaving the area. Its owner decided to install a cogeneration system but wanted to remain linked to the electric grid system to allow Con Ed to provide backup power as necessary. The utility agreed, but it imposed a standby fee equal to 75 percent of the maximum monthly amount Seal-Kap had used during the previous year, whether or not the company used any electricity. At that price it was cheaper for Seal-Kap to buy another power plant and completely uncouple from the grid. Even though the additional power plant would remain idle most of the year, it would still be a better investment than the cogeneration system plus Con Ed's stiff backup power rate.

So Seal-Kap uncoupled. Con Ed responded by approaching New York City. Con Ed argued that independent operations were profitable primarily because the manufacturer could avoid paying the 15 percent gross receipts and sales taxes imposed by the city and state. Con Ed argued that New York City would lose millions of dollars in tax revenue if independent power producers continued to uncouple from the grid system. The city agreed. It revised its tax schedule so that Seal-Kap's on-site power plant would be taxed at significantly higher rates than was Seal-Kap's previous, heat-only furnace. This action increased the company's taxes $3,000 per month, doubling the payback period of the initial investment.

A number of observers believe that the utility's skirmish with Seal-Kap was only the beginning of a major nationwide struggle between the electric utilities that rely on gigantic central plants and the office buildings or factories that want to produce a portion of their own power to reduce their expenses. New York City became a laboratory for experimentation with new technologies and new organizational forms because of Con Ed's high prices, the size of the city's buildings, and the relatively high heating load.

Richard Stone, manager of the Big Six Towers, a 12-acre cooperative complex in New York City that consists of seven towers, each 18 stories tall, and a small shopping center, was interested in cogeneration for his complex for a number of years. But not until the 1977 blackout in New York City did the members of the co-op realize that "utilities don't have a monopoly on reliability." Richard Stone and several others established the National Urban Energy Corporation, which was to provide financing for apartments and office buildings to convert to cogeneration. Like Seal-Kap, the Big Six complex management originally wanted to inter-connect with the grid system, but Con Ed opposed such an arrange-ment. So Big Six added another power plant and handled the high summer peak during its first year with no problems. The National Urban Energy Corporation planned to install two more cogeneration systems in 1981 and has been discussing projects with people in Topeka, Kansas; Warminster, Pennsylvania; and Orange, New Jersey. To Richard Stone, who is also president of the corporation, self-reliance is the wave of the future. "The economies of scale for electric generation no longer ap-ply," he said in an interview in 1981. "The pendulum is swinging toward decentralization."[3]

PURPA: Opening Up the Grid System

Cogeneration could be a profitable technology even when uncoupled from the grid system. From the vantage point of soci-ety as a whole, however, it is inefficient to duplicate power plants, as disconnections from the grid system have required—the grid system, by connecting many power plants and serving many customers, allows the necessary reserve capacity to be reduced. Moreover the economics of small-scale power plants using water or wind power, unlike cogener-ation, are completely dependent on the sale of electricity to utilities.

To encourage the use of cogeneration and renewable resources for power production, Congress enacted legislation that abolished the monopoly electric utilities have had over power generation; the Public Utility Regulatory Policies Act of 1978 (PURPA) requires utilities to pur-chase electricity from independent power producers. Furthermore, utilities must provide them backup power at low prices. Finally, PURPA exempts most independent power producers from state and federal regulation. They are not burdened with the cumbersome paperwork necessary for conventional utilities.

The act also prohibits utilities from owning more than 49 percent of an independent power producer and establishes a maximum size for plants qualifying for the incentives PURPA provides.

Congress also took steps to make the new plants profitable. The price a utility charges its customers is based on investments in power plants and transmission lines incurred long before, when interest rates were much lower and construction times much shorter. New power plants can be extremely expensive. Therefore, the electricity they generate is extremely expensive. But when a new power plant begins operation, the high cost of that plant's electricity is rolled into the total cost of electricity from all existing power plants. As a result, the customers' rates increase only slightly. Thus they might be five cents per kilowatt hour (enough to light a 100-watt bulb all night) even though the electricity from the new power plant costs nine cents a kilowatt hour. To encourage the rapid development of the energy-efficient small power plants, Congress specifically ordered utilities to pay the same price to the developers as they would have had to pay to bring an additional power plant on-line. This directive is crucial to the success of small power plants; if it is obeyed, the price paid the developers for new power will almost always be higher than the price the customer now pays for utility-generated power. In utilities jargon, the "avoided costs" (avoided by the utility) will be higher than the "average costs" (to the consumer).

By this directive, the federal law required the electric utility to pay the small power producer what the utility would itself have to pay to bring the new power source on-line. Congress was very clear that the costs to be avoided may be in the distant future. For example, an electric utility which owns a source of hydroelectric power and which is offered the sale of electric energy from a co-generator or small power producer might offer a very low price based on the low costs of hydropower. The purchase of independent power may, however, delay or eliminate the need to rely on new fossil-fueled power plants in the future. The utility, according to Congress, should pay the higher, avoided, costs of constructing fossil-fuel plants to the small power producer.

The New Hampshire Public Service Commission was the first to establish a purchase price for independently generated electricity. In 1979 it established a price of four cents per kilowatt hour, more than double the going rate utilities were paying. A year later New Hampshire raised the price to almost eight cents a kilowatt hour, and shortly thereafter Vermont established even higher rates. PURPA and the state actions created an industry. By forcing utilities to pay premium prices for electricity generated from cogeneration or renewable resources, PURPA created an instant guaranteed demand.

In the field of energy-efficient power generation, much of the activity has been in cogeneration. A small industry already existed for that technology. But renewable resources also have become lucrative. The Federal Energy Regulatory Commission concluded in 1980 that 90 percent of the more than three thousand retired small hydroelectric facilities might potentially be redeveloped, each with an average capacity of about 500 kilowatts. Many of these sites lie within city limits, because city sites originally were selected specifically for the availability of water power for commerce and to drive the early industries. The rush to claim sites along fast-flowing streams and rivers in some instances reached feverish levels. Journalist John McPhee comments in a *New Yorker* article, "It is possible that in 1897 less action was stirred by the discoveries in the Yukon. There was a great difference, of course. The convergence of the Klondike was focused. This one—this modern bonanza—was diffused, spread among countless localities in every part of the nation. As a result, it was a paradox—a generally invisible feverish rush for riches."

The rewards could be quite attractive. "If water were falling at twenty-five feet where the annual flow was 400 cubic feet per second, it could turn modest turbines that could turn small generators that would earn, at six cents a kilowatt-hour, about two hundred thousand dollars a year,"[4] McPhee conjectured. Prospectors searched New England for cities that contained in their names the word "falls": Haines Falls, Hoosick Falls, High Falls, Hope Falls. Auburn, New York, discovered half-a-dozen dam sites within its boundaries; Ann Arbor identified four; and Franklin Falls, New Hampshire, identified ten. The combination of attractive tax incentives for hydropower and high purchase prices from local utilities led to the formation of many small investment companies that developed tax shelters for such wealthy investors as Essex De-

149

velopment Associates in Lawrence, Massachusetts, Continental Hydro Corporation in Boston, and American Hydro Power Company in Villanova, Pennsylvania.

To develop a site, one has to be issued a permit from the Federal Energy Regulatory Commission. Initially this process proved very time-consuming, but in 1980 FERC streamlined the paperwork for plants that generate fewer than 5,000 kilowatts. In addition FERC reversed a 60-year-old policy of preference for applications by municipalities. For sites that potentially can generate 5,000 kilowatts or less, the cities now compete equally with private companies—and the competition for permits is intense. Sometimes two, three, or even half-a-dozen private and public entities have submitted applications for the same site. If all applications are equally worthy, the federal government awards the permit to the first applicant.

FERC receives hundreds of applications. The BSR company in Vermont, the Kimberley-Clark Corporation in Wisconsin, the Madison Paper Company in Maine, and the Tupperwear Division of Dark Industries in Rhode Island have submitted applications, as have the cities of Patterson, New Jersey; Columbus, Ohio; Martinsville, Virginia; Gonzales, Texas; and Muscatine, Iowa.

Increasing electricity prices, as they change the cost effectiveness of development strategies, and new technologies, as they develop, allow cities to install turbines in their own water mains. Colorado Springs, population 185,000, has two turbines along the collection pipelines that carry the city's water supply from the north and south slopes of Pike's Peak. With a capacity of 6 megawatts, these water mains generate about 1 percent of the city government's electrical requirements. New York City uses 1.5 billion gallons of water daily. Eighteen reservoirs in upstate New York deliver the water through three main aqueduct systems, which range in width from slightly more than 13 feet to about 19 feet and which have a flow rate of two to five feet per second. The main tunnels funnel water from large storage reservoirs to the city. In 1981 New York City initiated a study to determine the amount of electricity it could generate by installing turbines in strategic locations.

Some utilities have been supportive of cities' using their water departments to generate electricity. In fewer cases have they been supportive of cities that try to establish municipally owned utilities as mechanisms to harness large amounts of electricity from existing dam sites. The conflict between Central Vermont Public Service Company and the city of Springfield, population ten thousand, illustrates the problem. Springfield decided to investigate the feasibility of harnessing the river running through it to generate electricity. If this could be done, it could radically change Springfield's relationship to the investor-owned utility in the area, Central Vermont Public Service Company—instead of a buyer of electricity, the city could be a seller. Springfield's town manager, Paul McCarthy, believes the city has had an advantage in being home to many machine-tool industries and therefore "heavily salted with people who either are engineers or are familiar and comfortable with the vocabulary and methodology of engineering analysis. This factor, perhaps more than all others, has proven over the last four years to be critical in the development of this project."[5] The citizens of Springfield voted in March 1975 on a $57.8 million bond issue to finance the new hydroelectric plant. Central Vermont Public Service Company, which serves 60 percent of the state, vigorously opposed the project. Thomas F. Hurcomb, vice president for external affairs of the utility, viewed it as the first step in a Balkanization process. "If we continue to break down," he said, "we come up with what we had 50 or 60 years ago, of a hundred or more utilities, which was the condition at one time in the state of Vermont. I believe that will make the planning process more difficult. I believe it will make energy more expensive. I do not think that the course we should be following is continually to break down into smaller energy groups."[6]

The residents of Springfield overwhelmingly approved the bond issue, but in 1977 the Vermont Supreme Court overturned the vote. State Senator Chester Scott remembers the period: "We recognized in the beginning that we were going to be up against a tremendous battle from the private utility. We recognized that their resources were endless in terms of money and in terms of staff. We were not disappointed. The campaign against our project made the Normandy invasion pale by comparison."[7] The town had to vote again. Just before the vote five selectmen addressed a letter to the townspeople, urging their reaffirmation of the project. The letter said, "Yes, things have changed dramatically since 1975. . . . 'This project is no longer just desirable. It's a moral imperative.'"[8] More than half the Springfield voters entered the

151

ballot booths, and almost three out of four supported the bond issue again. Senator Scott saw the vote as the first of many steps toward energy independence. He foresaw a future similar to that envisioned by Hurcomb, but he was much more sanguine. "It is my feeling," Scott remarked, "that the 'centralist' concept is no longer a viable solution, but rather our help is going to come from many diverse sources such as wind, solar, water, solid waste recovery, hydrogen gas production et cetera."[9]

Decentralizing the Fuel Supply

While new power plants are under construction, communities are beginning to tap into the fuel sources that are locally available. Communities are drilling gas wells everywhere. Sometimes the wells tap natural gas deposits. In other cases the wells are drilled in landfills, where they bring out methane gas generated by the decomposition of solid waste. In still other instances methane generated from sewage treatment plants is gathered for useful work; garbage and plant matter are being turned into liquid fuels for vehicles, and electricity and heat are being generated from direct sunlight. Communities are beginning to harvest the wood and wood waste within or near their borders. Finally, as the technology matures for converting low-temperature heat for useful applications, communities are using the earth's heat itself as a fuel supply.

One of the bumps on communities' road to fuel self-reliance is that, in an era of scarce fuel, tapping any fuel source involves tradeoffs. Solid waste that is burned or converted to alcohol is not available for recycling into raw materials, although in many instances recycling saves more energy than does direct conversion. Communities that rely on wood are having to confront the ensuing air pollution problem stemming from the thousands of household wood stoves and the competing demand for wood by the paper-products and home-building industries. Another of the difficulties typically encountered is technical; communities tapping geothermal resources discover that in some states these are regulated as mineral resources and, in others, as water resources.

Drilling for Gas

The deregulation of natural gas after 1978, phased in over the seven-year period ending in 1985, ushered in gold-rush excitement similar to that caused by PURPA over hydro sites. Wells producing only a small amount of gas suddenly have become economically attractive. At 1981 prices, the equivalent of two barrels of oil a day would give an annual gross income of $30,000.

The American Public Gas Association estimates that more than six thousand small and medium-sized cities may be sitting atop untapped but economical natural gas supplies. Under a pilot program funded by the Department of Energy, Pleasant Grove, Alabama, population five thousand, was the first to strike paydirt, in January 1980. By the end of that year, it had three producing wells. Trinidad, Colorado, where 40 percent of the town's ten thousand residents live on fixed incomes, began exploratory drilling in 1980, and by early 1981 the community appeared able to provide a significant portion of its needs with its own wells. Youngstown, Ohio, population a hundred forty thousand, leased municipal property to a private contractor for energy exploration. The property could yield more than 330 million cubic feet of natural gas annually, enough to heat two thousand to four thousand homes, about 10 percent of Youngstown's residences. By the end of 1980 ten wells had been drilled at Youngstown's Municipal Airport, and land at the city's other airport, Lansdowne, was also leased for drilling. The city receives $2 to $5 per acre per year plus a percentage of the gross revenue received by the contractor and as much as two hundred thousand cubic feet of gas for its own use. When all 15 wells are up and operating, Youngstown estimates it could receive $80,000 annually. The gas must first be offered to local industries at the fair market price, insulating them from any such future supply cutoffs as those that ravaged the industries in the mid-1970s.

Some cities also have discovered that they manufacture—naturally—a gas with heating properties similar to those of natural gas. Methane is generated as organic matter decays. A hundred forty million tons of garbage is deposited each year into open dumps or landfills, and the seepage of gas from landfills has been a source of concern for many city and county officials. Local governments are now turning this natural production to their advantage. Los Angeles drilled 14 wells in existing landfills in 1979 and now pumps out about one billion cubic feet per year. Brooklyn Union Gas operates several methane recovery sites in New York City and estimates that major landfill sites in the company's service area could supply almost 15 percent of its customers' needs. Dozens of methane recovery operations have sprung up around the nation, from Mountain View, California, to Shreveport, Louisiana, to Pompano Beach, Florida. In New York City, Coop City, a major cooperative apartment complex, is situated next to a large landfill, and as part of its ongoing program of energy self-reliance, the cooperative has arranged with the city to do exploratory drilling for methane there. If the drilling proves successful it will provide the fuel for the complex's cogeneration systems and will complete the association's independence from imported energy.

Sewage treatment plants also generate methane naturally. Traditionally the gas is burned off; flames shooting out of their gas stacks are recurring signs of waste. In some cases, the gas is used to warm the facility's digesters and heat the buildings. As the cost of natural gas increases, sewage authorities find expansion of their methane recovery operations economically attractive. Los Angeles County's Sanitation Authority, for example, now uses methane to provide almost three-quarters of the electric power needed to operate its sewage treatment facility, replacing electricity that had cost more than $7 million a year.

Gas, either natural gas or methane, can be used to fuel vehicles, as well. Several cities, spurred by the gasoline shortages in 1979, have begun to convert emergency vehicles to the use of two fuels—natural gas or methane in addition to gasoline. The city of Greeley, Colorado, converted its municipal vehicles to operate on compressed natural gas (CNG). The driver can change from CNG to gasoline while driving by simply pushing a switch on the dashboard. Greeley estimates it will save about $1 million between 1980 and 1985 by converting more than a hundred vehicles to operate on CNG. C. William Hargett, the director of public works of Greeley and a professional engineer, lists the following advantages: (1) natural gas contains no additives or solvents and, being a dry fuel, does not contaminate engine oil; (2) because natural gas is a vapor, the results are smoother operation, quicker starting, and no vapor lock; and (3) auto emissions are dramatically reduced—carbon monoxide by 37 percent, hydrocarbons by 37 percent, and oxides of nitrogen by 53 percent.

The Eaton School District, located seven miles north of Greeley, converted 13 school buses to CNG in mid-1980. It not only gained 60 to 70 percent savings in fuel costs, but according to Stan Scheer, assistant superintendent, the CNG is safer. "Natural gas is lighter than air," Scheer writes, "and as a result dissipates very rapidly when released into the atmosphere. Gasoline puddles on the ground when spilled and produces explosive vapors. The flash point of gasoline is around 480° F. Natural gas has a flash point just above 1,200° F."[10]

Some cities have begun to use methane gas in their transportation systems. Municipal fleets in Fort Collins, Colorado, population seventy thousand, and Modesto, California, population one hundred thousand, now run on methane. Modesto estimates that the methane costs about 35 cents per gallon of gasoline equivalent to produce. A plant that uses all the sewage of the city could generate the equivalent of eighteen hundred gallons of gasoline equivalent per day. Modesto's two hundred municipal vehicles consume about eleven hundred gallons per day. Modesto's staff advises other cities, however, that their city may have a greater production than comparably sized cities because local canneries dump large amounts of organic waste into the sewage stream during the canning season.

The more feedstock cities can find for their methane digesters, the more gas they can generate. Modesto found an ideal source in its local canneries. Lamar, Colorado, designed and built a bioconversion facility that will consume the waste from fifty thousand feedlot cattle and produce more than one million cubic feet of methane daily. This fuel will supplement the city's natural gas utility and provide one-third to one-half the energy needs of the residents of the Arkansas River Valley.

One company, Calorific Recovery Anaerobic Process (its acronym, appropriately, is CRAP), is turning manure from a hundred thousand head of cattle at feedlots in Guymon, Oklahoma, population eight thousand, into methane. The methane is sold to People's Gas Company, a Chicago gas utility. In the ever-changing world of energy, Chicago's homes are now in part heated from the manure of Oklahoma's cows.

Solid Waste: Garbage to Energy

In 1976 the Mohawk Rubber Company approached Salem, Virginia, population 23,500, with an attractive proposition. The company needed an alternative to natural gas. It offered to furnish a building site adjacent to its factory and to Salem's garage, if in return the city agreed to burn its garbage and sell steam to Mohawk for the cost of natural gas or No. 2 fuel oil. The city agreed. But just as it was about to issue $2 million in bonds to finance the operation, its attorneys advised the city that tax-exempt bonds could not be used to finance the steam production part of the process. Another business, Reynolds Materials, was invited to join the partnership. Reynolds agreed to establish a facility for separating ferrous metal, glass, and aluminum cans from the refuse before they enter the incinerator. It agreed to pay for the installation of the facility and all maintenance costs greater than the first $1,500 a year in return for all the aluminum it recovered; Reynolds and Salem would share equally in revenue from the sale of other recyclable materials. Everyone appears satisfied with the arrangement. According to one Salem official, "We have an option to purchase the equipment at half price in five years, or at the end of ten years it will automatically become the property of the city. We are earning income instead of spoiling the earth with landfill, and we are saving the natural resource—natural gas—by producing steam. We have been very, very fortunate along the way."[11]

Others have not been quite so fortunate. Resource recovery plants have been beset by mechanical problems. The technology to separate the waste materials has not functioned well. And because solid-waste volume and composition change literally from hour to hour, to design continuous processing systems is extremely difficult. But the biggest problem has been that local officials, encouraged by the federal government, have built plants that are just too big. The larger the plant, the more garbage it needs to operate economically. Ironically, the justification for building the plants is the short supply of petroleum, and the major problem faced by these facilities has been an inadequate supply of trash. When private capital finances a city facility, the city could be required to pay a penalty in the future if garbage volume decreases. Hempstead, Long Island, has such an arrangement. New Orleans has agreed to keep the volume and composition of its solid-waste stream unchanged for 20 years.

Another problem is that, as scrap materials become more valuable, small businesses and households begin to withdraw the most valuable parts of the waste stream for their private gain. This leaves to the resource recovery facility the least valuable materials. Local governments, to protect themselves against such eventualities, have sometimes resorted to coercion. To facilitate the marketing of revenue bonds funded by the sale of steam from its resource recovery plant, the city of Akron and the Ohio Water Development Authority required all waste collection within the city's limits to be dumped at the resource recovery plant. When Akron passed Ordinance Number 841-1976, it became the first city in the nation to outlaw recycling. In upstate New York, in 1981, Monroe County was in the process of constructing a major resource recovery plant when its largest city, Rochester, population two hundred seventy thousand, began to consider a bill that would effectively ban the sale of nonreturnable bottles. The director of solid waste for the county advised Rochester's city manager that "the establishment of any sort of bottle bill in the city of Rochester or the county of Monroe is not recommended at this date with the implementation of the Monroe County Resource Recovery Facility. The resource recovery facility is equipped to remove glass, aluminum and light ferrous metals from the solid-waste stream. This law would greatly modify the influx of glass, aluminum and light ferrous metals to the recovery facility and may deprive the facility of certain anticipated revenues by the sum of these recovered products."[12]

The issues in the controversy over solid-waste recovery are similar to those in the wood industry. What is the best use of our solid-waste stream? Some, like Neil Seldman, waste expert at the Institute for Local Self-Reliance, believe that the greatest amount of energy can be generated by recycling, not burning, our trash. Making a can from recycled aluminum saves 95 percent of the energy used to make a can from bauxite; making paper from recycled materials saves 75 percent of the energy required to make paper from wood. Similar reductions occur with the use of scrap glass and other materials.

Solid waste is also an ideal feedstock for making alcohol to be used as a transportation fuel. About 65 percent of municipal solid waste is

157

cellulose, consisting of lawn clippings, leaves, and newspapers. The difficulty with using this cellulose is that until recently there has been no economical way to convert the cellulose into alcohol. But in 1981 Gulf Oil announced the development of a mutant enzyme that lowers the cost of converting cellulose to sugar and then to alcohol—lowers the cost sufficiently to warrant Gulf's building the first solid-waste–to–alcohol plant, outside Richmond, Virginia. Gulf expects to separate the metals and glass from the waste stream mechanically. The remaining noncellulosic waste, such as meat and bones, will pass through the process unaltered, because the conversion takes place at relatively low temperatures, about 150° F. Also because of the low temperatures, plastics, too, will remain as part of the residue, and they can be strained out at the end of the process.

Alcohol, such as that produced from solid wastes, can be mixed with gasoline to fuel vehicles or used alone in modified vehicles. If the alcohol is to be mixed, all of the water in it must be removed (otherwise the water will separate out, and the carburetor will not function effectively). Alcohol with no water is called anhydrous alcohol and is more expensive to make than alcohol with a 5 percent water content. Yet the latter can be used to provide 100 percent of a vehicle's fuel if modest modifications are made to the engine. Gulf hopes to generate 50 gallons of alcohol from each half ton of cellulose. The average person throws away each year about a ton of solid waste; if two-thirds of this is cellulose, a household of three could generate about 50 gallons of alcohol. For comparison, an automobile that gets 50 miles to the gallon, already possible in 1981, would use a maximum of 200 gallons per year. Alcohol for urban vehicles can be homegrown. And it has the additional advantage of not polluting.

As is the case with sewage treatment plants, communities may find other sources of garbage. Carbondale, for example, has a local dairy that generates sufficient whey wastes to yield about 90,000 gallons of alcohol a year. That is enough to provide 100 percent of the needs for 450 cars, about 3 percent of Carbondale's vehicle population.

Rediscovering the Value of Wood

Much human and solid waste is generated inside city limits. Wood, for the most part, is not. But wood or the land area to raise woody plants, is found near many cities. Little doubt can exist that the nation has the wood available to meet a significant share of its energy needs. In 1980 the Michigan Public Service Commission concluded that the state could "generate all of its electricity from dead and decaying wood fiber, logging residues, mill wastes, forest thinnings and surplus annual growth, with ample megawatts to spare."[13] In 1975 the Governor's Task Force on Wood as a Source of Energy reported that "enough surplus, unmerchantable wood fiber grows in Vermont forests each year to provide fuel for a substantial portion of Vermont's annual energy and heating needs."[14] The Government Accounting Office reported in 1980 that if the 600 million tons of wood residue annually available from the nation's forests were burned to generate electricity, heat, and steam, it could halve the nation's oil imports. If this were accomplished, the portion of total energy used in this country that is supplied by wood would rise from 1.9 percent in 1980 to almost 15 percent.

With rapid increases in the price of oil, and then in natural gas, wood has regained its popularity as a source of heating. Industrial and institutional users of fuel wood helped triple the nation's wood-energy consumption in the 1970s. Five million residences joined the swelling ranks of wood users in the late 1970s, increasing wood's contribution to the energy consumed nationally to the level near 2 percent at which, in 1980, wood surpassed nuclear fission in production of energy used domestically.

But many people are concerned about this explosion in wood consumption. Some worry that the economics of whole tree use encourages clear-cutting, which robs the forests of the nutrients gained from the decomposition of leaves and branches. Slash also helps to shade the ground and enhances the soil's capacity to retain moisture.

Others worry about air pollution. Wood does not yield the sulphur-gas pollution of coal, but it can still generate pollutants. Much of the wood burned in residential stoves is wet and unseasoned; green wood burns at a lower heat efficiency and coats chimneys with creosote. Creosote is the flammable residue of unburned gas and particulate matter.

In Missoula, Montana, half the residents use wood for a part or all of their space heating needs—wood accounts for more than a quarter of the city's total energy consumption. And a study completed in 1980 concluded that Missoula's worsening air pollution problem was substantially aggravated by particulate matter from wood stoves. Albuquerque reports similar trouble with pollution from wood stoves. Even picturesque Vail, Colorado, has had to shut down its ski slopes some mornings because of poor visibility, even though each new dwelling unit constructed since 1979 is limited by ordinance to one stove or fireplace.

Some observers believe that, even though the supply of wood might be sufficient for its use as fuel, its supply is not sufficient to meet every need of society. If the object is to use wood to save the greatest amount of energy, the highest and best possible use of wood would be in structures. Steel floor joists require 50 times more energy to manufacture than joists made of wood. Aluminum siding uses 20 times more energy than wood. Bricks are 25 times more energy intensive to make than boards and shingles.

The next most energy-economic use of wood would be for paper. Its use for fuel rates only third. The competition for the wood supplies may prove intense. Herbert Hunt, director of power resources for the municipally owned Eugene Water and Electric Board, in Oregon, has described his difficulties in getting adequate quantities of wood for power generation. "Over the years, there's been a significant change in wood residue. Mills are using narrower blades; they're using pulp mills to process some waste; they are using waste to heat mills. We are now short of wood waste and having to burn coal. I believe we're in for a shock in the future. Our mill operators are going to find a profitable way to use any and every part of the tree."[15]

Competing interests arose when the municipally owned utility in Burlington, Vermont, at population forty thousand the largest city in the state, decided to convert to wood. In 1977 the Burlington Electric Department converted one coal-fired unit to wood—it uses about 25,000 tons a year. Thomas Carr, the company's generating plant superintendent, spent only half the $50,000 the utility had allocated for the conversion. "It was easy," Carr said. "There's nothing to it, really. No new technology is required."[16] Matchbook-size wood chips are dumped by conveyor belt into the kiln. The 10-megawatt facility generates electricity for two cents a kilowatt hour, much cheaper than nuclear power and one-third less expensive than burning coal. Burlington's voters overwhelmingly approved an $80 million bond issue to take the next step and build a 50-megawatt wood-fired plant. This had a number of advantages. Not only would it insulate Burlington from oil disruptions, but the fuel money that previously had left the state hereafter would be retained. "We'll be spending $30,000 a day here for fuel," estimates General Manager Robert Young, "and all that money will be staying right here in Vermont, strengthening our local economy."[17]

However, the plant will need half a million tons of wood a year, the equivalent of a forest area the size of Burlington itself, so not all the wood can be acquired in the immediate vicinity. The neighboring town of Winooski worried about the substantial number of vans, each carrying a payload of 22 tons, traveling down its main street. Winooski City Attorney William Wargo argued before the Public Service Board against approving Burlington's application for a permit to truck its wood along Winooski's streets. "Even an ideal transportation schedule would present an unbearable burden," he noted, "not only on traffic congestion but on road conditions, on safety, on air quality and on the noise level as well."[18] Burlington modified its transportation plans to bring in 75 percent of its wood by rail. And there were other concerns. One report on the wood situation in Vermont concluded, "A 50-megawatt plant . . . will pre-empt most of the present surplus of low-quality wood in northern Vermont and will limit the use of this wood for small-scale power generation, domestic or commercial heating, or materials fabrication. . . ."[19]

The Burlington plant is scheduled to be completed in 1982. Its use will move the utility toward energy self-reliance. But the central issues concerning the use of wood highlighted by the construction of that plant will be discussed increasingly in the coming years. Some observers believe that the most efficient use of wood as a fuel would be burning it, but in three- to five-megawatt boilers, using cogeneration to produce electricity and heat, rather than in a large centralized facility. Others think that the use of wood as fuel might go the way of oil use. Bangor forester Lestor DeCoster has been quoted as saying, "The forest products industry is plenty worried that while this housing slump is holding forth, a huge chunk of the forest—a chunk it is going to need when the slump ends—will have been allocated to energy. There's a saying that oil is too valuable to burn, let's make things out of it instead. Well, that saying may soon enough apply to wood."[20]

Wood can be converted into other fuels and then burned in furnaces. Bud Rowell's 72-unit, four-story brownstone apartment building in Windsor, Vermont, was to his knowledge in 1981 the only apartment building in the world heated by a wood gasification system. He decided in the winter of 1979–1980 that he either had to raise rents by $50 per unit or find a better way to heat than oil. He purchased a wood gasifier, the smallest one he knew of. To accommodate the gasifier and the truckloads of wood chips it burns, Rowell purchased a large garage across the street from his apartments. Each load is 85 cubic yards of fuel; the building uses 32 loads each winter. The chips are fed into the system automatically on a conveyor to a large dryer that removes about 45 percent of their moisture. They are then burned in an oxygen-deficient atmosphere. This releases volatile gases; the gases in turn are burned with oxygen, to power a conventional boiler. Rowell's unit produces 2 million Btus at maximum operation and the fuel to operate it costs 85 percent less than the oil he would otherwise use.[21]

The increased attractiveness of wood as a fuel source has led to experimentation with a wide variety of woody plants. The University of Arizona has turned tumbleweed into logs, and in southern Texas scientists are examining possible uses for mesquite. In Wainaku, Hawaii, the BioEnergy Development Corporation has attained yields of 120 barrels of oil-equivalent energy from one acre of eucalyptus trees.

Morton Fry, president of the 300-acre Miles Fry and Son Nursery in Ephrata, Pennsylvania, claims the winner in the energy derby will be the fast-growing hybrid poplar. The poplar's life span is 35 years. It is self-regenerating. After an initial, fourth-year harvest, the poplar can be harvested every other year, and its yield is about ten pounds of wood per tree every year. This translates into a thousand to fifteen-hundred gallons of ethanol or butanol per acre. "Those guys licking their chops out there in the Midwest corn fields thinking they are going to be the Texas of the future don't even know this is coming," says Fry.[22]

But poplars have their critics also. Richard Archer, dean of the Department of Design at Southern Illinois University, claims that after several years the poplars' deep roots will extract so much of the soil's trace minerals that their growth will be retarded, unless significant infusions of mineral supplements are made.

The list of plants that could yield large quantities of fuels per acre appears endless. The jojoba bean is being planted on thousands of acres in California for its oils, and the honey locust tree is considered capable of providing fertilizer, fuel, and food even while interplanted with more traditional crops.

Few cities have the acreage to raise their own significant quantities of woody fuels, although some western cities do have hundreds of acres that could be used—and other cities have set aside land as open spaces or for agricultural uses that might permit limited farming. Yet for many cities plant matter is a reachable resource nearby.

Geothermal Energy:
Tapping the Earth's Heat

The deeper you go below the surface of the earth, the hotter it gets. The ground becomes 1° F. hotter for every 75 feet you descend, until reaching 6,400° at the earth's core. While much of the core's heat is retained there, pockets of heat have accumulated near the surface of the earth in fractures of the earth's crust. Scientists calculate that stored in the land of the United States, from the surface to six miles deep, are more than 25 million quadrillion Btus of heat. (The total energy consumed by the nation in 1979 was 80 quads.) Although only a small fraction of this heat will ever be technically and economically accessible, it is an immense resource, and it is stored in a surprisingly large proportion of the country.

Geothermal deposits are of four principal types: "dry" steam, hot water reservoirs ("wet" steam), geopressurized zones, and hot dry rock. Among them, dry steam is the cheapest and most exploitable. Surface water becomes dry steam when it seeps underground, is heated to steam by molten rock, then rises by convection back to the surface, escaping through well pipes or fractures in the earth in a hissing cloud. However, dry steam fields are relatively rare geological oddities. The Geysers Power Plant, near Santa Rosa, California, has been producing electricity from natural steam since 1960, but it remains the only commercial operation in America that is turning earth heat into electricity.

When rain water seeps into the earth it is occasionally trapped in giant underground "reservoirs" of porous rock. In volcanic and earthquake-prone areas of the world, such as California's Imperial Valley, these reservoirs sometimes sit atop hot pockets of magma like kettles of water over a fire; when a well digger's drill hits the reservoir, the boiling, pressurized fluid races up the pipe, roaring out in a flash of steam and hot water—what's called wet steam.

163

Geopressurized zones, like those found in Texas and Louisiana, contain pockets of hot brine under abnormally high pressures two to six miles below the surface of the earth. To drill to such depths is extremely costly, but the investor who is successful gets a bonus: the tapped brine contains vast amounts of marketable methane gas.

Strata of hot, dry rock, found in some volcanic regions closer to the surface than are geopressurized zones, contain geothermal energy that can be extracted by another method. Cold surface water can be injected into man-made fractures in such a rock field, circulated to absorb the heat stored in the stones, and then extracted. A project in New Mexico has demonstrated the technical feasibility of this method. The collected heat, typically greater than 350° F., is then released in a heat exchanger, where it causes a liquid that boils at low temperatures—such as freon—to vaporize. The vapor then can be used to turn the blades of a turbogenerator.

Geothermal heat is usually distributed from a central source. This is called district heating, and it is operating in Boise, Idaho, population a hundred twenty thousand. There, as many as four hundred businesses and single-family homes have been heated by two producing wells for about a century. The city is currently expanding the system to heat 1.5 million square feet of office space and two thousand residences.

Klamath Falls, Oregon, population thirty thousand, heats more than five hundred homes geothermally. It also heats a hospital, a nursing home, and a dairy creamery (the heat is used to pasteurize the milk). Klamath Falls is currently installing an extension of the system that will heat 14 government buildings and 11 blocks of residences, at a cost half that of using oil heat.

El Centro, California, population twenty-three thousand, will soon use geothermal energy from a well to heat and cool the city's 13,000-square-foot community center. If that proves economical, the city, situated 120 miles east of San Diego, plans to tap the adjacent 13.5-square-mile geothermal reservoir to expand the system. An initial feasibility study estimated that 78 percent of all the energy consumed in the residential and commercial sectors of El Centro could be replaced with geothermal energy.

The more that scientists investigate the nation's geothermal resources, the more they find. Eliot Allen Associates, a firm of energy specialists based in Salem, Oregon, discovered several hundred cities in the West each having a warm-water well within a five-mile radius. In other words, these cities already have demonstrated that warm water is available. Eliot Allen Associates also found 89 cities in the state of Washington alone that have potential for geothermal heating. Evidence indicates many potential sites in other parts of the country, as well, depending on the depths explored. Edgemont, South Dakota, discovered 125° F. water at 3,000 feet. St. Mary's Hospital in Pierre, North Dakota, found 106° water at 2,176 feet.

If the water is hot enough, it can be used directly for space heating or water heating. If it is warm but not hot enough for direct applications, its temperature can be boosted with heat pumps. For example, in many locations the ground water is used as a heat source; its temperature stays relatively constant year-round, between 47° and 74°, depending upon the location.

In St. Paul, the Tower Square complex, containing one million square feet of office and hotel space, is capitalizing on the constant 53° F. of area ground water. The water works for both heating and cooling because at 53° it is cool enough to assist the conventional cooling system, and yet many Btus of heat energy are extracted from it. The system works in this manner: three wells pump as many as 4,800 gallons per minute of well water from an aquifer 365 feet beneath the site into the heat pump/chiller units at a basement level of the office towers. These devices warm or cool the water, according to the season's requirements, for use in the buildings.

Even small housing subdivisions are tapping the earth's heat. John Jones, a mechanical engineer in Dayton, Ohio, and owner of Jones Heating and Cooling, has constructed hundreds of homes that combine use of direct solar heat with geothermal heat. Water from the earth is supplied to a house's water-to-air heat pump, where heat is extracted from it to warm the house. The cooled water is returned to the earth and is again heated, continuing the cycle. When air conditioning is required, the cycle is reversed: the heat pump, instead of extracting heat from the water, extracts it from the house and transfers it to the water to cool the house. The heated water is then returned to the earth to be cooled. Jones says this system has reduced heating costs by as much as 80 percent.

165

Using Direct Sunlight:
A Question of Space

By the early 1980s hundreds of urban communities were drilling into landfills, installing turbines in their water mains, burning their trash, and installing cogeneration systems in office buildings and factories. Yet these activities have touched only small parts of the cities; most members of the local populations have not been directly affected by the projects.

The key to energy generation that is decentralized is the technology to convert direct sunlight into electricity or heat. The solar collectors used for this conversion are now affixed to several hundred thousand buildings throughout the country; they are being used to generate high-temperature steam for industrial processes or electric generation, and they are also used to generate heat sufficient to operate cooling systems. But the technology that clearly has captured America's imagination is the one that weds our fascination with electricity to our desire for solar-derived energy independence—the photovoltaic or solar cell. As was mentioned in the beginning of this chapter, solar cells have dropped in price so rapidly that most observers believe they could become competitive at the household level by the mid-1980s. Some believe that solar cells, which generate only electricity, will give way rapidly to solar cogeneration devices, in which the collector surface is used to generate heat and electricity just as the fossil-fuel cogeneration systems do. This capacity can triple the amount of useful work we get from a surface.

If a single-family detached house's rooftop is oriented correctly, sufficient solar cells can be installed not only to generate all the household's energy needs but to have enough left over for an electric vehicle. We may see the car treated as a household appliance, like the refrigerator or the hot-water heater. Indeed, John F. Long Homes in Phoenix, Arizona, unveiled an entirely solar-electric house in May 1980. And Long plans to build another hundred units like the first one. His first units are subsidized by the federal government in order to evaluate how they work interconnected with the electric grid system, but Long believes that very soon household rooftop power plants will become a routine item. People who purchase one of his homes now have the option of purchasing an electric vehicle at the same time. It can be recharged by surplus power from the home's solar electric cells. At present, Long offers three car models to choose from: a Datsun B310 sedan, a Chevrolet Citation, and a Chevrolet Luv pickup, all priced competitively even after the conversion from gasoline to electricity.

We might see a different relationship in the future between house and car. When the vehicle runs low, it plugs into house current. When the house's batteries are exhausted during an emergency, it has a back-up in the electric batteries of the car. This symbiotic relationship is another example of integrated systems.

The key to significant energy production in cities appears to be the availability of surface area accessible to direct sunlight. And one factor in the availability of sunlight is urban density. Can direct solar energy generate a significant portion of a densely populated area's requirements?

Population densities in our largest cities vary dramatically. Although most people think of the skyscrapers of Manhattan as typifying American cities, its density does not. The population per square mile on that small island is more than 20 times that of the average city with at least a hundred thousand residents. The handful of very densely populated cities are situated in the mid-Atlantic and northeastern states. Ten of the 18 cities that have population densities greater than 15 people per acre are in the corridor between Boston and Washington. But 70 percent of the urban population lives in cities with fewer than six people per acre.

Even in our densest cities, however, a surprising amount of solar energy can be collected. A study of Boston concluded that up to half of its year-round housing units have sunlight falling on the roofs or south-facing walls for six hours or more on December 21, the day of the year when the sun hangs lowest in the sky and thus the time when access to direct sunlight would tend to be most diminished. The south-facing walls of two-story buildings (one-fifth of Boston's buildings) have the greatest access to sunlight. Of the buildings with four stories or more (half the buildings), only one in four has good access to sunlight; the tall buildings tend to be situated in parts of the city that contain other tall buildings and therefore are susceptible to shadows thrown by their neighbors.

Boston is among the older, vertical cities. The newer, western cities are characterized by very low densities and, consequently, greater ac-

167

cess to solar energy. The Jet Propulsion Laboratory has evaluated the potential for rooftop photovoltaics in the San Fernando Valley of California, a populous part of the Los Angeles area. It concluded, "For the sixty-five square mile study area the results showed that with half the available flat and south-facing roofs used and assuming the availability of energy storage, 52.7 percent of actual energy demand could have been met in 1978 using photovoltaic collectors."[23]

For new housing subdivisions, designs can accommodate both high densities and sufficient access to direct sunlight. Averaging results from six different sites, architects Ralph Knowles and Richard Berry of the University of Southern California concluded that 52 dwelling units could be constructed on an acre, for a density of more than a hundred people per acre, and still have excellent access to direct sunlight on the roof and south-facing walls.[24]

Even at sites in those cities that lack sufficient space on roofs or walls to support significant producing solar equipment, a great deal of space may be available nearby. One 1968 study concluded that, in central cities with populations greater than a hundred thousand, almost one quarter of all privately owned land was vacant.[25] That amounted to almost as much land as was devoted to housing, and more than twice as much as was devoted to commerce and industry. A 1971 survey of 86 cities evaluated the amount of buildable land available for development. It eliminated from consideration all plots that were less than one-quarter acre, yet still found available more than one million acres of vacant and usable land.[26]

Storage: What to Do
When the Sun Doesn't Shine

Almost every home is already equipped with a device for storing heat. A 40-gallon hot-water tank can retain hot water for about 24 hours. Larger tanks, set in the ground and well insulated, can retain heat for many months. The ability to store heat between seasons is crucial if direct sunlight energy is to provide significant heat, especially in northern climates. Although the average yearly amount of solar energy falling on a rooftop all year might indeed be great enough to supply a large proportion of the household's needs, the sun is not always available precisely when we need it. In the winter not only is the sun's energy less intense, but more days are cloudy. Seasonal storage systems allow us to store the heat of the summer sun for use during the winter.

Storage systems on a community-wide scale boast several attractive features. Larger tanks hold more water at less cost per family than small tanks. And because in tanks of increasing size the volume of water they contain increases proportionally more than the tanks' total surface area, increases in volume also exceed concomitant increases in the cost of construction materials. Moreover, the larger the body of water contained, the smaller is the proportion of the water actually exposed to the air, and thus the smaller the heat loss.

Another of the advantages to storage facilities built large is that they can take advantage of a community's load diversity. People vary in the times of the day they use energy, so an adequate storage system designed for one household would have to be of a size that could handle wide fluctuations in demand. But a tank designed large enough for a community compensates for the variations in individual demand. Consequently, community-sized storage facilities can be smaller than the sum of the sizes of individual household storage systems.

The heat retention quality of a large body of water—sometimes called a solar pond—can be enhanced by adding table salt. The salt divides the pond into layers with different salt densities. When solar radiation penetrates the water, the light is converted to heat and the heat is trapped in the bottom saline layer. Two factors prevent the heat from rising and escaping. First, the salt in the densest layer limits its movement. Second, the middle boundary layer—the density and salinity gradient—acts as an insulating blanket. The salt thus increases the effectiveness of a solar pond's dual functions as solar collector and storage system.

The city of Miamisburg, Ohio, population seventeen thousand, built its own salt pond in a community park. The small pond (180 by 120 feet) was put into operation in 1979. Total construction costs ran about $70,000 ($3.20 per square foot). Its plastic bottom liner and eleven hundred tons of salt accounted for the largest share of the capital expenditure; operation and maintenance now costs about $1,400 a year. At the end of February, when a layer of ice floats on the surface of the pond, the water at the bottom is still 83° F. By the first day of summer it

169

is warm enough to heat the city's outdoor swimming pool. In early October the pool closes, but the pond has heat enough to warm a nearby recreation building for three more months. The cost, according to Layton Wittenberg, analyst for the U.S. Department of Energy, is less than $9.15 per million Btus, less than that of fuel oil.

Solar ponds also can be used to generate electricity, by heating a fluid under pressure until it vaporizes. The vaporized fluid passes through a turbine or piston engine, where it is allowed to expand and so produces mechanical motion. After the expansion stage, the vaporized fluid is cooled and the cycle begins again. A 150-kilowatt Rankine engine has been generating electricity from a 70,000-square-foot pond in Israel since 1980, and in Gila Bend, Arizona, a Rankine engine gets heat from concentrating solar collectors and generates power to pump water for irrigation. At its June peak the system can pump more than ten million gallons a day.

A method has been developed, too, to use for cooling. Ted Taylor, a physicist who once contributed significantly to America's nuclear-power program, calls them "ice ponds." He demonstrated the concept in Princeton, New Jersey: water sprayed into the air in a fine mist during the winter froze into accumulations of porous ice about 20 feet thick. In January and February Princeton produced and stored several hundred tons of ice in a plastic-lined, 15-foot-deep pond with an insulated surface. Then, in the summer, the ice was used to air condition a building adjoining the pond.

Ted Taylor convinced his neighbors in the unincorporated town of Damascus, Maryland, population seven thousand, to consider installing a solar heating and cooling system using ponds. He estimated that 33 acres of solar ponds 25 feet deep would be required, after energy conservation measures were taken, to heat Damascus's residential buildings. To provide heat for the town's commercial buildings the area of the ponds would have to be increased by 20 percent. The total water needed for space heating would be 230 million gallons, about equal to the annual total consumption of water by the town.

A study of Northampton, Massachusetts, population thirty thousand, concluded that an average pond area of about 2.5 acres—about 100,000 square feet—would be necessary to supply a hundred homes with space and water heating. About 495 acres, or two-thirds of a square mile of pond area, would be necessary to supply all the low-temperature hot-water and space heating needs of the community as well as its lighting and appliance requirements.

Some researchers are investigating the possibility of using natural water-storage tanks rather than building new ones. More than 60 percent of the surface area and 75 percent of the population of the continental United States rests on underground water aquifers. The amount of groundwater contained in the upper half mile of the continental crust of the United States is estimated to be nearly 20 times greater than all the water in the nation's rivers and lakes. Charles Meyer, in a report to General Electric on heat storage wells, noted, "Geologists and ground-water hydrologists agree without hesitation that hot water can be injected into the ground, stored and recovered. This is intuitively obvious because sand and rock are good thermal insulators and there is an enormous amount of storage space in the groundwater aquifers that underlie most of the United States."[27] One computer model indicated that about three-fourths of the heat stored still can be recovered after 180 days. James Calm, analyst at the Argonne National Laboratory, observes that using these heat storage wells would reduce the surface area required for drilling and operating wells: "The insulation is already in place," he comments.[28]

Once storage systems are in place, any heat source can be tapped. Solar energy is one possibility, but cogeneration, waste heat, or any other energy source also could be used. This diversity of suppliers increases the attractiveness of storage systems to communities of widely varying resources.

Putting the Pieces Together

All energy systems have separate but interrelated components. Energy is generated, distributed, and consumed. In some cases it is also stored. And each of these components of energy systems has characteristics of its own; for example, distribution systems will probably always be owned by public or private monopolies, because whether gas, oil, heat, or electricity is being distributed, to have redundant pipelines or grid systems is wasteful. In this section we will examine how the components interrelate in the systems that have been discussed.

Storage systems tend to be more economical the larger they are—

171

yet at some point the economies of scale are exhausted. The Northampton energy study recommended building 2.5-acre solar ponds. The Damascus energy study envisions 7-acre ice ponds. Probably, the best use of storage systems will be to serve one block or one small neighborhood, rather than an individual household or an entire city.

For our power plants, the scale that is most economical depends largely on the type of technology and fuel used. Technologies that directly convert sunlight into heat or electricity have the greatest potential for decentralization. An individual building's rooftop, walls, and canopies are the best sites for photovoltaics or solar collectors. Yet, as the Boston solar-access study determined, many buildings will not have adequate solar access. In those cases, solar energy systems will be more centralized—at the end of the block served, or even in an outlying area. Among other technologies based on renewable sources that have some scale economies, wind power is a particularly apt example.

Wind power has not been discussed in this chapter. The reason is that few urban areas appear able to use this power source. Lincoln, Nebraska, which has established setback requirements for wind turbines based on the maximum distance a blade might be thrown in case of an accident, requires a 100-foot setback for a 5-foot diameter blade and a 385-foot setback for a 40-foot diameter blade. Boulder County requires a setback equal to the height of the tower. The density of urban areas is such that these setbacks allow room enough for wind turbines in few locations.

Wind turbines, however, have two characteristics that make large systems attractive; first, the power generated by a turbine varies as the cube of the wind speed. Thus if the wind speed doubles, the power generated increases eight times. This ratio makes it highly profitable to install the machine on the one particular piece of a vicinity's land that has the highest winds. This is the reason that energy prospectors are rapidly buying up the windiest land areas in the nation, just as they are buying up the fastest-flowing rivers and the most productive farmland. Second, the power output also varies as the square of the blade diameter; if the blade diameter doubles, the power generated increases four times—so relatively large machines become economically attractive. However at some point, not yet known, the economies of scale are overcome by the increased engineering complexities of very large blade diameters. Wind farms in Hawaii are installing 4,000-kilowatt machines while developers in the state of Washington are using 2,000-kilowatt machines, and in New Hampshire an operational wind farm is a forest of 50-kilowatt machines. The 1980s will yield a great deal of information as to which size is most effective.

Cogeneration systems, too, generate energy less expensively the bigger they are. Whether significant scale economies exist is unclear, however, in systems that produce more than 1,000 kilowatts. This is about the energy used by five hundred homes, the number in a small neighborhood.

Although the data are sparse, we can draw preliminary conclusions from the various energy activities throughout the country. The systems of the future might furnish energy for more than a household but for fewer residents than occupy a city or region. Denis Hayes, former director of the Solar Energy Research Institute, testified before Congress in 1980 that "right now we don't have very good ways of handling things at that level, the neighborhood level, the community level. Something less than Manhattan Island but more than your house."[29] Except for systems that use direct sunlight, neighborhood-level storage, distribution, and generation systems do appear well justified.

In designing an energy system, forgetting the demand side of the picture is an error easy to make. Unfortunately, too many designers have discovered only after the fact the harmful results of this omission. For example, district heating systems are designed to meet the predicted demand—the diameters of pipes and the sizes of the heat exchangers inside the buildings are determined by the demand to be met. But as energy prices rise, it becomes increasingly economical to reduce dramatically, if not to eliminate, buildings' heating requirements and so the overall demand for heat. Robert Timmerman, a consulting engineer based in Boston and an expert on district heating, believes most existing buildings already have the capability of conserving so much heat that sufficient energy for their use is given off as waste heat by their lights, machinery, and workers. Instituting conservation only after the district heating system is in place, however, would undermine the system's cost effectiveness.

This problem will be avoided if conservation investments are made before the system is designed. Such investments should be sufficient to institute all those measures that will save energy at a rate less than the cost to generate it.

The energy systems we build for the future should be more resilient and more flexible than those designed in the past. Once again, district heating systems provide a good illustration. Contemporary district heating systems in the United States distribute steam. Thus they can put to use only those sources of waste heat that have very high temperatures. Yet many observers believe that lower-temperature hot water is a better transport medium. Steam systems, because of their high temperature and pressure, have such high heat losses that if they transport steam only half as far as hot water is carried with the same operating parameters, the heat losses from the two will be equal. Low-temperature hot-water systems also have the advantage that they can use the less expensive plastic pipes and heat exchangers. To compare: the cost of laying a six-inch steel pipe under a sidewalk or roadway can be $1,000 per installed foot; the cost for plastic pipes running through the basement walls of attached buildings can be less than $50.

The primary advantage of lower-temperature distribution systems, however, is that they significantly broaden the number of potential suppliers. Jack Gleason, an urban planner and author of a book on European district heating systems, has written widely on the advantages of low-temperature systems for precisely this reason. Waste heat from appliances and solar energy can add to the supply of heat for such systems.

The city will be intimately involved in almost all humanly scaled energy systems. It will have to enact ordinances protecting future solar access for those installing solar energy systems on their rooftops. It will have to change land-use planning regulations to permit attached greenhouses. It will have to grant franchises to district heating companies that need to cross streets or alleys. Some observers, like Helge E. Nurmi, assistant project manager of the Belle River Project for the Detroit Edison Company, believe the involvement of municipalities should go much further. After supervising district heating in Sweden, he told a group of utility engineers and planners in 1980 what he had learned. Nurmi was "particularly interested in why . . . [there is a] rapid growth rate of district heating in Europe as compared to the stagnation in North America." He doubted that it was a matter of technology. Rather, the

Europeans had resolved the institutional problems involved in financing and operating district heating systems. Here, private utilities will not invest in such systems, because the return on investment is too low. But the benefits to the society as a whole are great. Nurmi concludes, "Europeans found out the same truth 25 years ago. The Europeans, through the independent actions of many cities, began to build district heating systems with public funding." For Nurmi, "city governments are the key to district heating construction."[30]

The PURPA legislation creates a guaranteed market for independently produced electricity; as a result of this legislation and the rapid maturation of new technologies, we can expect the number of power plants to increase dramatically in the near future. This number had remained constant between 1920 and 1980—we only traded four thousand small power plants in 1920 for four thousand giant power plants in 1980. But with cogeneration, wind turbines, hydroelectric plants, and photovoltaics coming on-line, fifty thousand power plants may be operating by the mid-1980s and millions by the mid-1990s. That explosion of power producers is what many utilities fear. And while the city develops its genuine self-interest in encouraging decentralized energy systems, the utility companies are pursuing their opposite interest.

In March 1981, the same month the PURPA regulations were to go into effect, Judge Harold Cox of the Southern District Court of Mississippi sided with the Mississippi Power and Light Co., the state of Mississippi, and the Mississippi Public Service Commission in declaring PURPA unconstitutional. Cox argued that PURPA constitutes a "direct intrusion" by the federal government into the affairs of the state of Mississippi. Proclaimed Cox: "The sovereign state of Mississippi is not a robot or lackey which may be shuttled back and forth to suit the whim and caprice of the federal government."[31] Cox's decision cited no legal precedent after 1935. It was a modern reversion to the days before federal agencies had authority over electric distribution.

Immediately after the Mississippi decision, the public service commission in Georgia ceased PURPA proceedings. Utilities in Louisiana, Mississippi, and several New England states immediately withdrew offers to purchase independently produced power.

Some utilities went even further. The Potomac Electric Power Company submitted a legal brief to the District of Columbia Public Service Commission claiming that not only was the commission no longer required to implement PURPA as a result of the Mississippi decision, but that it in fact had no authority to do so. PEPCO went back to the 1926 case of *Public Utilities Commission of Rhode Island* v. *Attleboro Steam and Electric Company* to support its contention that "local regulation over any sale of electric energy to PEPCO is constitutionally impermissible" because it interferes with "interstate commerce." The Attleboro case, PEPCO conceded in its brief, "directly resulted in the enactment of the Federal Power Act."[32] Thus utilities are beginning to argue that if the federal government leaves the utilities field, the state governments can no longer enter it.

Utilities are reacting not only to PURPA but to the whole range of new, potentially decentralizing technologies. Often the battleground is the state legislatures; non-home-rule cities must be given specific authorization from state legislatures before they can undertake new projects, and utilities have been fighting any expansion of municipal authority in the energy area. A bill to allow the city of Bellingham, Washington, to develop a district heating system passed the state senate but failed as a result of a tie vote in the house. In Idaho, the state legislature rejected a bill that would have allowed three municipalities to finance new power-generating facilities with revenue bonds.

Power companies, as one Wyoming newspaper noted, "are simply reluctant to play ball with new competitors." "They own the whole restaurant," says Idaho Public Utilities Commission President Perry Swisher of the power companies, "and here comes some guy wanting to sell his damn hot dogs out in front."[33]

Cities are fighting back. One tool is use of the franchise authority to gain concessions from private utilities; although some franchises granted in the early part of this century are perpetual, many have 20-year to 40-year periods. So ascertaining a franchise expiration date can be an opening point for negotiations with local utilities. A surprising number of franchises are expiring in the next few years. For example, 40 franchises are expiring in the Florida Power and Light Co. service area between 1980 and 1984. These franchise areas brought in about a quarter of all the company's energy sales during 1979.

Our eventual achievement of energy independence is by no means assured—in fact, the road by which we approach it is tortuous. General Electric, the company formed when Thomas Edison sold his own corporation in the late 1880s, has already developed a rooftop photovoltaic roof shingle. By the mid-1980s, when we reroof our homes we could not only be protecting ourselves from the elements but converting one of the elements—direct sunlight—to useful work. Yet in the same period the federal government is moving ahead with plans to launch solar-power satellite systems. These orbiting power plants will link millions of solar cells in arrays, as large as half of Manhattan Island, that will beam down microwaves to central earth-based receiving stations, from which the electricity will be distributed regionally. Thus, using the same fuel source—sunlight—and the same technology, we could have the most decentralized or the most centralized form of electric generation in history.

The technical potential for energy independence can now be considered a given; the question of the political and institutional aspects of decentralizing energy generation has become much more important. But one other factor may be more influential than any of these: money. Without capital, the dreams of the cities mentioned in this chapter will be stillborn. How do we finance the transition to energy independence?

CHAPTER **8**

Financing
the Transition

Money alone sets all the world in motion.

Publius Syrus

Energy independence costs money. Communities will
have to attract huge amounts of investment capital to increase the efficiency of their buildings, vehicles, and equipment and to construct and
operate humanly scaled energy production systems. Moreover, this investment capital must be attracted even as other parts of the economy
compete vigorously for capital. Yet the quantity of the capital is only one
important ingredient in a successful transition to energy independence.
Equally important are the terms of the capital. To finance the transition
to energy independence, mechanisms will have to be evolved that allow
the borrower to benefit immediately.

The individual household or business cannot achieve energy self-
reliance because of its limited access to capital markets. Some households and businesses are too poor; banks and stores will not extend
credit to poor people. Those with income sufficient to get credit can
borrow only relatively small amounts for very short time periods at very
high interest rates, sometimes to their disadvantage. For example, suppose I currently pay $500 a year for energy to heat my building, and
energy prices are increasing 10 percent annually. I borrow $1,000 at 18

percent interest, repayable in three years, and invest in storm windows, caulking, weatherstripping, and insulation. My energy bill declines by $200 the first year. However, I spend more than twice this amount to repay the loan that first year and continue to spend more to repay the loan than I save in energy during the three-year repayment period. In the fourth year, when the loan is paid off, I pay 50 percent of the amount I would have been paying for energy had I not made the conservation investments. But few individual investors are willing to wait that long to get a benefit.

On the other hand, if I could borrow the same amount of money, at the same interest rate, but repay the loan in ten years rather than three years, my loan payments would be equal to my energy savings. The goal for the tools of finance is to allow us immediate benefit, and this can be accomplished in many ways—by stretching out loan periods, by reducing the interest rate, or by any of many other means. Individual homeowners and businesses cannot develop such mechanisms. But each of us is a part of larger networks, larger collectivities that do have the power to borrow large amounts of money and channel them into energy self-reliance investments. There are two organizations to which we each belong that operate on the local level and that are expressly required to take into account the public interest and public welfare. One is the municipal corporation, the city. The other is the energy utility.

Our collective monthly energy payments form a huge and stable flow of capital for the energy utility. That guaranteed stream of revenue allows energy corporations to attract investment capital to finance gas, oil, and coal exploration and the construction of new power plants. The previous chapter explored how consumers of energy are redefining themselves as producers. Ratepayers, too, are shedding the consumerist mentality. They are beginning to see their monthly payments as investments and themselves as investors with the right to decide what type of energy future their payments will help to finance.

Similarly, taxpayers are realizing that local governments can become powerful allies in channeling capital to local energy projects. The purpose of the municipal corporation is to promote the general welfare, and, as we shall see, in the long run financing energy self-reliance is one of the best ways to promote the general welfare.

179

The Utility as Financing Agent

Seattle, Washington, became in 1975 the first city to endorse the right of an electric utility's customers to control the future investments of the utility. The superintendent of Seattle City Light and Power, the fourth largest municipally owned electric utility in the nation, had recommended to the city council that the city purchase a share in two nuclear power plants to be built by a consortium of Washington cities. The superintendent argued that the additional generating capacity would be necessary to meet the rising demand for electricity in the 1980s. The city council approved the request.

But a formidable citizens' organization threatened legal action if the council did not investigate alternatives to the new power plants. Times had changed. The citizens argued that so long as the cost of electricity had declined (as had been the situation from 1910 to 1970), to build new power plants and promote consumption was sensible. But since 1970 the production cost and the selling price for electricity were rising. Building new power plants can cost as much as $5,000 per household. The council members, after listening to their constituents and looking more closely at the figures involved, agreed to investigate alternative investments. Four months later the *Seattle 1990* report was completed.

The *Seattle 1990* report quantified the costs of saving electricity by installing weatherstripping or storm windows compared to the costs of generating electricity from nuclear power plants that would begin operation in the mid-1980s. The report concluded that the owner of an electrically heated home could save electricity more cheaply by investing in attic insulation than by having the same amount of money invested in a new power plant. Since either strategy increases the supply of available electricity, the terms "saved" and "generated" can be used interchangeably. If we reduce the amount of electricity needed to keep a house warm through a winter, we can build another house without adding a new power plant.

The city council accepted the report's conclusions and reversed its vote. It withdrew from participation in the power-plants consortium. Instead, it adopted a city policy favoring conservation. (A historical footnote on this decision: the cost overruns of the nuclear plants from which Seattle withdrew had by 1980 become so huge that the state legislature ordered an analysis of the fiscal health of the Washington

Public Power System and an evaluation of whether the possible default on its bonds would harm the credit rating of the state of Washington itself.)

Unfortunately, the *Seattle 1990* report was both right and wrong. It was correct in the conclusion that to save is more economical than to produce. It was wrong, however, in assuming that the populace defines the term "economical" in the same way the report's authors did, or in the same way that the utility does. In financial terms, the utility and the homeowner or businessperson live in separate worlds.

The utility borrows money at lower rates, since a banker charges less interest on loans of $1 million than on loans of $1,000. Not only does the utility pay less for its money, but it borrows for longer periods. Utility bonds are normally issued for 10 to 20 years, compared to the average home improvement loan of three to five years.

Another difference between the individual and the utility is in the planning perspectives of the two. The utility's planning horizon is 10 to 20 years. It takes into account future energy prices and construction costs when evaluating potential investments. The customer, on the other hand, plans for the short term. He or she wants a quick payback. The utility evaluates an investment over the life of a power plant, while the homeowner or businessperson wants an investment that repays itself in two or three years.

A more subtle but crucial difference in perspective is that the customer evaluates an energy-related investment on the basis of the current price the utility charges for energy. But the current utility bill actually gives the wrong signal. The amount we pay for electricity reflects the past cost of power plants rather than their future cost. And the difference between the current (average) cost and the future (marginal) cost of electricity is particularly pronounced in the Pacific Northwest, where the hydroelectric potential has been largely exhausted and new power must come largely from coal or nuclear plants. The hydroelectric plants were built many years ago, when interest rates and construction costs were low, and now, of course, their fuel is nearly free. Because the price charged customers reflects the utility's current costs, electricity generated from the hydroelectric facilities is extremely inexpensive. In 1975 it cost a penny per kilowatt hour, compared to a national average of 3.5 cents per kilowatt hour for electricity.

Electricity from a new coal or nuclear power plant, on the other hand, will cost about ten cents per kilowatt hour (figuring all the costs of building and operating the plant divided by the total amount of electricity to be generated over the life of the plant). When a new power plant begins operation, the expensive electricity it generates is blended into the supply of much less expensive hydroelectricity, and the costs are averaged. Thus, although the customer's utility bill will increase, the increase will not completely reflect the added capacity's high cost.

If the customer pays a relatively low price for energy, he or she will tend to postpone or minimize investments that save (or produce) energy. Even if the energy savings to be had are significant, the low price of energy use means the dollar savings of conserving it will be nominal for the consumer. For the utility companies, however, investments in conservation are compared not to the current energy price but to the price of generating additional energy from new power plants. Suppose a new power plant generates electricity at ten cents per kilowatt hour, but attic insulation saves energy at a cost of three cents per kilowatt hour. The utility's customers will save money if the utility's investment is in attic insulation.

The customers may save money with this conservation strategy. But will the stockholders? To answer that question we must turn to the heart of the utility's balance sheet—the rate base.

The Rate Base

Seattle's utility is owned by the city. There are no stockholders; the city council acts as the board of directors. Most electricity and gas in this country, however, is generated and distributed by investor-owned utilities. These utilities are generally allowed to make money only on investments related to the generation and distribution of energy. These investments are called the utility's rate base. Other expenditures, such as those for administration, labor, and fuel, can be repaid through rate charges but no additional return can be earned on them. The regulatory commission determines what investments can be included in the rate base and the rate of return that the utility can earn on the rate base.

A utility raises capital in two ways—by borrowing it and by selling stock. A part of the capital comes from selling corporate bonds—in effect, corporate IOUs. This portion constitutes the debt carried by the utility. The other portion of capital comes from selling ownership shares in the company—what's called the equity capital. Although utilities typically have a capital structure that consists of about 60 percent debt and 40 percent equity, for convenience assume a utility has 50 percent debt and 50 percent equity. Suppose bondholders receive 14 percent interest and stockholders receive 16 percent return in the form of dividends. On a fifty-fifty weighted basis, the overall return on the rate base would fall exactly between 14 percent and 16 percent, or at 15 percent. If such a utility invests $1 billion in a new power plant it can earn $150 million.

On the one hand, a utility is constrained from adding too much debt to its capital structure, because at some point bond rating agencies would become wary about the company's debt position and downgrade the credit-worthiness of future bond offerings. When this occurs, the utility must pay a higher interest rate to attract capital, and this affects its balance sheet adversely unless the utility can get a higher return on its capital from the regulatory agencies—that is, unless it can raise its rates. On the other hand, stockholders are concerned about a company's issuing more stock to raise capital if the earnings of the company do not increase. If the value of the company remains steady but more shares are outstanding, the value of each share of stock is reduced. Thus the capital structure of the utility tends to stay in equilibrium.

For many years, regulatory commissions would not permit conservation investments to be included in the rate base. No profit could be earned on them. But the situation has changed dramatically in the last few years. In early 1981 *Business Week* could announce in a headline, "California Utilities Ordered to 'Unsell' Electricity." Some regulatory commissions have even allowed utilities a slightly higher rate of return on conservation investments as an incentive. But others believe that the utilities have sufficient incentive already. A utility that invests $1 billion to construct a new power plant earns a return on the investment each year. But this is a paper return. It is carried on the books but is actually not taken until the power plant begins operation. Thus to many potential investors or bondholders, the new-plant return is phantom, uncertain. Compare conservation investments, which begin earning a return in a few months—they can begin to enter the rate base immediately.

183

Conservation investments also are less risky than investments in new power plants.

By the early 1980s the traditional regulatory structures were changing. In some states the regulatory commissions have intervened to mandate investment policies on the part of regulated utilities. In other states the legislatures have ordered the regulatory commissions to encourage utilities to invest in conservation or renewable energy technologies. And in still other states the utilities themselves have requested permission to initiate pilot financing programs. From state to state the examples of financing mechanisms vary significantly. But all have been based on the concept that the customer and investor would be served best by investment in the lowest-cost energy alternative.

In 1977 Pacific Power and Light, an investor-owned utility based in Portland, Oregon, received permission from the Oregon Public Service Commission to implement a financing program that would allow customers to invest in energy conservation measures at little or no cost. Under this program a customer requests a utility representative to examine his or her house and evaluate the cost effectiveness of various conservation measures. The measures—including attic insulation, water-heater blankets, weatherstripping, caulking, and shower or faucet flow restrictors—that would save electricity for the area at less expense than the cost of building a new power plant are approved for financing. The customer selects a private contractor to perform the work. The utility pays the contractor directly, after the job is completed and passes inspection. The homeowner pays nothing. The utility adds the amount of the loan to its rate base and earns a profit on it. When the house is sold (to other than a relative), the seller repays the loan, with no interest, and the investment is removed from the rate base.

By 1981 this type of financing had become available in five states. It allows the homeowner to reduce electrical demand at virtually no cost. The homeowner repays the loan, but only when the house is sold. Since the original cost of the equipment for conservation will certainly be included in the selling price, the effective cost to the homeowner is zero. The stockholders are satisfied because the investment earns the same return as investments in new power plants; the ratepayers are satisfied because the program moderates future rate increases.

Sometimes utilities lend money directly to their customers. In 1978

184

the Tennessee Valley Authority initiated a program to finance the installation of a thousand solar hot-water systems in Memphis. To attract
people to the program, TVA arranged financing that allowed the customer to repay the loan from energy savings. To develop the financing,
the TVA staff investigated typical Memphis electric hot-water heating
bills and estimated that the average ratepayer was spending $15 per
month for electricity to heat water. A solar heating system could provide
about 75 percent of that electricity, at an installed cost of $2,000; the
customer, then, could afford to pay about $12 per month for the solar
system and come out about even in the first month of operation. As
electric prices increase, the savings will also increase.

To be repaid with a monthly payment of $12, a $2,000 loan has to be
for 20 years at 3.75 percent interest. Since the TVA borrowed money at
about 7 percent interest, its contribution to the financing plan was the
difference between the cost to TVA of borrowing money and the cost at
which it lent the money to the customer—about $800 over the 20-year
period. Thus one could say that TVA is actually investing $800 of its own
money to encourage solar hot-water heating. However, if by installing a
solar hot-water system TVA can postpone building one kilowatt worth of
new electrical generating capacity and one kilowatt of capacity costs
$2,000, then TVA would have a net system savings of $1,200.

TVA achieves this saving only if it can guarantee that capacity will be
displaced. The solar water systems could actually save energy without
displacing capacity—the reason is that to predict exactly when a solar
collector will be generating heat is impossible. TVA's greatest demand is
for electric space heating in the winter. Suppose that during a particularly cold period, when people are using a maximum amount of electric
energy for heating, several consecutive overcast days cause the solar
heating system to produce little or no energy. The solar customer
would use back-up electrical power, at precisely the time all the other
customers are demanding a large amount of electricity. To be prepared
for such a contingency, TVA would have to keep electrical capacity on
reserve just in case the solar customer needs it. The solar heating system
would therefore displace no capacity: TVA would still have to construct
and maintain a reserve power plant even if it were to be used only a few
days or even a few hours a year.

To justify the low-interest loans, then, TVA had to be able to count on the solar water systems' not using electricity during peak demand periods. It accomplished this objective by requiring solar buyers to install oversized storage tanks and timers. The timer prevents a customer from purchasing electricity during peak times, thus guaranteeing a drop in peak demand. An oversized storage tank allows the customer to use electricity during off-peak times to generate heat that can be stored for several days.

TVA also offers a comprehensive energy audit to all commercial and industrial customers. The audit estimates the potential for cogeneration, solar energy use, and the use of other renewable resources. Staff engineers spend 50 to 60 hours on each survey. The property owner receives estimates of the potential energy savings in fuel and dollars, the cost of implementing the energy conservation measures, and the payback time for each investment. TVA will rebate the full cost of the audit to any customer who achieves at least 75 percent of the potential savings. And TVA will lend as much as $100,000 to commercial and industrial customers who wish to install measures recommended in a full audit. Private firms cannot obtain loans for items with a payback period greater than three years unless they first make the improvements with payback periods of three years or less. The interest rate on the loans is TVA's cost of borrowing money plus one percent to cover administrative costs. The loans are made for terms of up to ten years.

A 1980 study by the California Public Utilities Commission concluded that, although deferred and low-interest or no-interest loan programs were useful, they have not attracted as much citizen response as had been expected. California decided to imitate the private sector's use of rebates. Consumers apparently are attracted more by getting a rebate at the moment of sale than by attractive financing terms when they buy such items as automobiles or appliances. In 1980 the California commission ordered its four major electric and gas utilities to offer programs to finance solar hot-water systems in existing buildings. Each utility was given specific goals. For example, San Diego Gas and Electric's three-year goal was to install solar hot-water systems in seventy-eight hundred single-family electric homes and twenty-five hundred single-family gas homes. In addition it was to install nineteen thousand solar heating systems in multifamily units. To those participating in the program who used electric water heaters, SDG&E paid $20 per month for three years, for a total rebate of $720. It gave the same monthly payment, but for four years, to customers installing solar heating systems that displaced gas-fired hot-water systems, for a total of $960. By the middle of 1981 SDG&E had already filled its three-year goal for single-family gas homes and by the end of the year was expected to fill its electric water-heating quota.

Northern States Power Company, a Minneapolis utility, announced in 1981 a program to encourage the purchase of high-efficiency appliances. It will pay up to half the additional cost of a high-efficiency air conditioner or refrigerator compared to the cost of one that has average energy efficiency. Thus, if an air conditioner that uses the average amount of eletricity costs $1,500 and a higher-efficiency air conditioner costs $2,000, the utility will pay up to $250 to the customer. By helping customers purchase appliances that use less electricity to perform the same function, NSPC is reducing the need to construct more expensive power plants.

In the Pacific Northwest, the Bonneville Power Administration, a federal agency, is taking the concept of buying conservation to its furthest extent. Congress enacted legislation in 1980 that provides BPA with as much as $1.2 billion to invest in either energy conservation or new power plants, whichever is less expensive. According to the provisions of the legislation, popularly known as the Regional Power Act, BPA must purchase conservation whenever the cost is within 10 percent of the cost of any alternative power generation technology. In descending order from conservation, BPA must finance electric generation from renewable resources, from high-efficiency techniques (for example, cogeneration), and, last, from conventional thermal-electric power plants. BPA has developed a price schedule for various energy-related measures. For example, it will pay a commercial enterprise $1 for every fluorescent bulb replaced with a more efficient bulb. It will pay several hundred dollars to a local utility (which can then pass on the payment to the customer) for every home that is weatherized, and it will pay municipalities for every street light they convert to high-efficiency bulbs.

By mid-1981 tens of millions of dollars were being redirected from power plants to investments in storm windows, solar collectors, energy efficient appliances, and insulation. No utility had yet made a billion dollar commitment to energy independence, and the amount invested nationwide in energy-efficiency improvements still represents only a tiny fraction of the tens of billions invested each year in new power plants. But even though the financing programs have been in existence only a few years, many state regulatory commissions and utilities are advocating utility financing as an effective tool for encouraging cost-effective energy independence investments. The trend is toward greater involvement by the energy utility in channeling capital for energy self-reliance.

The Municipal Corporation as a Financing Agent

Municipal corporations are endowed with political authority by their state constitutions or state legislatures to promote the general welfare of their inhabitants. Energy has become a key factor in that welfare. Disruptions in the supplies of oil and gasoline, natural gas, and coal during the 1970s severely disrupted local economies. The municipal corporation uses large quantities of energy to provide such basic services as police and fire protection, water, sewage treatment, and street lighting. And in the past generation the city government has expanded its authority considerably beyond the delivery of basic services. It is now an oversight authority for local development, and increasingly the link between development and energy becomes more pronounced.

To give one example, the Congress enacted the Clean Air Act in the 1970s. The act ordered the Environmental Protection Agency to establish maximum pollution levels for air quality basins. Regions that exceed the maximum levels can add no new housing or industry unless the additional pollution is offset by reduced pollution from some other source within the region. Because almost all pollution is caused by the consumption of energy, in furnaces, power plants, or vehicles, the local and regional planning agencies have begun to encourage energy efficiency as a way to allow more business development.

There are other links between energy payments and local economic vitality. The dollar spent for energy in a locality disappears from it rapidly, because the energy we consume comes from Texas, Mexico,

Nigeria, Alaska, or Saudi Arabia. It is transported in tankers and pipelines owned by a dozen or so global oil corporations. The energy is delivered to us by way of power plants situated outside cities, or by way of pipelines that are owned by utilities, or by independent oil dealers. Therefore, few of the jobs created in the energy industry are local, and little of the money spent to generate new energy sources circulates in the local economy. To create a job in the electric-utility industry costs more than $200,000, compared to $20,000 for a manufacturing job and $10,000 for a job in the service sector.

Analyses of the paths taken by energy payments in the District of Columbia, in Northampton, Massachusetts, and in Carbondale, Illinois, determined that on average only 10 to 15 cents on the dollar remains in the city. This compares to between 75 cents and $1.25 returned for every dollar paid in federal taxes. By 1981 many communities yearly spent the equivalent of $1,000 per person on energy. And the future holds no prospect that prices will level off. Cities have become alarmed at the potential for their well-intentioned economic development efforts to be thwarted by rising energy prices. Franklin County, Massachusetts, found that in order to keep up with projected energy price increases, it would have to attract a new business as large as its largest employer every year. Only then would increase in income, from an expanded labor force, keep pace with the decrease in income caused by rising energy prices.

Communities that reduce their spending for imported energy thereby increase the amount of money they can spend for other purposes that may be more beneficial to the local economy. Moreover, when a community invests in conservation or solar technologies, it is spending money on businesses that tend to be locally based. Dollars spent for storm windows, caulking, energy audits, weatherstripping, and solar collectors tend to go to local businesses.

Municipal corporations have some of the same advantages that energy utilities have in financing energy self-reliance. Both can borrow large amounts of money for long durations. Both do long-range planning. Both take account of future energy costs, and both can include in their cost-benefit equations the benefits to their members of reduced energy demand. But cities have one advantage that investor-owned utilities do not have; they can borrow money at tax-exempt rates. Be-

189

cause owners of municipal bonds pay no federal taxes on the interest received, the bond owners will accept an interest rate lower than they would on other bonds. An investor in the 50 percent tax bracket who buys a taxable bond (issued by the federal government or a private corporation) paying 15 percent interest will pay half the interest income to the federal government; the effective return on the investment is then reduced to 7.5 percent. If the same investor purchases a tax-exempt bond carrying an interest rate of 9 percent, the actual return to the investor will be higher.

The attractive tax-exempt status of municipal and state bonds has been the target of criticism for many years. To many critics these bonds are little more than tax loopholes for the rich. If a wealthy investor avoids paying taxes, the rest of the taxpayers will pay a little bit more to make up the loss. Tax exemption is justified by its supporters by the fact that the funds are used for worthy public purposes. The problem is that the definition of "public purpose" has become increasingly blurred. Originally it was restricted to the laying of sewer or water lines or the building of roads or docks; in other words, the construction of facilities to be used by broad sections of the public. But in the 1930s a number of states began to issue industrial development bonds. These bonds financed private developments to encourage industries to locate in the deep South. The courts generally approved the use of tax-exempt status for these bonds on the basis that, even though private interests made a profit on the bonds, the public also gained from the increased health of the local economy.

However, the pressure to expand the use of industrial revenue bonds increased as interest rates and inflation rates rose. The interest paid on tax-exempt bonds is typically one-third lower than the interest paid on taxable bonds. When a taxable bond pays 3 percent, a tax-exempt bond pays 2 percent. When taxable bonds pay 15 percent, as was the case in 1981, tax-exempt bonds pay 10 percent. As the spread widens, the money saved by using tax-exempt financing grows substantially. A company borrowing $1 million for ten years would have to pay out almost $400,000 more on a 15 percent interest bond than on a tax-exempt bond.

Congress has twice intervened to limit the purposes for which tax-exempt securities can be used. In the late 1960s Congress prohibited the use of tax-exempt financing for projects that benefit private businesses except for specific types of projects (such as resource recovery plants, docks, or housing), or for relatively small projects. In 1980 Congress again intervened—this time to restrict the rapidly growing practice of issuing tax-exempt bonds to finance home mortgages. Congress was concerned that cities were financing expensive homes for wealthy families. It restricted the use of tax-exempt bonds for mortgages on single-family, owner-occupied houses to a set amount until 1984, after which such bonds could not be issued at all.

The concern about the abuse of tax exemption for home mortgages was understandable, but, unfortunately, Congress included home improvement loans and energy-related improvements in its restrictions. The argument against using tax-exempt bonds to finance home mortgages was that it put cities in direct competition with local financing institutions. Financing was available from traditional sources for home mortgages, although at high interest rates. The length of the mortgage usually was identical whether it was financed through a savings and loan association or through the city. But in the case of energy-efficiency improvements, tax-exempt financing would not compete with alternative sources of financing; local financial institutions are indifferent to the relatively small loans given for energy conservation, and they are wary of the relatively new technologies for power generation at the household or small-business level. The loans that are made for these carry not only very high interest rates but short terms. So the case for limiting the use of tax-exempt bonds for financing conservation or solar technologies is much weaker than the arguments against using tax-exempt financing for the purchase of new homes.

The restrictions on the use of tax-exempt financing for energy improvements on single-family, owner-occupied dwellings was not the first limitation Congress had imposed. The Crude Oil Windfall Profit Tax Act of 1980 was passed early in that year. The act was designed not only to impose a tax on oil but to distribute a portion of the tax's revenues to encourage development of various alternative energy sources. The tax incentives for conservation already in effect were not raised, but Congress enacted a provision that disallowed a homeowner or businessperson who used tax-exempt financing to invest in conservation or solar energy from also taking advantage of the federal tax incentives.

The rationale was that the customer, by using both the tax incentives and the tax-exempt financing, was "double dipping" into the federal treasury. Yet once again Congress appears to have ignored the fact that accelerating energy self-reliance was the purpose of the act, and the provision actually reduces the means available to encourage conservation and the use of solar energy. As a result of this provision, a number of state and municipal governments delayed issuing tax-exempt bonds until they studied the tradeoff between tax-exempt financing and the use of tax incentives.

Local and state governments issue two types of tax-exempt securities. General obligation bonds are backed by the taxing authority of the government. If the bond is in danger of default, the city or state guarantees that it will raise taxes to make up the deficit. Revenue bonds are not backed by the taxing power but by the revenues generated by the specific project to be financed, such as turnpikes' tolls and the user fees charged by water utilities.

Because of the somewhat higher risk involved in revenue bonds, they offer a slightly higher interest rate than general obligation bonds. States traditionally put a ceiling on the total value of general obligation bonds and require a majority (in some cases two-thirds) approval by local voters for their issuance. There is no ceiling and no vote requirement for revenue bonds. Municipalities have been issuing increasing proportions of revenue bonds in recent years, partly because the cities need not go to the voters for approval of that and partly as a result of tax limitation movements. In such states as California and Massachusetts, where voters have amended the constitution to restrict property tax increases, general obligation bonds have become risky investments.

The ability to issue tax-exempt bonds is controlled not only by the federal government but by state legislatures. Just as utilities have to gain the permission of the state regulatory commission to finance energy conservation or solar energy, so the municipal corporation must ask permission of its state legislature to authorize the use of tax-exempt bonds for energy-related projects. In some cases, such as in Washington, the state constitution is particularly restrictive in the use of tax-exempt financing that results in private gain. Since low-interest financing of conservation or solar energy collection clearly results in private gain, often a constitutional amendment is necessary before a city can embark on a financing program. Seattle could not begin its aggressive financing program until the citizens of Washington approved such a constitutional amendment in 1980.

Seattle gained approval from a constitutional amendment to establish a bonded financing program. In late 1980 and early 1981 the city of Baltimore issued $5 million in general obligation bonds; two-thirds of the voters approved the issuance of these bonds, to be used to finance conservation investments in local residential units. Baltimore has home rule status in Maryland and did not need the state legislature's permission to issue such bonds. Minneapolis and St. Paul received state authorization in mid-1981 and, at the time this book was being written, were about to issue bonds to finance energy conservation measures.

Cooperation of the Cities and Utilities

By the early 1980s energy utilities were gearing up to expand their pilot financing programs into large-scale offerings. Municipalities were beginning to set up financing systems through their housing rehabilitation authorities (as was the case in Pittsburgh) or their water departments (as in Santa Clara, California) or through various city and noncity agencies. Sometimes the two institutions, the energy utility and the municipality, pooled their resources.

The nation's largest utility, Pacific Gas and Electric, worked out an arrangement with three mid-sized California cities—Merced, Davis, and Chico, each with about thirty thousand residents. PG&E's program was designed to reduce a summer peak demand largely for air conditioning. The giant utility offered to pay each city $10,000 for every 1 percent reduction in peak energy consumption, up to a maximum of $100,000. The program was to be in effect for two summers. So if a city's residents saved 10 percent the first year and an additional 10 percent the second year, the city would receive two $100,000 checks.

The first summer all three cities achieved their goals. From June through September 1980, Merced, Davis, and Chico reduced peak electric consumption by 13, 22, and 17 percent, respectively, for a total reduction of 15.3 million kilowatt hours.

St. Paul and Minneapolis worked out arrangements with their local investor-owned utilities. Each city developed a different program. In St. Paul, the city issued $1 million in revenue bonds to finance loans to residents for conservation. The Northern States Power Corporation contributed $650,000 for loan money and an additional $150,000 to cover the costs of setting up a separate "energy bank." The utility lends money at a simple 6 percent interest rate and is repaid when the homeowner sells the house, as in the plan in operation in Pacific Power and Light's service area. In ten years NSP estimates it will have been repaid its initial loans, generating $1 million—counting principal and interest. Meanwhile, the city will lend the money received from issuing bonds at an interest rate to cover its own debt payments. When a city issues a bond, it agrees to pay back the interest in monthly or yearly installments, but the principal is not due until the bond comes to maturity. Thus St. Paul will be receiving $133,000 each year for loan repayments but will pay only $100,000 each year in interest on a 10 percent $1 million loan. At the end of ten years, NSP pays off the $1 million bond issued by St. Paul.

In Minneapolis, the city government issued several million dollars in bonds to finance conservation loans. The local gas utility, Minnegasco, gives a rebate of $100 to those receiving the loans.

Encouraging Decentralized Electric Generation: The Utility as Buyer of Power

So far we have discussed the concept and the actuality of energy utilities' financing conservation or solar technologies. With neither conservation nor solar energy use is the household or business generating electricity to be sold back to the utility—but with cogeneration or renewable resources, surplus power can be produced. And as a result of federal legislation passed in 1978, electric utilities, both public and privately owned, must purchase power generated by independent producers by these methods. The law requires utilities to pay a new producer a price that reflects the amount that would have to be spent to bring a new power plant on-line.

In 1981 most state regulatory commissions and city councils were developing the prices that would be paid to independent power producers. Because of one provision of the federal legislation, cities that own their own electric utilities could play an important role in setting this price. Although more than two thousand cities own their electric utilities, more than fifteen hundred of these have no generating capacity; these cities own the grid system but no power plants. They buy all their power from outside suppliers on the basis of long-term contracts, at the wholesale price of power.

Under the provisions of the federal law, a city that owns its grid system but has no generating capacity has the choice, with the independent power producer's consent, to purchase the power itself or to transmit the power to its bulk supplier at a nominal cost to the producer. It appears to be in the interest of the independent producer for the city utility to pass on the electricity to its supplier. If the city utility purchases the independently produced power for itself in place of bulk power, it pays a rate based on the wholesale price for bulk power, which is relatively low. The price the city pays for the new power, being based on a low rate, would be thus very low. However, if the bulk supplier were to purchase the power, it would pay a price based on the cost of the next power plant it was planning to construct—a considerably higher rate.

Cities that own their own electric distribution systems can use them as powerful tools for setting the prices paid for on-site-generated electricity. The higher the price, the greater the attractiveness of such a venture. Traditionally, when utilities build new power plants, they do so in remote areas, importing large engineering and construction firms to perform the work. Small power plants, in comparison, can be situated within a city to play a beneficial role in the local economy—the city can then help redirect the investment capital that would have been spent outside the community to investments within its jurisdiction.

Where Does the Capital Come From?

The objective of any financing mechanism is to attract as much capital as possible from outside the community. Utilities and municipal corporations cannot print money; they must attract its investment. Someone has to purchase municipal or utility bonds. Someone has to put money in the bank that can be lent for solar development or conservation. Where will the capital come from?

Some of it can come directly from individual households. In San Francisco the Solar Center, a solar installer, advises those in the local area or around the country who want to encourage solar technologies that they should invest in an account at a local savings and loan association—the Continental Federal Savings and Loan Association—earmarked specifically for solar energy. The accounts return investors the same interest rate obtainable in any other financial institution, but this savings and loan association agrees to use that money only for loans to the owners of single-family and multifamily homes for solar installations. The savings and loan association also agrees that it will charge an interest rate lower than comparable institutions charge and it will extend the terms of the loan far beyond those of the typically short-term loans offered by other financial institutions. In the first year of the energy fund, $500,000 in loans were extended.

We discussed before the ability of the city to issue tax-exempt bonds to finance energy self-reliance measures. Typically these bonds are sold in large denominations to wealthy investors or underwriting firms; a municipal bond may cost a minimum of $5,000. But in September 1978 the township of East Brunswick, New Jersey, population forty thousand, became the first locality to issue "minibonds." These bonds sold for $100, $500, or $1,000, making them attractive investments for local residents. The city was, in effect, creating a tax shelter for moderate-income residents. A savings account in 1978 paid 5 percent interest annually, and the interest income was taxable. The municipal bond paid 7 percent interest, and the interest income was exempt from taxation. So the municipal bond generated income like a savings account getting 12 percent interest, assuming the investor was in the 33 percent tax bracket.

Mayors view minibonds as a way not only to give residents a tax break but also to involve citizens in local projects and to build civic pride. "We wanted to give citizens a piece of the rock," one official in Ocean County, New Jersey, said after the county sold $1 million in minibonds in early 1979.[1] After a $500,000 "citizens subscription" bond sale in December 1979, Mayor Thomas P. Ryan of Rochester, New York, explained, "In addition to getting a tax-free yield, the citizens investing in these bonds will be directly helping to create jobs, improve downtown and make the city safer."[2]

Another source of investment capital is public or private pension funds. Pension funds are the most rapidly growing source of investment capital in the nation today. There are more than $500 billion in pension assets and almost $160 billion in state and local government employees' pension funds.

Pension-fund participants have in recent years demanded much more say in how their pension funds are invested. Traditionally participants have been concerned only that money has been invested wisely so that they could be assured of adequate monthly revenue when they retired. But as pension funds have grown, the investment policy of the funds themselves have become a focus of attention. Although investment trustees are required to invest on behalf of the members of the pension—that is, present and future pensioners—and the investments must be of very low risk and relatively high return, great latitude exists within these guidelines. State governments have in recent years analyzed their pension portfolios and discovered to their chagrin that the vast majority of the funds were being invested outside their states, even though comparably secure and high-yielding investments could have been made within their states. Unions have discovered that a significant portion of their pension funds have been invested in nonunionized-company stocks and bonds.

Pension funds can be targeted very specifically to support certain types of activities. The carpenters' union, for example, has its pension fund invest in building mortgages only if the construction is done by union labor. Some corporations use their pension funds to purchase mortgages in certain geographic areas where they have high numbers of employees.

Local governments are also beginning to evaluate their investment portfolios, to determine how the funds can be invested to benefit the local economy while maintaining high quality in the portfolio overall. Most local pension funds are controlled by statewide investment managers, but a number of larger cities do control fairly large pension funds—St. Paul and Baltimore are examples.

Pension fund managers rarely purchase municipal bonds, because the funds are already tax-exempt; in effect, their lower interest rate would penalize pension funds for ownership. Nor do pension funds lend money directly. But they can purchase loans already made by local governments or financial institutions. That is, they can enter the secondary market.

Loans are bought and sold in national and global securities markets; about 20 years ago the federal government established a secondary market for home mortgages. Before, a savings and loan association that made a 30-year mortgage would not be able to relend that money until a sufficient amount had been paid in. But because in a secondary market the savings and loan can immediately sell the loan, the institution can replenish its funds and make additional mortgages. Governmental institutions such as the Federal Home Loan Mortgage Corporation purchase large numbers of mortgages; the number reduces the probability of major defaults. These institutions, in turn, issue certificates backed by the large numbers of mortgages. These certificates are sold to institutional investors, insurance companies, pension funds, and other large investors.

In 1980, for the first time in American history, the amount of money spent for housing remodelling and rehabilitation surpassed that spent for new house construction. Increasingly the government was pressed to establish a secondary market for home improvement loans. In early 1981 the Federal Home Loan Mortgage Corporation inaugurated a $200 million pilot program to buy home improvement loans, including loans for energy conservation or solar energy development.

A secondary market helps to replenish local funds. It also encourages the lender to extend the repayment period, because a lender selling a loan immediately is indifferent to its term. The Federal Home Loan Mortgage Corporation, for example, will buy loans of 5-, 10-, or 15-year duration.

The city of Baltimore established a secondary market with bond issues. It does not make the loans directly. Rather, a local financial institution makes them, with terms of seven years and 9.5 percent interest. The city then buys the loans at 8 percent interest. That is, the bank collects 9.5 percent interest but pays the city only 8 percent, which is enough to cover the costs of repaying the bond. The 1.5 percent difference is the profit for the bank. (An additional small charge to the borrower compensates the bank's costs for originating the loan.)

Arkansas Power and Light, an investor-owned utility, proposed to develop a secondary market in the following manner. It makes a customer a ten-year loan for, say, $4,000 at no interest for conservation. The utility then sells the loan to a local bank—for $1,800, the discount to make up for the fact that the bank is receiving no interest payments. The customer pays off the loan on his or her utility bill, and the utility sends the payments to the bank. Thus an original $4,000, ten-year loan, sold for $1,800, earns the bank the $2,200 difference—an amount equivalent to the money the bank would have earned on a $4,000 ten-year loan at a normal 18 percent annual interest rate. The utility finances loans only for conservation measures that can save energy at a cost lower than that to the company for the generation of more energy. The proposal was vetoed by the state legislature.

Limited Partnerships

Utility bonds, municipal bonds, and federally backed secondary-market certificates carry very low risk, if any, and have relatively good returns on investment. Some investors, however, are willing to accept a higher risk for the possibility of a much greater profit. In recent years, inflation, which pushes people into higher and higher tax brackets, and the enactment of a variety of tax incentives to encourage energy-related investments have led tax attorneys and accountants to devise projects that allow wealthy investors to "shelter" their taxes. The lawyers and accountants have created a hybrid business enterprise called a limited partnership. This type of business combines the attractive feature of limited liability, which traditional corporations have, with the ability to pass on tax benefits to individual investors, as conventional partnerships do.

In a partnership, an investor can use the business's investment tax credits, depreciation allowance, and interest deductions to offset his or her personal income tax liability. However, the partner also assumes personal liability for the business. A corporation's stockholders have limited liability—that is, the stockholders cannot personally be sued for business losses—but neither can the tax benefits received by the corporation be passed through to the stockholders; their profit comes from dividends and any rise in the value of their stock.

Limited partnerships are often called tax shelters because they allow investors in very high tax brackets to decrease their tax liability. For example, suppose a limited partnership forms to purchase a $500,000 power plant that uses renewable resources or produces heat and power. Such a limited partnership will usually have a general partner, a professional engineering firm or a contractor familiar with energy conservation or energy generation, and a number of individual investors or limited partners. In this case let's say the partnership has four investors, each putting up $50,000. The remaining $300,000 is borrowed. The limited partnership will qualify for the conventional 10 percent investment tax credit and an additional 10 percent energy tax credit if it meets certain criteria. The investor can deduct the considerable amount allowed for depreciation on new equipment and the interest on any loan used to finance the purchase of the equipment.

The combination of these various tax benefits makes such an investment very attractive to people in high tax brackets. The limited partners can immediately take a 20 percent, or $100,000, tax credit. This would be divided in proportion to each investor's investment; each of the four partners would be able to reduce his or her tax liability by $25,000. Thus the first year the investor receives a 50 percent return on investment, not counting the additional tax benefits from depreciation or interest deductions or the revenue from the sale of the power plant's products—heat and electricity.

Limited partnerships are often used to purchase equipment that is then leased to, for example, businesses or apartment houses. A lessee can often obtain equipment that provides energy-efficiency improvements for a monthly payment that is less than the price of the projected monthly energy savings. Leasing provides 100 percent financing to the property owner, along with flexible monthly payments and a deduction on the lease payments as a business expense. And leasing also permits the lessee to avoid the risk of investing in a technology that may become obsolete. If the system fails to produce the desired energy savings or if a better system becomes available, the owner can cancel the lease or trade in the outdated equipment for new equipment without having paid the full cost of the first system.

Complex Financing Strategies

Sometimes it is possible to combine a number of financing mechanisms to generate capital for local energy self-reliance. An example of this is being planned in Dade County, Florida, where tax shelters, leases, and power sales to private utilities are combined. Dade County will lease a cogeneration plant from a New Jersey engineering firm. The engineering firm will establish a limited partnership that owns the equipment; the attractiveness of the tax benefits to the partners allows them to lease the power plant to Dade County on terms that also are attractive, equivalent to Dade County's taking out a loan at 9 percent interest (its tax-exempt-bond interest rate at the time). Dade County operates the power plant. It receives an immediate income from using the waste heat to chill water that is used for air conditioning and from selling electricity to the local utility. The county estimates that it will make a net profit of $700,000 during the first year from the revenue generated by the sale of electricity and the savings in the electricity that would otherwise be needed to air condition its buildings. After ten years, Dade County can purchase the power plant for a nominal sum.

Sometimes the public-private tax sheltered arrangements can become quite complex. Oceanside, California, population sixty-four thousand, is developing such a mechanism. The city has established the Oceanside Municipal Solar and Conservation Utility to encourage the leasing of solar hot water systems by city residents. The city proposes to act as a consumer protection agency to guarantee the workmanship and integrity of firms that are leasing the systems. A limited partnership will be established to attract capital from investors eager to benefit from recent changes in the tax law. Because of these lucrative tax benefits the investors can lower the lease payments to the point where the residents could lease the system for less than he or she would have paid for energy if the solar system had not been installed. After a period of years the resident would be permitted to purchase the system for a nominal sum.

This type of arrangement benefits all participants. The resident obtains a solar hot-water system with no down payment, at low cost and at no risk. Investors can earn a 30 to 100 percent return on their money during the first year of the investment because of the tax-related benefits and the low-interest loan offered by the manufacturer. And the manufacturer increases sales.

Marketing Energy Independence

Money is necessary to achieve energy self-reliance. But money alone is not sufficient. Even when financing is structured so that the homeowner or businessperson can repay energy-related loans through energy savings, people will not inevitably take advantage of the loans. Energy self-reliance itself must be sold, marketed, promoted. An ethic of energy independence must be created.

The concept of energy self-reliance involves new roles for local utilities and local government; it also involves a new self-image for a city's residents. Rather than residents' viewing themselves only as consumers, they must see themselves as producers and investors. Energy self-reliance means, in part, accelerating the conversion of our buildings, our vehicles, our appliances to high efficiency. Suppose a new refrigerator has an energy-efficiency rate double that of the one a homeowner currently owns—the new refrigerator costs $350 and saves $50 per year in electricity compared to the older model. The return on investment is about 14 percent, but since the return is tax-free, it is equivalent (for someone in the 30 percent tax bracket) to a savings account that pays 20 percent interest. That is by far the highest return from any nonspeculative investment today. It is true that the investment is not liquid; it cannot easily be converted into cash. But then one has a new refrigerator. A similar argument could be made for trading in the old gas guzzler for an energy-efficient automobile.

We are in a peculiarly advantageous historical period. In light of the new energy prices, our buildings, vehicles, and appliances are remarkably inefficient; one result is that financing mechanisms can be developed to allow the investor a handsome profit while allowing the borrower to repay the loan through energy savings. Indeed, some professional engineering firms have embarked on a "shared savings" program based on just this strategy. A firm audits a commercial building free. It then pays for the installation of energy conservation measures. The client pays nothing if no savings of energy costs ensues, but if it does occur, the engineering firm gets half the savings for a certain period of time. This system works precisely because a small investment right now can yield a high degree of energy conservation, and because energy prices are increasing so fast.

Obviously cities and utilities will have to decide what type of conservation measures or generating plants they will finance. The supply of capital, like the supply of energy, is finite, and there are many competing bids for it. One attractive feature of investments in energy, however, is that, unlike most public investments, the benefits can be quantified with a high degree of precision.

When cities and utilities aggressively pursue energy self-reliance to gain the benefits for their taxpayers and customers, they soon discover that energy efficiency goes far beyond the installation of a storm window or a solar collector. It is a design principle. It has to do with the way we produce our goods and services and the way we handle our wastes, the way we design not only our buildings but our communities. As energy efficiency becomes a central design principle, cities will begin to reconstruct their physical plants to minimize the amount of energy consumed. In the process, the ecological city will emerge.

CHAPTER 9

The Ecological City

We wring material from the earth, we use it,
and after its span of life it disperses by
rot, fire, or corrosion back into the earth,
into the air, or into the sea. It may not
again become sufficiently reconcentrated
by natural forces to the point of industrial
usefulness for geologic ages. Wherever we
are able to shorten this cycle, we are able
to use materials more intensively with less
net drain on what the earth still provides.

Paley Commission Report, 1952

America's cities are built on nineteenth and early twentieth century technologies. The giant industrial cities were products first of the coal-fired steam engine, which centralized industry and created the economic rationale for densely populating the cities. Then, the density of people and industry in those great cities outstripped the capability of the environment to handle their wastes. Huge amounts of water, fuels, and food had to be imported just to keep the city alive. And so the city was transformed from a self-sufficient community into a parasitical creature, dependent on great public-works projects for its survival. Chicago, for example, reversed the flow of the Chicago River so that it would not pollute drinking water from Lake Michigan; Los Angeles brought water from hundreds of miles away to build a city in the desert.

The steam engine gave way to the steam turbine and the central electric power station. Alternating current, developed by Tesla in the 1880s, allowed power plants to locate anywhere and deliver electricity anywhere. And alternating current, along with another invention, the internal combustion engine, exploded the densely populated core of the city, spreading the fragments over the countryside. Anywhere a road could be built, anywhere a power line could go—and that was just about everywhere—a town could be built, or a factory, or a housing subdivision. People no longer needed to live near their workplaces.

And people no longer bought products from nearby small businesses. No longer did the bread come from the local bakery or the beer from local breweries. Business grew larger as production systems grew larger, driven by the power unleashed by the use of concentrated fuels. Distribution lines lengthened. Whereas in the nineteenth century only the richest homeowners could afford to grace their buildings with marble brought from far-off places, in the twentieth the typical home builder imported materials that collectively had traveled tens of thousands of miles.

There was, to be sure, a reason that things came from so far away. Manufacturing facilities were located near the richest ore deposits. Steel plants were located near coal and iron deposits. Paper companies were located near forests. Agricultural enterprises were located where the soils were best and the growing seasons the longest. But as the century wore on, the richest ore deposits were exhausted, and lower grade reserves were mined. Much more rock had to be pulverized to get less useful material, and oil wells that were only a few hundred feet deep at the turn of the century became several miles deep by mid-century. The farms became ever more productive, but the amount of energy required to get the vegetables to market rapidly increased so that by the mid-1970s we were consuming more energy to transport the produce than to grow it.

In the 1970s, the unprecedented rise in energy prices brought home the cost of the parasitical cities and long supply lines. Rising energy prices encourage moving production and consumption closer together, shortening distribution systems. They encourage us to recycle our used products and wastes in order to capture the energy embodied in them during the conversion of the original virgin material into the final product. And rising energy prices encourage us to develop integrated systems, in which production, consumption, and disposal are only points on a continuum.

The rising prices of fossil fuels encourage not only the more efficient use of fuel but the use of renewable energy sources, such as direct sunlight. Unlike coal, uranium, natural gas, and oil, renewable fuels are widely distributed naturally, lending themselves to energy-generation facilities that also are widely distributed. So rather than moving petroleum ten thousand miles to heat our homes, direct sunlight can be converted to heat at our own points on the map—our households.

The pending exhaustion of our richest fossil fuel deposits is only a part of a larger raw materials problem. To prepare for future shortages in key materials, industry is working in two ways: first, developing technologies that recycle materials; second, developing techniques for expanding the ability of such abundant materials as sand and plant matter to substitute for those in short supply. Both kinds of development encourage more localized production systems. As we substitute abundant materials for scarce ones, extractive and conversion industries will tend to become more regionalized. Sand, for example, is an almost ubiquitous material. Plant matter can become a substitute for petroleum as a source of industrial chemicals.

These abundant materials will not be located within city limits, but they will be found close by. The city will still import the raw materials—the transportation lines, however, will be greatly shortened. Recycling encourages a more central role for cities. Since urban areas are our major repositories of post-consumer scrap and human waste, they will logically become the focal points for recycling efforts.

Rising energy and materials prices also encourage local self-reliance. And modern science makes it possible; the harnessing of concentrated fuels a century ago sparked a tremendous outpouring of scientific discovery. At first scientific techniques were used to create crude technologies that tried to subdue nature. But later, especially after World War II, the physical sciences gave way to the biological sciences as the leading edge of modern knowledge, and this led us in turn to a new view of the world, from the linear, mechanistic physics of Newton to more systemic biological concepts. We used to see a car only in a mechanical way, as a vehicle that moved people around. But now we realize its effects on the larger system. Its pollutants decrease the amount of sunlight striking the surface of the city. And vehicles shaped and sized the way ours are demand a large amount of road surface; Los Angeles devotes 65 percent of its land area to the car's needs, and urban planners ordinarily set aside a quarter to a third of the land area of a city for the automobile. By paving over large areas of soil inside the city, the ground's ability to absorb and retain rainfall is reduced and this increases the difficulty of treating the torrential flood of waters that therefore mingles with human wastes in our waste-water treatment systems.

In retrospect, the 1970s may be remembered as the era during which the exponential depletion of our natural resource base ran head on into the exponential expansion of our knowledge base. We had used older scientific principles to fashion technologies that had an immense impact on the environment, and at the same time newer scientific developments allowed us to monitor those impacts and design new technologies to minimize or avoid raw material depletion. The ten-story coal shovel that moves mountains aside to dig for coal represents the old. The tiny solar cell sitting on the rooftop generating electricity represents the new.

Modern science plays a critical role in the expansion of the three key industries of the energy-efficient and resource-efficient era: energy conservation and renewable energy technologies, recycling, and communications. Advances in these industries come not from mining more ore or building larger factories but from applying accumulated wisdom to do more with less. Businesses within these industries are competitive only in as much as they can increase productivity by consuming fewer raw materials. Energy conservation depends on getting a greater amount of useful work out of a given unit of energy. Recycling depends on minimizing waste. Communication depends on making increasingly efficient use of the nondepletable electromagnetic spectrum.

The combination of modern science with energy-efficient planning may change the way we relate to our surroundings—the way we think of ourselves, our homes, and our communities. Within a few years, for example, our rooftops will not only protect us from the elements, but with the installation of photovoltaic shingles will convert one of the elements, direct sunlight, into electricity to power our homes and our cars. The earth will be seen not only as a foundation for our buildings but as a source of heat to warm our homes and offices. The aquifers that run beneath our communities may become not only sources of drinking water but storage tanks for heat.

As the new technologies enter our homes and offices, as the new biological ways of thinking proliferate, communities may begin to think of themselves as part of a complex natural system, not as something separate. As Sir Frederick Soddy, an English scientist, once commented, "Men in the economic sense exist solely by virtue of being able to draw on the energy of nature." We used to draw on the energy of nature by digging up concentrated sources. Fossil fuels are, after all, nothing more than the fossilized remains of plants that used sunlight to generate energy through the process of photosynthesis. Modern science teaches us how to use the energy generated by nature daily to meet our needs. We are moving, then, into a biological, scientific, communications age. The implications are profound. The new awareness of the interrelationship of the different parts of the urban environment could lead us to abolish the compartmentalization that plagues our cities. Sanitation systems, water systems, energy systems, communications systems could all be seen as a part of a comprehensive whole, a natural resource utility. The advent of home computers gives citizens the capability not only to retrieve large amounts of information but also to analyze and correlate that information. This ability to understand the human, capital, and natural resources in the community and the future impact of current actions could generate a new role—the citizen-planner.

Transporting Materials and Goods: Closing the Loop

The tomato the Bostonian eats, even in season, usually comes from Florida, Mexico, or California. The steel in the office buildings in Phoenix comes from Ohio or Pennsylvania. The oil that heats the homes of New Yorkers comes from Saudi Arabia, while that used to heat the homes of San Franciscans comes from Alaska.

One effect of rising energy prices, however, is to encourage us to reduce the movement of materials—to move toward local self-reliance. About one-third of our raw materials consist of fossil fuels; as our communities use energy more efficiently and shift to such renewable resources as wind or direct sunlight or plant matter, the transportation required for fuels will drop significantly.

But rising energy prices lead to more than reduced movement of fossil fuels. They also induce materials recycling. According to Harvard geologist Harvey Brooks, the extraction and processing of raw materials accounts for about two-thirds of all industrial energy use in the United States, or about 25 percent of all energy consumption. A finished product contains within it, in effect, all the energy used to mine the virgin ore, to transport it to the refinery, to process the refined material into a finished product. When we recycle a product, we save all that energy. The energy required to produce a ton of steel from urban waste is only 14 percent of that needed to produce a ton of steel from raw ore; for copper the figure is 9 percent, and for aluminum, about 5 percent.

Recycling saves more than energy—it saves materials, and it reduces air and water pollution. As scrap materials have become more valuable, the infant recycling centers of the early 1970s have grown into major industries. Some industries, like glass and paper, have developed factories that operate on 100 percent scrap material. Scrap industries, like any manufacturing businesses, locate near their source of supplies, and since our urban areas are the major storehouses of post-consumer scrap, they are becoming the centers for future scrap industries.

A city of two hundred thousand annually throws away the amount of copper produced by a small copper mine, the amount of aluminum taken from a modest bauxite deposit, and as much paper as comes from a medium-sized timber stand. Until recently, the millions of tons of municipal waste were thrown away together. But the new value of recycled products is already enticing communities to encourage or even require businesses and residents to keep the major materials separate. Several paper companies have already announced that future plants will be built only in communities that recycle aggressively.

Solid waste is only a part of the municipal waste stream. Our human wastes contain millions of tons of nutrients useful for soil conditioning. One of the reasons that human-waste recycling is becoming increasingly common, despite the difficulty of handling sludge and the opposition of neighbors, is that rising energy costs have made incineration—one of the most favored methods of disposal—too expensive. About nine million dry tons of sludge are produced nationally each year, more than double the estimates of six years ago, and sludge output is expected to increase another 25 percent before this century's end. As sludge is dried and spread on surrounding farmland, and vegetables are grown on the land, the production and consumption and disposal systems become part of the same closed loop.

The concept of recycling goes beyond the use of scrap to the creation of integrated systems, in which the wastes of one process become the raw materials for another. Indeed, in an energy-efficient society the very word waste will lose its present meaning; very little will be literally thrown away. We have already seen how the increasing price of energy has made economical the use of the heat as well as the electricity generated by the combustion of fuel in power plants, doubling the useful work gained from a unit of energy. Communities and industries are searching for ways to use the previously discarded heat from power plants and manufacturing processes. The city of Ottawa, Kansas, population eleven thousand, for example, is investigating the feasibility of using waste heat from its two municipally owned power plants to produce alcohol. "Since we'd be operating the project without fuel costs," says Ottawa City Manager Robert Mills, "we could net between 20 and 25 cents a gallon or up to $3 million a year."[1] If Ottawa reaches that objective, it would net revenue almost equal to its present operating budget.

Integrated systems are changing the way we see traditional operations. Fort Collins, Colorado, population ninety thousand, processes the methane gas generated from its sewage plant for use in automobiles. Much of the municipal vehicle fleet now has a dual fuel capacity. At the flip of a switch the driver can change over from gasoline to methane. The other product of the sewage plant is nutrient rich sludge. This fertilizes 600 acres of corn growing on city owned land. Far sighted city manager John Arnold hopes to convert a portion of the corn crop to alcohol to fuel still more municipal cars. Fort Collins used to pay to throw away its raw materials. Now it uses them to generate revenue. The city has transformed a waste disposal facility into a production plant.

Integrated systems and recycling can reduce considerably the amount of raw material and energy we need to sustain our communities. Obviously, though, recycling cannot meet all our material needs. We will need virgin materials to supplement recycled materials. But as material shortages become more pronounced, we will substitute more abundant materials for those in short supply and substitute renewable resources for those that are exhaustible. As a result of advances in science, we can do both, and as we do, the materials system can become more local—the new materials will be more dispersed throughout the country.

One material that is becoming increasingly useful is common sand—silicon dioxide. Silicon constitutes 27 percent of the earth's crust. It is the only commodity produced in every one of our 50 states. It is found in a significant number of our 3,000 counties.

Silicon, besides being the basis of the electronics and glass industries, is already replacing metals. For example, glass fibers are beginning to replace the traditional copper wires in the communications industry. A typical copper telephone cable is three inches thick, weighs less than nine pounds per foot and carries about thirty-two thousand telephone conversations at one time. A comparable glass cable is one-half inch thick (most of that is plastic filler), weighs one-tenth of a pound per foot, and carries forty-eight thousand telephone conversations at once. It is also easier to maintain, needs only one-third as many amplifiers as copper (with which amplifiers must be installed every 1.5 miles to increase the signal) and costs half as much as copper wire.

The National Academy of Science, in a report on the potential for nonmetallic substances to replace scarce metals, foresaw a major role for the forms of glass. They are, the study noted, "remarkably versatile materials used hardly at all in proportion to their potential abundance. The properties of glass include excellent corrosion resistance and very high intrinsic strength." The crystal structure of silica and silicate minerals, "each with attendant special physical properties, already provides a basis for future substitutions for the scarce metals."[2] Low-density special glass can now be made stronger than most metals. Glass-ceramic materials have been made having flexural strength up to 200,000 pounds per square inch, comparable to many metal alloys.

A silicon-based economy will be one part of our raw material base. The other part will continue to be based on carbon. But instead of taking carbon from the fossilized remains of prehistoric photosynthesis, we will use plant matter more directly. Before cheap petroleum supplies were discovered, after World War II, the use of agricultural crops as industrial materials was explored a great deal. Henry Ford was one of the major supporters of the exploration. In 1935 Ford and three hundred other leaders of agriculture, industry, and science formed the Farm Chemurgic Council. Its major objective was the gradual absorption of the domestic farm surplus by domestic industry. It announced, "The program of the Farm Chemurgic Council is founded on the timely unfolding of Nature's laws through which modern science has placed new tools in the hands of men, enabling a variety of surplus products of the soil to be transformed through organic chemistry into raw materials usable in industry. Basic research has progressed sufficiently for the commercial application to begin without delay. Here lies a new frontier to conquer that challenges the genius of science, the courage of private industry and the productive capacity of agriculture."[3]

Henry Ford succeeded in making plastics from soybeans during World War II. But cheap petroleum supplies after the war eclipsed the infant industry based on converting plant matter into industrial chemicals. More recently, however, the rising price of petroleum, and therefore of petroleum-based products, has revived interest in agricultural factories. Advances in enzymatic technologies combined with the aggressive interest in alcohol conversion has added to the revival—we are rapidly approaching a time when we will be able to supply ourselves with alternatives to oil-derived chemicals for making fertilizers, plastics, clothes, dyes, paints, and tens of thousands of other products.

Recycling will transform our urban areas from consumers into providers of raw materials. In addition, the substitution of widely accessible resource materials—those that are locally available—for those imported from far away will in effect move the farms, wells, and mines closer to urban populations. That is, the substitution will allow local producers to do more of their business locally. This market expansion in turn allows new local manufacturing, processing, and assembly operations to develop. But such development can take place only if the new, small factory can make a product or provide a service that costs no more than the imported good. Probably, it can. To begin with, industries that use scrap materials cost less to start than those that use virgin materials. A typical traditional steel mill can produce five million tons of steel annually. But the fastest-growing sector in the domestic steel industry is of plants that use 100 percent scrap steel, and electric furnaces that consume only 20 percent of the energy used in the conventional plants. These reprocessing plants produce as little as three-hundred thousand tons annually. Surprisingly, even in traditional manufacturing industries far fewer economies are achieved by building large factories than one would expect. Indeed, the size of the average factory in the United States has not increased at all in most industries since World War I. Tiny factories can produce products at prices competitive with those of much larger factories; and, returning to the advantages of local supply, the less one has to produce to be economically healthy, the less one has to sell outside the local area.

The energy situation, rather than marking the end of industrial civilization, has opened up a new development path. The movement of raw materials will decline markedly as communities begin to use modern science to convert such common materials as sand, plant matter, and sunlight into useful products. Two of the fastest growing industries in the world right now are founded on the principle of doing more with less: energy conservation is based on increasing the amount of useful work we gain from consuming a unit of energy; recycling's goal is to minimize waste.

But the most rapidly growing industry of all is also an industry upon which all other parts of the economy are based—knowledge and communications. As we reduce the movement of materials, we increase the movement of information by electronic means.

Transporting Electrons: Harnessing the Electromagnetic Spectrum

The phenomenal growth of the electronics and communications industries is well known. A computer that filled a room and cost half a million dollars in 1959 can now fit on one's fingernail and costs $5. In 1960 Standard and Poor's register of industrial companies had no "Semiconductor and Related Devices" category; in 1970, 85 companies were listed in that category, and in 1978, 147. In 1975 the world's first computer store opened in Los Angeles. By 1978, 700 such

213

stores operated in the United States alone. Already, computers exist that speak, that listen, that read.

The growth of the electronics, computer, and communications industries is based on the ability to get more productivity out of fewer raw materials. The objective is to store more information on a given area. Every two years, the semiconductor industry quadruples the amount of memory that can be stored for the same price. Indeed, Carl Sagan in his book *The Dragons of Eden* estimates that the logic of a human brain is equivalent to ten thousand billion elementary electronic logic circuits; if his estimate is accurate, some computer experts believe, within 20 years we will be able to buy enough electronic logic to match the human brain for less than $1 million—perhaps for only a few thousand dollars.

The hardware of communications systems is increasingly energy efficient as more capability is packed into a silicon chip. But even more compelling a case can be made for the energy efficiency of the electronics industry when we realize that the fastest-growing component of the communications industry is not in hardware at all but in software, or programming. The programmer's goal is to tell the computer to analyze and retrieve information in the fewest steps possible, that is, with the smallest number of electronic actions. Since the programmer's work is sitting and thinking, the programming industry is literally based on food calories. Thus the fastest-growing part of our entire economy is based not on the consumption of raw materials or on energy at all, except for food energy. Could one make the case that advances in science have actually allowed us to revert to an agricultural society?

We can now ship vastly greater quantities of electrons from one part of the globe to another using much less energy. The road upon which our electronic freight travels is the electromagnetic spectrum. The way we have broadened the use of this spectrum is comparable to going from country dirt roads to the major interstate highways. But while automobiles have become more and more resource-consuming over the years, taking up more and more of the road, the advances in electronic transmission have allowed us to use less and less of a lane to accomplish the same purpose, and allowed us to continue to open more lanes of this natural highway. In the early 1980s we are using light itself to carry information. These light waves can carry ten thousand times the information carried by telephone technology in 1919, and at far less energy consumption. We have learned to harness electromagnetic waves of higher and higher frequencies (shorter and shorter wavelengths). The higher the frequency, the more information each wave can carry. We have moved from being able to transmit a pale imitation of the human voice via telephone to stereophonic music to the transmission of black and white and then color pictures to the transmission of billions of bits of electronic information that can be translated into sounds, pictures, or words.

The electromagnetic spectrum is not, however, infinite. As we widen our use of its frequencies we begin to bump into other users. At the World Administrative Radio Conference in 1979, the developing countries expressed their concern about the use of microwaves to beam down energy from orbiting solar power satellites. They feared that the wide beams would interfere with their ability to use communications frequencies. We need not look to the skies to see evidence of overlapping frequencies. Heart pacemakers can now operate on the body's own electricity. But those wearing pacemakers must be alert to the presence of microwaves leaking from ovens or transmitting stations.

The spectrum is not infinite, but it is nondepletable. Harvey J. Levin of Resources for the Future wrote in 1971, "Insofar as it is free from depletion upon use, the spectrum has characteristics of a sustained yield (flow) resource of a unique sort, perhaps most similar to solar or water power."[4]

That we could exhaust the potential of the electromagnetic spectrum appears unlikely—it is a constantly renewable highway for transporting information. This aspect of the nature of the resource is crucial, because an energy-efficient society is a knowledge-intensive society. And knowledge increases as communications increase. Scientists learn from other scientists. Policymakers learn from other policymakers. Cultures learn from other cultures. The propagation of knowledge cross-fertilizes the world, fostering a greatly compressed learning curve.

The discovery that the electromagnetic spectrum is a major source of wealth comes at a propitious time for municipalities; they have the authority to issue franchises for cable television. A century ago, cities learned of the value of the electricity franchise and slowly gained an ability to design franchises that enhanced the public welfare. The communication franchise is more complex, but the municipality's ability to create an instrument that can improve the quality of its citizens' lives has never been greater.

Changing Roles in
the Energy-Efficient City

The 1980s will prove exceptionally interesting as changes in technology and natural resource-use wash over the society. We will change the way we look at our households, our communities, and our cities.

For example, with the advent of residential rooftop solar cells that are grid-connected, we will be able to sell electricity to the local utility. The house will become a revenue producer. Traditional jurisdictions will overlap. Already, for example, the electric utility industry, in the wake of the decline in electrical demand and of the legalization of independent power production, is undergoing an active internal discussion about its future. Alex Radin, executive director of the American Public Power Association, advises the more than two thousand publicly-owned utilities that they must broaden their functions. They should become full-service energy planners, "a concept derived from the premise that the consumer is interested in certain services provided by energy—that is, heating, cooling, lighting, operation of various appliances, etc.—rather than obtaining electricity per se. Consequently, the objective of the utility should be to provide these services in the most economical or most 'cost effective' means possible, whether or not they involve the use of electricity."[5] The utility will assist homeowners and businesspersons to achieve satisfactory individual comfort levels inside their buildings and to have light sufficient to read and work. The utility will satisfy the need rather than supply a given commodity.

But, as we have learned, the concept of energy efficiency now embraces much more than direct fuel conversion. It is more than anything else a design principle. It is more economical to redesign the refrigerator to preserve food while consuming less energy than it is to build new power plants to operate traditionally inefficient refrigerators. It takes less energy to recycle an aluminum can than to manufacture a new one from virgin ore. Will the electric-utility-turned-energy-service-corporation provide architectural assistance to housing developers? Will it become directly involved in land-use planning at the local or regional level? Will it push for energy-efficiency standards for appliances? Will it become involved in planning efficient transportation systems? If it takes on these new functions, it trespasses on the authority of other institutions, such as the city planning department, or the private manufacturer, or the independent design and planning firm.

One of history's ironies is that, just as we are examining the role of monopolistic energy utilities, the original franchises extended to these utilities by local governments are expiring. Many franchise agreements were granted during the 1920s, when state public-service commissions were just getting established and when the utilities spilled over city and state lines and formed giant holding companies. These franchises began expiring in the 1960s, and in the 1980s a great number will come up for renewal. During the process of negotiating franchise renewal, communities can help to shape the future energy utility.

Even if the energy utility restricts its future functions to direct energy generation, distribution, or storage, it will still overlap the jurisdiction of other utilities. Who has authority over the underground aquifers? Already a number of energy researchers are testing the potential for these aquifers to store thermal energy. Most water departments get drinking water from surface water. But as the need for water increases, they are tapping into underground supplies. Should the city water department coordinate activities related to energy and other functions that could use the underground water systems? In many states, riparian rights laws were developed to guarantee downstream water users sufficient water if someone upstream tapped the river. Who will monitor riparian rights to underground aquifers?

Our concept of the rights and responsibilities of private property will probably change in the coming years. Already, as cities begin to understand the value of living systems, they are enacting ordinances that encourage benign environmental activities. In 1972 the city of Palo Alto, California, rezoned almost 5,000 acres within the city as open space to be used primarily for agricultural purposes. After an exhaustive study of the changing legal principles underlying the concept of private property, two attorneys concluded, "Basically we are drawing away from the nineteenth century idea that land's only function is to enable its owner to make money." Increasingly, the attorneys argue, the courts are considering not only the question "Will this use reduce the value of surrounding land?" but also "Will this make the best use of our land resources?"[6]

How will we decide the value of land? Some scientists are starting to quantify the economic worth of living things. Howard Odum, a pioneering ecologist at the University of Florida, argues that trees in their natural state are worth more than $10,000 per acre, or more than $1 million over a hundred-year period—not counting inflation. "There are ecosystems," Odum writes, "capable of using and recycling wastes as a partner of the city without being a drain on the scarce fossil fuels. Soils take up carbon monoxide, forests absorb nutrients, swamps accept and regulate floodwaters."[7] Many others believe the value of living things cannot be estimated purely by their monetary worth. Chief Judge Brown of the Fifth Circuit Court of Appeals, in a comment on a case involving the authority of cities to ban nonreturnable bottles, indicated that city officials could take into account "the immeasurable loss from a silent spring like disturbance of nature's economy."[8]

The environmental movement has learned about the complexity of regulating dynamic technologies with local or national watchdog agencies. To protect living systems, society has developed voluminous regulations on every single piece of equipment used in many industries. More recently, communities have moved toward a simpler regulatory tool; they have established pollution ceilings under which a marketplace is allowed to develop. The first test of this concept has been the use of emission offsets in those parts of the nation where the air contains more than the maximum amount of pollutants. In such regions, no new development can take place without an equal or greater amount of pollutant being withdrawn from the air. One result is that industries that want to move into an area assist existing industries to reduce their pollutant emissions, so that with the new development the overall level will not increase.

Densely populated communities have begun to be concerned not only about the quality of the water they drink and the air they breathe, but about their continued access to vital resources. The electric power blackouts in the 1960s and 1970s demonstrated communities' total reliance on a product with distribution systems that are incredibly complex. In the winter of 1980–81, many cities and towns in Massachusetts were forced to close schools when a combination of circumstances delayed the shipment of natural gas to that part of the country. In northern New Jersey, apparently several teenagers opened drain valves in reservoirs; so much water was lost that the mayor of Newark declared a state of emergency.

Many observers believe that water, rather than energy availability, will become the major issue in the coming decade. In Florida, sink holes have appeared and swallowed parts of urban areas, the result of a dramatically dropping water table. For much of Florida's recent history, water was something to be eliminated. Swamps were drained and rivers rechanneled to make more area available for farming or building. But, according to the *Christian Science Monitor,* "By draining away its water, the state has destroyed its wetlands that provide the delicate balance that allows rainfall to seep into the underground water supply." Now, instead of draining wetlands, "the state government is fighting to protect and buy the remaining swamps."[9]

In fact, many people are already predicting that the battles over water in the 1980s will be more tumultuous than the battles over energy. The problems of scarce water in Arizona and New Mexico and southern California are well known, but the water issue affects the entire country. Because the water tables are dropping, salt water is seeping into the water supplies of towns in Cape Cod and Florida. Santa Cruz, California, in the northern half of the state, has already declared a housing-construction moratorium until the city can accurately inventory its ground-water resources.

Long distribution lines link the fates of disparate groups. Towns in New Mexico that want to increase their populations must work out new water-use plans that also benefit the farmers who need to tap the underground water and the industry that shares the same resource base.

In another unlikely combination of interests, the introduction of modern microprocessors spurs interaction by those who are linked electronically. For example, in 1979 two utilities in southern California, one public and the other private, linked several large commercial buildings electronically so that their electric demand could be monitored by a central computer. When the computer indicates that the overall demand is rising above an agreed-upon maximum, the building managers are notified and turn off certain systems temporarily to reduce the peak demand. The utility benefits by reducing its need for oil-guzzling back-up generators. The building owners, in return for this cooperative effort, share a portion of the system's dollar savings.

Shaping the Future Community

Three major forces work together to encourage local self-reliance. First, the increased cost and decreased availability of raw materials, including but not limited to fossil fuels, pushes us to substitute more abundant and renewable materials. This in turn encourages us to recycle our scrap products, to process materials at the local level, and to generate energy nearer the final customer. Second, the extraordinarily rapid development of new technologies, spurred in part by the exponential increase in scientific understanding and in part by rising resource prices, pulls us toward local self-reliance by allowing us increasingly to generate our wealth within our homes. Third, the electronics revolution, a part of the general technological advancement sweeping the nation, allows us to monitor our environment and understand our relationship to it. The electronics revolution also permits us to step outside our homes and communities and look back, to gain a different and perhaps more comprehensive perspective.

The increasing price of fossil fuels leads us to substitute more plentiful fuels, such as wood, water, plant matter, and direct sunlight. These fuels typically are more efficiently converted into useful energy at the local level. Rising energy prices also increase transportation costs, thereby encouraging us to recycle our products and limit the importation of materials from far away. The larger raw-materials problem reinforces recycling and leads to the substitution of sand and plant matter for iron ore and petroleum.

The cost of raw materials provides us the need to move toward local self-reliance; modern technology provides us the possibility. Technological advances allow us to convert sunlight directly into electricity, to create glass as strong as steel from ordinary sand, to convert plants into pharmaceuticals. The fastest-growing industries in the country are now those that are on the cutting edge of technological advance and those that use fewer and fewer raw materials and energy to produce the same amount of finished product.

The electronics revolution allows us to communicate with our environment, both man-made and natural, in unprecedented depth. We can monitor our environment and develop sophisticated feedback systems to make our communities more energy-efficient. We can more efficiently match the supply to the demand, using only as much of a resource as is necessary to satisfy a specific need. When daylight intensity reaches a certain level, the interior lights begin to dim. Community heat storage systems provide the right amount of heat for widely varying customers. Hydroponic plants are fed through automated drip irrigation systems that sense when the feeding is completed.

Electronics also gives us the ability to step outside of ourselves and look back. X rays and sound waves allow us to peek inside the human body and discover the interrelationships of its many parts. Infrared waves permit us to perceive our homes in a new way, identifying the heat losses. Video graphics can tell us quickly where our pipelines, sewer lines, and wires are located, how many flat roofs are available, and about the community's demographics. The new information expands our perspective. Just as the first space satellite pictures that showed the entire planet earth generated the "Spaceship Earth" metaphor, so our expanded images of our communities using the new techniques will change the way we relate to our surroundings.

There are powerful forces working to move us toward local self-reliance. But there is no inevitability that we will achieve that goal. Institutions change slowly. Habits and customs change even more slowly. When people redefine their functions and new institutions arise to take care of new desires and needs, old institutions feel threatened. Structural tensions arise. The tension between the old and the new is the catalyst for change in any society, but the gap between old and new is now growing wider, and therefore the kinds of change and the rapidity of change will become more profound.

Bertrand Russell once remarked, "Change is one thing; progress is another. Change is scientific, progress is ethical. Change is indubitable, whereas progress is a matter of controversy." Will we have change or progress? We can't know yet. But our cities—as the homes for the majority of our population, as the seats of government closest to the people, as the communities most interested in developments that foster local self-reliance—our cities will certainly be in the forefront in determining the answer.

Notes

Chapter 1

1. Howard Mumford Jones, *The Age of Energy* (New York: Viking Press, 1970).

2. Ralph Woods, *A Plan for Decentralization of Industry* (London: Longmans Green and Co., 1939), p. 32.

3. Jones, op. cit., p. 142.

4. Lewis Mumford, *The Culture of Cities* (New York: Harcourt Brace Jovanovich, 1970), p. 158.

5. John R. Ottensmann, *The Changing Spatial Structure of American Cities* (Lexington, Mass.: Lexington Books, 1975), p. 17.

6. Charles N. Glaab, *History of Urban America* (New York: Macmillan, 1967), p. 287.

7. K. H. Schaeffer and Elliott Sclar, *Access for All: Transportation and Urban Growth* (New York: Columbia University Press, 1980), p. 49.

8. Ibid.

9. Edward Hungerford, *The Story of Public Utilities* (New York: G. P. Putnam's Sons, 1928), p. 107–108.

10. Ibid.

11. Benjamin Briscue, "The Inside Story of General Motors," *Detroit Saturday Night*, Jan. 15, 22, 29 and Feb. 5, 1921, cited in James J. Fink, *America Adopts the Automobile*, 1895–1910 (Cambridge, Mass.: MIT Press, 1970), p. 310.

12. Bradford C. Snell, *American Ground Transport* (Washington, D.C.: Government Printing Office, 1974), p. 30.

13. Ibid.

14. Ibid.

15. Ibid., p. 31.

16. Ibid., p. 35.

17. Schaeffer and Sclar, op. cit., pp. 45–46.

18. Ibid., p. 47.

19. Woods, op. cit., p. 297.

20. Ibid.

21. Herrington Bryce, ed., *Small Cities in Transition: The Dynamics of Growth and Decline* (Cambridge, Mass.: Ballinger Publishing Co., 1977), p. 5.

22. Committee on Banking, Finance and Urban Affairs, House of Representatives, *Compact Cities: Energy Saving Strategies for the Eighties* (Washington, D.C.: Government Printing Office, July 1980), p. 5.

23. Ibid., p. 7.

Chapter 2

1. Sheldon Novick, "The Electric Power Industry," *Environment*, Nov. 1975, p. 34.

2. Charles N. Glaab and A. Theodore Brown, *A History of Urban America* (New York: Macmillan, 1967), p. 92.

3. Charles F. Phillips, Jr., *The Economics of Regulation* (Homewood, Ill.: 1969), p. 83.

4. Martin Glasser, *Public Utilities in American Capitalism* (New York: Macmillan, 1957), p. 92.

5. Ellis L. Armstrong, ed., *History of Public Works in the United States: 1776–1976* (Chicago: American Public Works Association, 1976), p. 3.

6. Marc Messinger, H. Paul Friesema, and David Movell, *Centralized Power: The Politics of Scale in Electricity Generation* (Cambridge: Oelgeschlager, Gunn and Hainz Publishers, 1979), p. 20.

7. Novick, op. cit., p. 35.

8. National Civic Federation, *Commission on Public Ownership and Operation, Municipal and Private Operation of Public Utilities* (New York, 1907), p. 24.

9. H. S. Raushenbush and Harry M. Laidler, *Power Control* (New York: New Republic, 1928), p. 119.

10. *Linn v. Borough of Chambersburg*, 160 Pa. 511.

11. Stiles P. Jones, "State Versus Local Regulation," *The Annals*, May 1914, p. 103.

12. Delos F. Wilcox, *Municipal Franchises* (Rochester, N.Y.: The English News Publishing Co., 1910), 1:vii.

13. Ibid., 2: 808–809.

14. Jones, op. cit.

15. Wilcox, op. cit., p. 704.

16. Novick, op. cit., p. 34.

17. *Congressional Record*, 66th Cong., 1974 (1925).

18. William M. Cafron, ed., *Technological Change in Regulated Industries* (Washington, D.C.: Brookings Institution, 1971), p. 54.

19. "Creating the Electric Age," *EPRI Journal*, March 1979.

20. Amory B. Lovins and L. Hunter Lovins, "Energy Policies for Resilience and National Security," unpublished draft, 1981, p. 49.

21. Ibid., p. 50.

22. Cafron, op. cit., p. 71.

23. Messinger et al., op. cit., p. 53.

24. *Otter Tail Company v. United States*, 93 S. Ct. 1022 (at 1035), 1973.

25. *Public Power*, Nov.–Dec. 1979.

26. Ibid.

27. Ibid.

28. Berkshire County Regional Planning Commission, *Evaluation of Power Facilities* (Springfield, Va.: National Technical Information Service, April 1974).

29. *Environmental Law*, Vol. 9, p. 575.

30. Richard G. Stein, *Architecture and Energy* (Garden City, N.Y.: Anchor Press, 1977), p. 50.

31. Ibid., p. 50.

32. *Promotional Practices by Public Utilities and Their Impact Upon Small Business*, Hearings Before the Subcommittee on Activities of Regulatory Agencies Select Committee on Small Business, House of Representatives, 90th Congress (Washington, D.C.: Government Printing Office, 1968), p. 408.

33. Ibid.

34. Alex Radin, "Outlook and Insights," *Public Power*, Sept.–Oct. 1980, p. 6.

Chapter 3

1. Charles N. Glaab and A. Theodore Brown, *A History of Urban America* (New York: Macmillan, 1967), p. 55.

2. Ibid., p. 54.

3. ·Gerald F. Flug, "The City as a Legal Concept," *Harvard Law Review*, April 1980, p. 1107 n. 201.

4. Ibid., p. 71.

5. Arthur M. Schlesinger, "A Panoramic View: The City in American History," *Mississippi Valley Historical Review*, June 1940.

6. Glaab and Brown, op. cit., p. 86.

7. Ibid.

8. Ibid.

9. Ibid., p. 165.

10. John A. Fairlie, "Municipal Development in the United States," *A Municipal Program* (New York: National Municipal League, 1900), p. 10.

11. Mark I. Gelfand, *A Nation of Cities: The Federal Government and Urban America, 1933–1965* (New York: Oxford University Press, 1975), p. 10.

12. Ibid., p. 11.

13. John Foster Dillon, *Commentaries on the Law of Municipal Corporation* (Boston: Little, Brown and Co., 1881), pp. 115–116.

14. *City of Clinton v. Cedar Rapids and Missouri Railroad Co.*, 24 Iowa 455(1868).

15. *Hunter v. City of Pittsburgh*, 207 U.S. 161(1907).

16. Harry M. Trebing, *The Corporation in the American Economy* (Chicago: Quadrangle Books, 1970), p. 5.

17. Arthur Selwyn Miller, *The Modern Corporate State* (Westport, Conn: Greenwood Press, 1976), p. 39.

18. Alfred D. Chandler, Jr., "The Role of Business in the United States: A Historical Survey," cited in Eli Goldstone, Herbert C. Morton, and G. Neal Ryland, *The American Business Corporation*, p. 46.

19. Sheldon Novick, "Electric Power Companies," *Environment*, Nov. 1975, p. 36.

20. James Willard Hurst, *The Legitimacy of the Business Corporation in the Law of the United States, 1780–1970* (Charlottesville: University of Virginia Press, 1970), p. 70.

21. *City of Clinton v. Cedar Rapids and Missouri Railroad Co.*, 24 Iowa 455(1868). Two decades later the United States Supreme Court affirmed this doctrine, declaring, "The State . . . at its pleasure may modify or withdraw all [city] powers, may take without compensation [city] property, hold it itself, or vest it in other agencies, expand or contract the territorial area, unite the whole or a part of it with another municipality, repeal the charter, and destroy the corporation. All this may be done, conditionally or unconditionally, with or without the consent of the citizens, or even against their protests." [*Hunter v. City of Pittsburgh*, 207 U.S. 161(1907).]

22. *Santa Clara County v. Southern Pacific Railway Co.*, 1184 U.S. 394(1886).

23. *Wabash, St. Louis and Pacific Railway Co. v. Illinois*, 118 U.S. 557(1886).

24. Paul Studensky, *Public Borrowing* (New York: National Municipal League, 1930), p. 11.

25. Lewis Mumford, *The Culture of Cities* (New York: Harcourt Brace Jovanovich, 1970), pp. 184–185.

26. Kenneth Fox, *Better City Government: Innovation in American Urban Politics, 1850–1937* (Philadelphia: Temple University Press, 1977), p. xiv.

27. Ibid., p. 85.

28. Glaab and Brown, op. cit., p. 265.

29. Samuel Kaplan, *The Dream Deferred* (New York: Vintage, 1977), p. 31.

30. John Nolen, *New Ideals in the Planning of Cities, Towns and Villages* (Boston: Marshall Jones Company, 1927), pp. 133–134.

31. *Fischer v. Township of Bedminster*, 11 N.J. 194, 93 A. 2d 378(1953).

32. David S. Arnold, ed., *The Practice of Local Government Planning* (Washington, D.C.: International City Management Association, 1979), p. 46.

33. Urbanism Committee, National Resources Committee, *Our Cities: Their Role in the National Economy* (Washington, D.C.: Government Printing Office, 1937), pp. v–xii.

34. Peter Libassi and Victor Hausner, *Revitalizing Center City Investment* (Columbus, Ohio: Academy for Contemporary Problems, June 1977), p. 5.

35. *City of Saint Paul v. Dalfin*.

36. 89 Cal. Rpts. at 905, citing *Miller v. Board of Public Works* 234 P. 2d 381 at 383.

37. *Central Lumber Company v. Waseca*, 152 Minn. 201, 188 N.W. 275(1922).
38. Martin Glaeser, *Public Utilities in American Capitalism* (New York: Macmillan, 1957), pp. 120–121.
39. Richard J. Barnet and Ronald E. Muller, *Global Reach* (New York: Simon and Schuster, 1974), pp. 14–15.
40. *Fortune*, February 23, 1981.
41. Neal Peirce, "Smokestack Chasers Who Miss the Point," *Washington Post*, May 30, 1979.
42. Peter J. Bearse, "New Jersey's Economic Identity Crisis," *New Jersey Magazine*, July 1978.
43. Gigi Coe and Lane DeMoll, eds., *Stepping Stones: Appropriate Technology and Beyond* (New York: Schocken Books, 1978), p. 163.
44. Annmarie Hauck Walsh, *The People's Business: The Politics and Practices of Government Corporations* (Cambridge, Mass.: MIT Press, 1979), p. 120.
45. Ibid., p. 4.
46. Ibid., p. 6.
47. Libassi and Hausner, op. cit., p. 4.
48. Ibid.
49. *Washington Star*, Oct. 11, 1977.
50. *Kit Mar Builders, Inc. v. Township of Concord*, 493 Pa. 466, 268 A. 2d 765(1970).
51. *Beck v. Town of Raymond*, 394 A. 2d 847(1978).
52. *Southern Burlington County N.A.A.C.P. v. Township of Mount Laurel*, 67 N.J. 151, 336 A 2d. 713, 423 U.S. 808(1976).
53. Richard C. Bradley, *The Costs of Urban Growth: Observations and Judgments* (Colorado Springs: Pikes Peak Area Council of Governments, July 1973).
54. *Construction Industry Association of Sonoma Co. et al. v. City of Petaluma et al.*, 424 U.S. 934(1976).
55. Kaplan, op. cit., p. 84.
56. Fred Bosselman and David Callies, *The Quiet Revolution in Land Use Control* (Washington, D.C.: Council on Environmental Quality, 1971), p. 314.
57. Fred Bosselman, Duane A. Feurer, and Charles L. Siemon, *The Permit Explosion: Coordination of the Proliferation* (Washington, D.C.: The Urban Land Institute, 1977), p. ix.
58. *Planning*, Feb. 1981, p. 6.

Chapter 4

1. Mark I. Gelfand, *A Nation of Cities: The Federal Government and Urban America, 1933–1965* (New York: Oxford University Press, 1975), p. 22.
2. Urbanism Committee, National Resources Committee, *Our Cities: Their Role in the National Economy* (Washington, D.C.: Government Printing Office, 1937), pp. 52 and 54.
3. Quoted in *Greenbelt Towns* (Washington, D.C.: Resettlement Administration, Sept. 1936).

4. *Western City*, January 1980.

5. G. Ross Stephens and Gerald W. Olson, *Pass-Through Federal Aid and Interlevel Finance in the American Federal System, 1957–1977*, Vol. I (Kansas City: University of Missouri–Kansas City, August 1, 1979), p. 181.

6. Anthony J. Pascal, et al., *Fiscal Containment of Local and State Government* (Santa Monica: RAND Corporation, September 1979), p. 2.

7. Stephens and Olson, op. cit.

8. Rochelle L. Stanfield, "Building Streets and Sewers is Easy—It's Keeping Them Up That's the Trick," *National Journal*, May 24, 1980, p. 844.

9. Edward K. Hamilton, "On Nonconstitutional Management of a Constitutional Problem," *Daedalus*, Winter 1978, pp. 126–127.

10. *Cities and Energy*, November 24, 1980.

11. William Gorham and Nathan Glazer, eds., *The Urban Predicament* (Washington, D.C.: The Urban Institute, 1976), pp. 1–2.

12. Elinor Ostrom, ed., *The Delivery of Urban Services: Outcomes of Change* (Sage Publications, 1976).

13. Senator Mark Hatfield, "Submission to Republican Platform Committee," 1976.

14. *Fiscal Balance in the American Federal System*, Vol. 2, *Metropolitan Fiscal Disparities* (Washington, D.C.: ACIR, Oct. 1967), pp. 16–17.

15. Robert W. Poole, Jr., *Cutting Back City Hall* (New York: Universe Books, 1980), p. 23.

Chapter 5

1. A. Wolman, "The Metabolism of Cities," *Scientific American* 213 (1965), pp. 178–190.

2. Ralph Borsodi, *The Distribution Age: Study of Economies of Modern Distributing* (New York: D. Appleton, 1927).

3. Amory Lovins, "Renewable Energy and the City," Joint Hearings Before the Committee on Banking, Finance and Urban Affairs and the Committee on Interstate and Foreign Commerce, U.S. House of Representatives, October 16–17, 1979.

Chapter 6

1. ASHRAE 90–75 (New York: ASHRAE, 1975).

2. *Rain*, Oct. 1979.

3. Travis Price, personal communication, 1980.

4. Ibid.

5. *The Solar Law Reporter*, Sept.–Oct. 1980.

6. Ibid.

7. Ibid.

8. *Solar Law Reporter*, Nov.–Dec. 1979.

9. Eric Peterson, "Pathfinder Urban Solar Retrofit," unpublished manuscript, Washington, D.C., 1979.

10. *Wall Street Journal*, Sept. 3, 1980.

11. *Solar Law Reporter*, March–April 1981.

12. J. Tevere MacFadyen, "Finding Your Place in the Sun," *Passages*, March 1981.

13. Ibid.

14. Local Energy Policies Hearings, before the Subcommittee on Energy and Power, Committee on Interstate and Foreign Commerce, House of Representatives, May–June, 1978.

15. Bill Clement, personal communication, 1980.

16. Tom Valleau, personal communication, 1980.

17. Personal communication, 1980.

18. Mihailo Temali, "The 1980 St. Paul Mobilization," *The Neighborhood Works*, March 14, 1980.

19. Alice Murphy, personal communication, 1980.

20. Fran Koster, personal communication, 1980.

21. City of Cambridge, *Energy Use in Cambridge*, July 1980.

22. U.S. Department of Energy, *Energy Self-Sufficiency in North Hampton, Massachusetts* (Washington, D.C.: Government Printing Office, Oct. 1979).

23. Richard Archer, personal communication, 1981.

24. Paul Lattimore, personal communication, 1981.

25. Roger Hedgecock, personal communication, 1980.

26. *Solar Law Reporter*, Sept.–Oct. 1980.

27. Ibid.

28. *Solar Engineering*, Nov. 1980.

29. Sam Sperry, personal communication, 1980.

30. Personal communication, 1980.

Chapter 7

1. *Business Week*, April 6, 1981.

2. Amory B. Lovins and L. Hunter Lovins. "Energy Policies for Resilience and National Security," Unpublished draft, June 1981.

3. Doug Simpson, "Pulling the Plug on Con Ed: Big Six and Others Demonstrate Neighborhood Potential for Cogeneration," *The Neighborhood Works*, March 13, 1981, p. 1.

4. John McPhee, "Minihydro," *The New Yorker*, Feb. 23, 1981, p. 45.

5. Local Energy Policies Hearings Before the Subcommittee on Energy and Power Committee on Interstate and Foreign Commerce, House of Representatives, June 1978.

6. Ibid.

7. Ibid.

8. Ibid.

9. Ibid.

10. Memo from Stan Scheer, Assistant Superintendent, Eaton School District, Feb. 1981.

11. National League of Cities, *Environmental Report*, August 25, 1980.

12. Letter from Howard F. Christensen, Director of Solid Waste, to Peter Korn, August 4, 1980.

13. John G. Mitchell, "Whither the Yankee Forest?" *Audubon*, March 1981, p. 79.

14. Ibid., p. 80.

15. Ibid., p. 81.

16. *Mother Jones*, Dec. 1978.

17. Ibid.

18. Mitchell, op. cit., March 1981, p. 81.

19. Ibid., p. 81.

20. Ibid., p. 82.

21. *New Roots*, Nov. 1980.

22. Susan Schoenmaker, "Alcohol for the 80's: Hybrid Poplars Comes Out of the Woodwork," *Alternative Sources of Energy*, May–June 1980.

23. Jet Propulsion Laboratory, *Some Currently Available Photovoltaic System Computer Simulation Approaches*, Technical Report 5250–2 (Pasadena: U.S. Department of Energy, July 31, 1979).

24. Ralph Knowles and Richard Berry, *Solar Envelope Concepts: Moderate Density Applications* (Golden, Colo.: Solar Energy Research Institute, 1980).

25. *Land Use in 106 Large Cities, Three Hard U.S. Research Studies*, Study No. 2, Research Report No. 12 (Washington, D.C.: Government Printing Office, 1968).

26. Ray M. Northam, "Vacant Urban Land in the American City," *Land Economics*, Nov. 1971.

27. Charles F. Meyer et al., *Role of the Heat Storage Well in Future U.S. Energy Systems* (Santa Barbara: Center for Advanced Studies, 1980).

28. James Calm, *Heat Pump-Centered Community Energy System Development Summary* (Argonne, Ill.: Argonne National Laboratory, Feb. 1980).

29. Denis Hayes, Renewable Energy and the City, Joint Hearings Before the Committee on Banking, Finance and Urban Affairs and Committee on Interstate and Foreign Commerce, U.S. House of Representatives, Oct. 16, 17, 1979.

30. *District Heating*, 3rd Quarter, 1980.

31. *State of Mississippi v. Federal Energy Regulatory Commission*, Civil Action No. J79-0212 (c), U.S. D. Ct., S.D. Miss., February 19, 27, 1981.

32. March 23, 1980—Formal Case No. 757, "Memorandum of Points and Authorities of Potomac Electric Power Company," submitted to D.C. Public Service Commission.

33. Michael Moss, "Idaho's new energy source stumbles in the regulatory darkness," *High Country News*, March 20, 1981.

Chapter 8

1. "NJ County Minibonds Sell Out Fast," *American Banker*, April 3, 1979.
2. Thomas P. Ryan, statement, City of Rochester, N.Y., November 9, 1979, cited in Edward Anthony Lehan, "The Case for Directly Marketed Small Denomination Bonds," *Governmental Finance*, Sept. 1980, p. 4.

Chapter 9

1. Public Power Weekly Newsletter, Feb. 18, 1980.
2. *Materials and Man's Needs* (Washington, D.C.: National Academy of Sciences, 1975), pp. 57–59.
3. Ralph Louis Woods, *America Reborn: A Plan for 1969 Decentralization of Industry* (London: Longmans, 1939), p. 275.
4. Harvey J. Levin, *The Invisible Resource: Use and Regulation of the Electromagnetic Spectrum* (Baltimore: Johns Hopkins Press, 1971), p. 28.
5. Alex Radin, "Energy Services Planning," *Public Power*, May–June 1981, p. 6.
6. Fred Bosselman and David Callies, *The Quiet Revolution in Land Use Control* (Washington, D.C.: Council on Environmental Quality, 1971), p. 314.
7. Wilson Clark, "It Takes Energy to Get Energy: The Law of Diminishing Returns is in Effect," *Smithsonian Magazine*, Dec. 1974.
8. *Zabel v. Tabb*, 430 F.2d 199 200–201 (1970).
9. *Christian Science Monitor*, May 21, 1981.

Community
Energy Plans

The best way for a city to develop its own analysis of
its current energy situation and the steps necessary
to move toward energy independence is to examine
what others have done before. The following cities
had completed municipal energy plans
by mid-1981:

Ames, Iowa
Ann Arbor, Michigan
Auburn, New York
Austin, Texas
Bakersfield, California
Berkeley, California
Billings, Montana
Boulder, Colorado
Burlington, Vermont
Butte, Montana
Cambridge, Massachusetts
Carbondale, Illinois
Clearwater, Florida
Columbus, Ohio
Dayton, Ohio
District of Columbia
Eugene, Oregon
Fort Collins, Colorado
Helena, Montana
Kansas City, Missouri
Lincoln, Nebraska

Los Angeles, California
Madison, Wisconsin
Middletown, Connecticut
Minneapolis, Minnesota
Missoula, Montana
New York City
Northampton, Massachusetts
Palo Alto, California
Philadelphia, Pennsylvania
Pittsburgh, Pennsylvania
Portland, Maine
Portland, Oregon
Richmond, Indiana
Rochester, New York
Salem, Oregon
Santa Clara, California
Santa Monica, California
Seattle, Washington
Springfield, Illinois
Springfield, Vermont
St. Paul, Minnesota
Ukiah, California

Bibliography

CHAPTER 1
Shaping the Modern City:
From Wood to Coal to Petroleum

Abler, Ronald Francis, ed. *A Comparative Atlas of America's Great Cities: Twenty Metropolitan Regions*. Washington, D.C.: Association of American Geographers, 1976.

Abler, Ronald Francis, ed. *Boundary and Annexation Survey, 1970–1977*. Washington, D.C.: Bureau of the Census, 1979.

Jacobs, Jane. *The Death and Life of Great American Cities*. New York: Vintage, 1965.

Jones, Howard Mumford. *The Age of Energy: Varieties of American Experience, 1865–1915*. New York: Viking Press, 1971.

Mumford, Lewis. *The Culture of Cities*. New York: Harcourt, Brace, Jovanovich, 1938.

Mumford, Lewis. *The Highway and the City*. New York: Harcourt, Brace & World, 1963.

Ottensman, John R. *The Changing Spatial Structure of American Cities*. Lexington, Ky.: Lexington Books, 1975.

Snell, Bradford C. *American Ground Transport: A Proposal for Restructuring the Automobile, Truck, Bus and Rail Industries*. Washington, D.C.: Government Printing Office, 1974.

Sternlieb, George, and James W. Hughes, eds. *Post-Industrial America: Metropolitan Decline and Inter-Regional Job Shifts*. New Brunswick, N.J.: Center for Urban Policy Research, 1975.

CHAPTER 2
Facing the Grid:
From Neighborhood Power Plants
to Continental Grid Systems

Armstrong, Ellish L. *History of Public Works in the United States, 1776–1976*. Chicago: American Public Works Association, 1976.

Brown, Howard, and Tom Stromolo. *Decentralizing Electrical Production*. New Haven, Conn.: Yale University Press, 1981.

Glaser, Martin G. *Public Utilities in American Capitalism*. New York: Macmillan, 1957.

Messing, Marc, H. Paul Friesema, and David Morell. *Centralized Power: The Politics of Scale in Electricity Generation*. Cambridge, Mass.: Oelgeschlager, Gunn and Hain, 1979.

Novick, Sheldon. *The Electric War: The Fight Over Nuclear Power*. San Francisco: Sierra Club Books, 1976.

Promotional Practices by Public Utilities and Their Impact Upon Small Businesses. Hearings before the Subcommittee on Activities of Regulatory Agencies of the Select Committee on Small Business, House of Representatives, 90th Congress. Washington, D.C.: Government Printing Office, 1968.

CHAPTER 3
Governing the City:
Municipal Authority and Planning

Fordham, Jefferson B. "Local Government in the Larger Scheme of Things." *Vanderbilt Law Review*, June 1955.

Fox, Kenneth. *Better City Government: Innovation in American Urban Politics, 1850–1937*. Philadelphia: Temple University Press, 1977.

Frug, Gerald E. "The City as a Legal Concept." *Harvard Law Review*, April 1980, pp. 1059–1154.

Gelfand, Mark I. *A Nation of Cities: The Federal Government and Urban America, 1933–1965*. New York: Oxford University Press, 1975.

Kaplan, Samuel. *The Dream Deferred: People, Politics, and Planning in Suburbia*. New York: Vintage Books, 1977.

Kotler, Milton. *Neighborhood Government: The Local Foundations of Political Life*. Indianapolis: Bobbs Merrill, 1969.

Kotler, Milton. *The Disappearance of Municipal Liberty*. Washington, D.C.: Institute for Policy Studies, 1973.

Kramer, Howard D. "The Beginnings of the Public Health Movement in the United States." *Bulletin of the History of Medicine*, 21 (1947), pp. 352–376.

Long, Norton E. *The Unwalled City: Reconstituting the Urban Community*. New York: Basic Books, 1972.

Miles, Rufus E., Jr. *Awakening from the American Dream: The Social and Political Limits to Growth*. New York: Universe Books, 1976.

McBain, Howard Lee. *The Law and Practice of Municipal Home Rule*. New York: Columbia University Press, 1916.

McKelvey, Blake. *The Urbanization of America*. New Brunswick, New Jersey: Rutgers University Press, 1916.

Schlesinger, Arthur. *The Rise of the City, 1878–1898*. New York: Macmillan, 1933.

Walsh, Annmarie Hauck. *The Public's Business: The Politics and Practices of Government Corporations*. Cambridge, Mass.: MIT Press, 1978.

CHAPTER 4
Financing the City:
The Power of the Purse

Bahl, Roy, ed. *The Fiscal Outlook for Cities*. Syracuse, N.Y.: Syracuse University Press, 1978.

Bryce, Herrington J., ed. *Small Cities in Transition: The Dynamics of Growth and Decline*. Cambridge, Mass.: Ballinger Publishing Co., 1977.

Categorical Grants: Their Role and Design. Washington, D.C.: Advisory Commission on Intergovernmental Relations, 1977.

Hubbell, L. Kenneth, ed. *Fiscal Crisis in American Cities: The Federal Response*. Cambridge, Mass.: Ballinger Publishing Co., 1979.

Lovell, Catherine H. *Federal and State Mandating on Local Governments: An Exploration of Issues and Impacts*. Riverside, Calif.: University of California Graduate School of Administration, June 1979.

Pascal, Anthony J., et al. *Fiscal Containment of Local and State Government*. Santa Monica, Calif.: Rand Corporation, September 1979.

Reuss, Henry S. *To Save Our Cities: What Needs to be Done*. Washington, D.C.: Public Affairs Press, 1977.

Stephens, G. Ross. "State Centralization and the Erosion of Local Autonomy." *Journal of Politics*, Vol. 36, No. 1, Feb. 1974, pp. 44–77.

Stephens, G. Ross, and Gerald W. Olson. *State Responsibility for Public Services and General Revenue Sharing*. Kansas City, Mo.: University of Missouri–Kansas City, 1975.

Stephens, G. Ross, and Gerald W. Olson. *Pass-Through Federal Aid and Interlevel Finance in the American System, 1957 to 1977* (two volumes). Kansas City, Mo.: University of Missouri–Kansas City, August 1979.

The State of State-Local Revenue Sharing. Washington, D.C.: Advisory Commission on Intergovernmental Relations, Dec. 1980.

Tucker, Gilbert Milligan. *The Self-Supporting City*. New York: Robert Schalkenbach Foundation, 1958.

CHAPTER 6

The First Steps

Alschuler, John H., Jr. *Community Energy Strategies: A Preliminary View*. Hartford, Conn.: Hartford Policy Center, May 1980.

Becker, William S. *The Making of a Solar Village: A Case Study of a Solar Downtown Development Project at Soldiers Grove, Wisconsin*. Madison: Wisconsin Energy Extension Service, 1980.

Buchsbaum, Steven. *Jobs and Energy: The Employment and Economic Impacts of Nuclear Power, Conservation and Other Energy Options*. New York: Council on Economic Priorities, 1979.

Draft Action Plan. Seattle: Energy Ltd., Oct. 1980.

Energy Self-Sufficiency in Northampton, Massachusetts. Washington, D.C.: Department of Energy, Oct. 1979.

Estimating Energy Impacts of Residential and Commercial Building Development: A Manual. Bellevue, Wash.: Mathematical Science Northwest, Inc., Feb. 1979.

Franklin County Energy Study: A Renewable Energy Future. Amherst, Mass.: University of Massachusetts, May 1979.

Hayes, Gail Boyer. *Solar Access Law: Protecting Access to Sunlight for Solar Energy Systems*. Cambridge, Mass.: Ballinger Publishing Co., 1979.

Knowles, Ralph L. *Energy and Form: An Ecological Approach to Urban Growth*. Cambridge, Mass.: MIT Press, 1974.

Morris, David. *Planning for Energy Self-Reliance: A Case Study of the District of Columbia*. Washington, D.C.: Institute for Local Self-Reliance, 1979.

Okagaki, Alan. *County Energy Plan Guidebook: Creating a Renewable Energy Future*. Fairfax, Va.: Institute for Ecological Policies, 1979.

Olgyay, Victor. *Design with Climate: Bioclimatic Approach to Architectural Regionalism*. Princeton, N.J.: Princeton University Press, 1963.

Ridgeway, James. *Energy-Efficient Community Planning: A Guide to Saving Energy and Producing Power at the Local Level*. Emmaus, Penn.: The JG Press, 1980.

Schachter, Meg. *Creating Jobs Through Energy Policy*. Washington, D.C.: United States Department of Energy, July 1979.

Thompson, Grant P. *Building to Save Energy—Legal and Regulatory Approaches*. Cambridge, Mass.: Ballinger Publishing Co., 1980.

CHAPTER 7

Humanly Scaled Energy Systems

Application of Solar Technology to Today's Energy Needs (two volumes). Washington, D.C.: Office of Technology Assessment, June 1978.

Baylin, F., et al. *Economic Analysis of Community Solar Heating Systems That Use Annual Cycle Thermal Energy Storage*. Golden, Colo.: Solar Energy Research Institute, Feb. 1981.

Brown, Howard. *On-Site Generation*. New Haven, Conn.: Earth Metabolic Design, 1980.

Brown, Peter W. *Legal Obstacles and Incentives to Small Scale Hydroelectric Development in the Six Middle Atlantic States*. Concord, Mass.: Energy Law Institute, 1979.

Calm, J. M. *Heat Pump-Centered Integrated Community Energy Systems: System Development Summary*. Argonne, Ill.: Argonne National Laboratory, Feb. 1980.

Cogeneration: Its Benefits to New England: Final Report of the Governor's Commission on Cogeneration. Boston: Governor's Energy Office, Oct. 1978.

Community Systems: Energy Saving Programs for Communities. Argonne, Ill.: Argonne National Laboratory, Oct. 1979.

Gleason, Jack. *District Heating*. Washington, D.C.: Institute for Local Self-Reliance, 1980.

LaViale, Roger, III. *The Prospects for Developing Solar Ponds in Northampton, Massachusetts*. Amherst, Mass.: Hampshire College, May 1979.

Nadel, Steven. *Soft Energy Paths and Urban Areas*. Middletown, Conn.: Wesleyan University, Dec. 1979.

Ritschard, Ronald L. *Assessment of Solar Energy Within a Community: Summary of Three Community-Level Studies*. Berkeley, Calif.: Lawrence Berkeley Laboratory, Oct. 1979.

Shapiro, Michael. *Boston Solar Retrofits: SQTUDIES OF Solar Access and Economics*. Cambridge, Mass.: John F. Kennedy School of Government, Harvard University, Dec. 1980.

Sillman, Sanford. *The Trade-off Between Collector Area and Building Conservation in Annual Storage Solar Heating Systems*. Golden, Colo.: Solar Energy Research Institute, in progress.

CHAPTER 8

Financing the Transition

City Lights: A Handbook of Energy Conservation and Renewable Energies for City Homes. Boston, Mass.: Massachusetts Audubon Society, Nov. 1980.

237

Demonstration Solar Financing Program. San Francisco, Calif.: California Public Utilities Commission, Sept. 1980.

Energy Efficiency and the Utilities: New Directions. San Francisco, Calif.: California Public Utilities Commission, 1980.

Lamb, Robert, and Stephen P. Rapaport. *Municipal Bonds: The Comprehensive Review of Tax-Exempt Securities and Public Finance*. New York: McGraw-Hill, 1980.

Robertson, Chris, Michael Besal, J. Randle Shick, and Larry D. Strange. Carbondale: Shawnee Solar Project, 1981.

Sanger, John M., and Peter B. Epstein. *Municipal Solar Utilities in California: Marketing, Financial and Legal Issues*. Sacramento, Calif.: California Energy Commission, Aug. 1980.

Yudelson, Jerry, ed. *Making the Solar Loan: A Primer for Financial Institutions*. Golden, Colo.: Solar Energy Research Institute, 1980.

CHAPTER 9
The Ecological City

Blair, John M. *Economic Concentration: Structure, Behavior and Public Policy*. New York: Harcourt Brace Jovanovich, 1972.

Burns, Scott. *The Hidden Wealth and Power of the American Household*. Garden City, N.Y.: Doubleday, 1975.

Corbett, Michael N. *A Better Place to Live*. Emmaus, Penn.: Rodale Press, 1981.

Davis, W. Jackson. *The Seventh War: The Industrial Civilization in Transition*. New York: W. W. Norton, 1979.

Energy Service Corporations: Opportunities for California Utilities. Sacramento, Calif.: California Energy Commission, Dec. 1980.

Friend, Gil. *Closing the Circle: Waste Management, Nutrient Cycles and Regional Food Systems*. Washington, D.C.: Institute for Local Self-Reliance, 1978.

Materials and Man's Needs. Washington, D.C.: National Academy of Sciences, 1975.

Osborne, Adam. *Running Wild: The Next Industrial Revolution*. Berkeley, Calif.: OSBORNE/McGraw-Hill, 1980.

Renewable Resources for Industrial Materials. Washington, D.C.: National Academy of Sciences, 1976.

Seldman, Neil. *Municipal Composting*. Washington, D.C.: Institute for Local Self-Reliance, 1980.

Seldman, Neil N. *Economic Feasibility of Recycling*. Washington, D.C.: Institute for Local Self-Reliance, June 1978.

Index